Progress in Tourism, Recreation and Hospitality Management
Volume One

Progress in Tourism, Recreation and Hospitality Management

Published in association with the Department of Management Studies for Tourism and Hotel Industries, University of Surrey, UK.

Progress in Tourism, Recreation and Hospitality Management

Edited by
C. P. Cooper

Belhaven Press
A Division of Pinter Publishers
London and New York

First published in Great Britain in 1989 by
Belhaven Press (a division of Pinter Publishers),
25 Floral Street, London WC2E 9DS

British Library Cataloguing in Publication Data

A CIP catalogue record for this book is available from the
British Library

Library of Congress Cataloging-in-Publication Data

A CIP catalogue record for this book is available from the Library of Congress

ISBN 1 85293 023 3 (Volume One) ✓
ISSN 0952-5424

Typeset by Joshua Associates Limited, Oxford
Printed by Biddles of Guildford and Kings Lynn Ltd

Contents

List of contributors

Professor Brian Archer
Department of Management Studies for Tourism and Hotel Industries
University of Surrey
Guildford GU2 5XH
UK

Brian Archer is a Pro-Vice-Chancellor of the University of Surrey and Head of the Department of Management Studies for Tourism and Hotel Industries. His particular research interest is in planning and development and the economics of tourism.

Dr Gregory Ashworth
Geografisch Instituut
Rijksuniversiteit
Postbus 800
9700 Av Groningen
Netherlands

Gregory Ashworth is Reader in urban geography at the University of Groningen. He has taught and researched in the fields of urban recreation and tourism, especially in relation to urban conservation and development planning in Western Europe.

Dr John Fletcher
Department of Management Studies for Tourism and Hotel Industries
University of Surrey
Guildford GU2 5XH
UK

John Fletcher is Lecturer in economics at the University of Surrey. He is a consultant for the WTO and has undertaken numerous economic impact studies in Europe, the Caribbean and the South Pacific.

Professor Paul Gamble
Department of Management Studies for Tourism and Hotel Industries
University of Surrey
Guildford GU2 5XH
UK

Paul Gamble is the Charles Forte Professor of hotel management at the University of Surrey. In recent years he has conducted research on hospitality computer systems on which he has written widely.

Mr David Gilbert
Department of Management Studies for Tourism and Hotel Industries
University of Surrey
Guildford GU2 5XH
UK

David Gilbert is Lecturer in marketing and course tutor for the University of Surrey's Diploma/MSc in Tourism Marketing. He has worked in tourism for the private sector and his research interests and publications include country profiles, promotion planning and rural tourism marketing.

Professor George Glew
Hotel and Catering Research Centre
Huddersfield Polytechnic
Queensgate
Huddersfield HD1 3DH
UK

George Glew is Professor and Head of Department of catering studies, Huddersfield Polytechnic.

Dr Sue Glyptis
Department of Physical Education and Sports Science
Loughborough University of Technology
Loughborough LE11 3TU
UK

Sue Glyptis is Senior Lecturer in recreation management and leisure studies at the Loughborough University of Technology. She is involved in teaching and research in countryside recreation, leisure lifestyles and the recreation needs of different sectors of the population.

Mr Garry Hawkes
Gardner Merchant Ltd
Europe House
Bancroft Road
Reigate RH2 7RA
UK

Garry Hawkes is Managing Director of Gardner Merchant Ltd.

David Kirk
Department of Food and Hospitality Services
Sheffield City Polytechnic
Pond Street
Sheffield S11 WB
UK

David Kirk is Principal Lecturer in food engineering at Sheffield City Polytechnic. He has been involved in the development of catering technology as a discipline for the last twenty years.

Dr John Latham
Department of Management Studies for Tourism and Hotel Industries
University of Surrey
Guildford GU2 5XH
UK

John Latham is a mathematician. His special interest is tourism statistics, particularly the methodological aspects of data collection.

Dr Christine Martin
Management Centre
Emm Lane
University of Bradford
Bradford BD9 4JL
UK

Christine Martin is Lecturer in operations management at the University of Bradford. Her major research interest is in the area of tourism forecasting and the use of operations management techniques in the services industries.

Professor Robert Christie Mill
School of Hotel and Restaurant Management
University Park
University of Denver
Colorado
USA

Robert Christie Mill is Professor of Hotel and Restaurant Management at the University of Denver. He has written or contributed to seven books on the subjects of tourism and human resource management.

Dr Auliana Poon
Science Policy Research Unit
Mantell Building
University of Sussex
Falmer
Brighton BN1 9RF
UK

Auliana Poon is a researcher and consultant currently affiliated to the Science Policy Research Unit, University of Sussex and the University of the West Indies.

Dr Paul Reynolds
Department of Hospitality Management
Hong Kong Polytechnic
Hung Hom
Kowloon
Hong Kong

Paul Reynolds is Senior Lecturer in the Department of Hospitality Management, Hong Kong Polytechnic. He is currently researching multinational hotel groups and their strategies in China.

Dr Michael Romeril
Conservation Officer
Planning Department
States of Jersey
Jersey
Great Britain

Michael Romeril is conservation officer for the planning department, States of Jersey.

Dr Helena Snee
Cardiff Business School
UWIST
Cardiff
UK

Helena Snee is Lecturer in economics at the Cardiff Business School.

Professor Geoffrey Wall
Department of Geography
Faculty of Environmental Studies
Isiah Bowman Building
University of Waterloo
Ontario N2L 3G1
Canada

Geoffrey Wall is Professor of Geography at the University of Waterloo, Canada and is cross-appointed with the Department of Recreation and Leisure Studies.

Mr Trevor Ward
Horwath & Horwath (UK) Ltd
8 Baker Street
London W1M 1DA
UK

Trevor Ward is an associate director of Horwath & Horwath (UK) Ltd., consultant to the tourism, hotel and leisure industries.

Professor Stephen Witt
Department of Management Science and Statistics
University College of Swansea
Swansea
Wales

Stephen Witt is Lewis Professor of Tourism Studies at the University College of Swansea. His tourism research interests centre on demand forecasting and economic impact studies.

Editorial Preface

Progress in Tourism, Recreation and Hospitality Management is a new publication designed to provide an annual authoritative international review of research and major issues of current concern in the fields of tourism, recreation and hospitality management. The concept of Progress is to divide these fields into subfields of specialization and to publish annually a number of reviews so as to cover the entire field every three years. Certain fast-moving fields may be reviewed more frequently and shorter contributions such as particular regional approaches or views of practitioners will also be included. For the first two or three issues contributions have been invited from authors who are internationally recognized in their specialist field.

It is intended that Progress will provide leadership in research and become the established publication for researchers, students and staff in academic institutions as well as a source of reference and orientation for practitioners in both corporate and public organizations world-wide. In many respects, by basing Progress in the University of Surrey's Department of Management Studies for Tourism and Hotel Industries the achievement of these aims is facilitated. The department has a long pedigree in tourism, recreation and hospitality and has been influential in both formulating and contributing to the body of knowledge in these and related fields, not only by research but also through course development. The complement of experts in the department have been generous with their advice on the commissioning and reviewing of contributions for Progress.

Progress will provide 'state-of-the-art' reviews of research at the leading edge, while also in the early issues relating recent material to the more historic milestones of the fields' development. Progress thus aims to fill a gap in the tourism, recreation and hospitality literature. This gap has arisen with the rapid advance of the fields, an advance which creates both difficulties for researchers in consolidating material, and also stresses and strains within the fields themselves as a result of their immaturity.

For example, researchers in the tourism, recreation and hospitality fields have been handicapped in the past by a variety of factors (Britton, 1979; Dann, Nash and Pearce, 1988; Stockdale and Eldred, 1982). Firstly, the fields are bedevilled by conceptual weakness and fuzziness (Cohen, 1974). There is still confusion and no real agreement over terminology and this leads to a basic lack of rigour and focus. The fields sprawl inconsiderately across industrial sectors and academic subjects, reinforcing the need for a disciplined approach and the difficulties of keeping track of a fast-moving field. Problems with data sources in terms of both comparability and quality are also highlighted and therefore demand the development of particular methodologies to handle not only the fragility of the data sources but also the difficulty of studying man at leisure, a much more private pursuit than man the producer. Finally, many of these leisure pursuits are themselves relatively recent developments—international mass tourism for example—and only recently have they been considered worthy of serious business endeavour or academic study. Even now there is still much prejudice to dispel.

The fields lack the antecedents of mature subjects and this is reflected in research progress. Much research and published material is descriptive, often the one-off case study or problem-specific work, wrestling with measurement but in the past failing to make links and relationships (Sheldon *et al*., 1987). Attempts to build a core of theory and to make generalizations are rare and the fragmentation accentuates both the lack of direction and an organizing framework. As research progresses in the tourism, recreation and hospitality fields a balance of method and theory will be reached (Dann, Nash and Pearce, 1988) though at this point, some (articulated by Dean, 1988) argue that the search for abstract theory should give way to a critique of contemporary provision so as to refocus on the user. Finally the interdisciplinary nature of the fields emphasizes the many different points of view and has resulted in a somewhat loosely articulated body of work. There is therefore a continual need to draw material together and consolidate systematically and effectively in the search for direction. It is hoped that Progress will contribute to this debate and facilitate the ability to profit from and build upon past research.

The immaturity of the fields is reflected in the fact that the educational infrastructure and intellectual base is only now being put in place. This is particularly the case for tourism, with new departments often based on hospitality, sports science/recreation, food studies, business or single discipline departments such as geography. Certainly in the past the researcher was often institutionally isolated and there has been little cross fertilization between hospitality, tourism and recreation research. Research in each field has progressed from different camps and remained relatively isolated. Yet these camps, and indeed all service industry research, would benefit from a more integrated approach (Fedler, 1988).

The fields also embody a number of underlying tensions. For example, there is a tension between academic and applied approaches which is not only reflected in the course planner's training versus education debate, but also in the difficulties of attracting funding for academic research against the frustrations (and consequent loss of continuity and direction) of working from contract to contract in applied research. Recent research reviews highlight these two ends of the spectrum. A special issue of *Annals of Tourism Research* (1988, 15(1)) deals comprehensively with the methodological issues involved in pure research while Ritchie and Goeldner's (1987) *Handbook of Travel*

Tourism and Hospitality Research is a thorough review of applied research techniques for managers and researchers. In this volume Ritchie (1987) for example, elegantly links a typology of research with its role and location in the management decision-taking process. However, Sheldon *et al.* (1987) point out that there is little academic research carried out in the lodging industry and even applied research is not seen as a priority. There is also a tension between researcher and educator. Despite the fact that research feeds the body of knowledge, the applied and vocational nature of the fields has encouraged a division between those who research and those who teach (the latter consequently have little time to engage in research and gain no credit for it).

This new publication aims to progress the tourism, recreation and hospitality fields 'into a systematic and cumulative body of knowledge' (Goeldner, 1988) by drawing together research material and allowing teachers, researchers and practitioners to keep up to date with research findings, to profit from previous work and so to build effectively upon it.

References

Britton, R., 1979, 'Some notes on the geography of tourism', *Canadian Geographer*, XXXIII(3): 276–82.

Cohen, E., 1974, 'Who is a tourist? A conceptual classification', *Sociological Review*, 22(4): 527–55.

Dann, G. M. S., Nash, D., and Pearce, P. L., 1988, 'Methodology in tourism research', *Annals of Tourism Research*, 15(1): 1–28.

Dean, A., 1988, 'Researching leisure', *Leisure Studies*, 7(2): 195–9.

Fedler, A. J., 1988. 'Are leisure, recreation and tourism related?', *Annals of Tourism Research*, 14(1): 311–13.

Goeldner, C. R., 1988. 'The evaluation of tourism as an industry and discipline', paper presented to Teaching Tourism in the 1990s, Conference, University of Surrey, proceedings forthcoming.

Ritchie, J. R. B., Goeldner, C. R. (eds), 1987, *Travel, Tourism, and Hospitality Research: A Handbook for Managers and Researchers*, Wiley, New York.

Ritchie, J. R. B., 1987, 'Roles of research in tourism management, in Ritchie, J. R. B. and Goeldner, C. R. (eds), *Travel, Tourism, and Hospitality Research: A Handbook for Managers and Researchers*, Wiley, New York, pp. 13–21.

Sheldon, P. J., Juanita, C. L. and Gee, C. Y., 1987. 'The status of research in the lodging industry', *International Journal of Hospitality Management*, 6(2): 89–96.

Stockdale, J. E., Eldred, J. G., 1982, 'Research methods appropriate to the task', in Collins, M. F. (ed.), *Leisure Research: Current Findings and the Future Challenge*, Sports Council, London, pp. 15–29.

1 Demand forecasting in tourism and recreation

S. F. Witt and C. A. Martin

Introduction

It is widely recognized that one of the most important functions of the manager at all levels in an organization is planning, and planning creates a substantial need for forecasts. Reliable forecasts of tourism and recreation demand are essential for efficient planning by airlines, shipping companies, railways, coach operators, hoteliers, tour operators, food and catering establishments, providers of entertainment facilities, manufacturers producing goods primarily for sale to tourists and other industries connected with the tourism and recreation markets. Such forecasts are also of great interest to governments in origin and destination countries, and to national tourist organizations.

Both the *need* for forecasts and the importance of *reliable* forecasts have been stressed by several authors working in the tourism and recreation fields. For example, Gunn (1987, p. 5) says: 'Of interest to many tourist businesses is increasing the ability to make forecasts. Decisions on the purchase of new generations of equipment, new sites, and new technology may rest on predictions of increased demand for a specific tourism service or product.' Wandner and Van Erden (1980, p. 381) point out that: 'Since governments and private industry must plan for expected tourism demand and provide tourism investment goods and infrastructure, the availability of accurate estimates of international tourism demand has important economic consequences.' Finally, Archer (1987, p. 77) notes the key role of forecasts in the planning process and emphasizes the importance of accuracy:

Forecasting should be an essential element in the process of management. No manager can avoid the need for some form of forecasting: a manager must plan for the future in order to minimize the risk of failure or, more optimistically, to maximize the possibilities of success. In order to plan, he must use forecasts. Forecasts will always be made, whether by guesswork, teamwork or the use of complex models, and the accuracy of the forecasts will affect the quality of the management decision.

Forecasts are needed for marketing, production, and financial planning. Top management needs demand forecasts for implementing long-term objectives; lower echelons of management require forecasts to plan their activities over a more limited horizon. In the tourism industry, in common with most other service sectors, the need to forecast accurately is especially acute because of the perishable nature of the product. Unfilled airline seats and unused hotel rooms cannot be stockpiled and demand must be anticipated and even manipulated.

Considerable benefits derive from an accurate forecasting system. If forecasts of tourism/recreation demand are too high, then firms in related industries will suffer; for example, there may be empty seats on airplanes and coaches, empty rooms in hotels, unoccupied apartments, unused hire cars and so on. It is likely that in general capital investment will be excessive, the labour force will be too big and excess stocks will be held of goods normally sold directly to or used by tourists. If, on the other hand, forecasts of demand are too low, then firms will lose opportunities; for example, there may be insufficient hotel accommodation or too few flights to cater for all those wishing to visit a certain area at a given time. Even if supply can be expanded to a limited extent at short notice, this is likely to impose additional costs on firms as, say, less efficient aircraft are used and excessive overtime is worked.

A broad range of techniques is available for demand forecasting in tourism and recreation, and overviews of possible forecasting methods (of varying degrees of detail) are provided by Archer (1976, 1980, 1987), Burton (1981), Calantone *et al.* (1987), Duke (1981), Sheldon and Var (1985), Uysal and Crompton (1985), Van Doorn (1984a), Vanhove (1980), and the World Tourism Organization (1978). This review discusses the main forecasting techniques which are used in the tourism/recreation fields.

Univariate time-series methods

Univariate time-series methods are non-causal quantitative techniques, and assume that a variable may be forecast without reference to the factors which determine the level of the variable—past history on the forecast variable is simply extrapolated. Univariate time-series methods determine future values for a single variable through a process of identifying a relationship for past values of the variable. Thus a great problem with forecasting by extrapolation is that it presupposes that the factors which were the main cause of growth in the past will continue to be the main cause in the future and that may not be the case. In an industry as highly volatile as international tourism, and one that is influenced by so many factors, trend extrapolation is a technique that should be used with extreme care.

It is rarely possible to justify time-series models on the basis of theory. The reasons for their use are essentially pragmatic; they often generate acceptable forecasts at low cost. Furthermore, univariate time-series methods may be used where causal models are inappropriate on account of lack of data or incomplete knowledge regarding the causal structure.

Although time-series extrapolation models are 'naïve' in the sense that the impacts of the forces which determine the behaviour of the time series are not taken into account, they often predict relatively well. Indeed Barnard (1971) found in his study that when forecasting overseas visits to the UK, non-causal quantitative models provided more accurate forecasts than econometric (causal) models. More recently, Martin and Witt (1989) found that when comparing the forecasting accuracy of econometric models with several time-series extrapolation models over many data sets, the econometric models performed relatively poorly, even though the form of the causal model was quite sophisticated compared with many earlier econometric models of international tourism demand.

Moving average (arithmetic)

In a survey of tourism practitioners and academics, Martin and Witt (1988b) found that the most widely used univariate time-series forecasting techniques were moving average and exponential smoothing. The arithmetic moving-average forecast is very easy and cheap to compute; the data for previous periods are added together and divided by the number of observations to give an average figure, and then as a new data point becomes available this is included in the set, the oldest observation is removed and a new average is calculated. For seasonal data with seasonality of s periods, a moving average s periods long is free of seasonal effects. The moving average forecast for periods $t + 1$, $t + 2$ etc. is given by:

$$(1) \quad F_{t+2} = F_{t+1} = [x_t + x_{t-1} + \ldots + x_{t-s+1}]/s$$

where

x_t is the value of a time series in period t
F_{t+j} is the moving average forecast of x_{t+j} (i.e. the forecast for j periods ahead), and
s is the length of the seasonal cycle.

The moving average model (1) attempts to estimate the non-seasonal portion of a time series. It is not applicable to series containing steps or trends (as is often the case with tourism data), as these would cause the moving average to lag behind the movement of the data. Thus, for example, if tourism demand were increasing the method would underforecast. If a trend were present in our time series, it would be necessary to difference the data to remove the trend before applying the moving average technique.

Exponential smoothing (exponentially weighted moving average)

Exponential smoothing models provide a relatively simple set of forecasting methods that tend to perform well in practice. As they are cheap to compute, smoothing models are well suited to high-volume applications. Provided that the previous period's parameters are given as a starting point, smoothing models can be cheaply re-estimated for each period, and this procedure tends to give better forecasts. The simplest smoothing method is single exponential smoothing; more complicated methods include adaptive smoothing, Brown's double exponential smoothing and Holt-Winters' double exponential smoothing.

Single exponential smoothing

The single exponential smoothing model in effect attempts to reduce forecast error by correcting the last period's forecast by a proportion of the last period's error:

(2) $F_{t+1} = F_t + k(x_t - F_t)$

where

x_t is the value of a time series in period t
F_{t+1} is the single exponential smoothing forecast of x_{t+1} (i.e. the forecast for one period ahead) and
k is a constant, such that $0 < k < 1$.

Equation (2) states that the forecast for period $t + 1$ is given by the forecast for period t plus a proportion (k) of the forecast error for period t. This equation may be rewritten to give:

(3) $F_{t+1} = kx_t + (1 - k)F_t$

Single exponential smoothing methods are only applicable to stationary series, i.e. to data without steps, trend or seasonality components and with constant variance. If a trend were present in our time series it would be necessary to difference the data so that we could subsequently apply the single exponential smoothing technique. If seasonality were present in our time series (as is almost certainly the case if monthly or quarterly tourism/recreation data are under consideration), it would be necessary to seasonally difference the data prior to forecasting using single exponential smoothing. Finally, a data series exhibiting changing variability may be rendered stationary in the variance by applying the logarithmic transformation.

Adaptive smoothing

A modification of the single exponential smoothing model is adaptive smoothing. Here, instead of using a constant value for k, the value of this parameter changes in accordance with the forecast error. When the forecast error is large, the value of k in equation (3) is set close to 1 so that the forecast adjusts rapidly towards the previous actual value. When the forecast error is small, the value of k is set close to 0 so that the forecast remains almost unchanged.

Adaptive smoothing models, in common with single exponential smoothing models, are only applicable to data series that are stationary in the variance and that do not exhibit trend or seasonality. However, whereas single exponential smoothing models are only applicable to data without steps, adaptive smoothing models can accommodate sudden upward or downward steps in a series.

Double exponential smoothing—Brown's model

Whereas single exponential smoothing and adaptive smoothing are not suitable for time series containing a trend, this is not the case with double exponential smoothing models. Brown's (1963) double exponential smoothing method produces forecasts containing both a constant level term and a linear trend term. In general, the forecasts produced by Brown's double exponential smoothing method tend to be better than applying single exponential smoothing to a series that has been transformed to render it stationary in the mean.

Double exponential smoothing—the Holt–Winters' model

Brown's double exponential smoothing method is not suitable for use with seasonal data, but the Holt (1957)–Winters' (1960) double exponential smoothing method is specifically designed to be used with time series exhibiting seasonality. The Holt–Winters method produces forecasts containing a constant level term, a linear trend term and seasonal factors.

Trend curve analysis

Trend curve analysis (TCA) is widely used in tourism/recreation forecasting situations. In general, regression analysis is used to find a curve of best fit through time-series data which is then projected forward into the future. TCA is relatively quick and easy to use and, using transformations, can be employed to produce forecasts from data showing a range of patterns, for example straight-line progressions, exponential growth or patterns that display a gradual approach to a saturation level. A variety of trend expressions is shown below:

(4) Linear $\qquad Y = a + bT$
(5) Constrained hyperbola $\qquad Y = T/(a + bT)$
(6) Exponential $\qquad Y = ae^{bT}$
(7) Log-log $\qquad Y = aT^b$
(8) Semi-log $\qquad Y = a + b\log T$
(9) Modified exponential $\qquad Y = ae^{b/T}$
(10) Hyperbola $\qquad Y = a + b/T$
(11) Modified hyperbola $\qquad Y = 1/(a + bT)$
(12) Quadratic $\qquad Y = a + bT + cT^2$
(13) Log quadratic $\qquad Y = e^{(a + bT + cT^2)}$

where

Y is the forecast variable
T is the time period
$e =$ 2.718 and
a, b, c are coefficients to be estimated using regression analysis.

TCA gives equal weight to all data. This can be problematical if there is a sudden change at the end of a series. Regression analysis will try to fit a curve to all the data so a forecast may pay little attention to new and important variations.

Curve-fitting methods should not be used blindly. Forecasters should choose the shape of the curve to be projected before using analytical methods to find the best fit, as several curves may yield a reasonable fit to the data series, but do not produce the same shape or forecast. Trend analysis is therefore best viewed as a three-part process. The first part is the selection of the general shape or expression to represent the trend to be forecast. The second part of the process uses regression analysis to fit the chosen expression to a historic pattern. The quality of the fit should be checked by visual comparison of the time series and the forecast. The final stage of trend analysis produces a forecast by extrapolating the trend equation.

Tie-Sheng and Li-Cheng (1985) provide an example of the use of TCA in the area of tourism forecasting. They examine domestic tourism in China; their study focuses on the number of tourist visits to Hangzhou, and an exponential trend model is employed to generate forecasts.

Decomposition methods

The observed values of a time series are usually the result of several influences, and here we are concerned with isolating and measuring those parts of the time series that are attributable to each of the components. Customarily time-series variations are considered to be the result of three or four basic influences: secular trend, seasonal variations, irregular or random changes and possibly cyclical fluctuations.

Classical decomposition

The starting point of the classical decomposition approach is that the observation of the time series at period t, x_t, can be represented as:

(14) $x_t = T_t \times S_t \times I_t$

where

T represents the trend value

S represents the seasonal component

I represents the irregular (unpredictable) component and

t represents the time period.

Sometimes an additional longer-term-cycle component is added to the classical decomposition model, but often this factor is ignored. This can be justified if there are insufficient data to detect it and that may well be the case with tourism/recreation series.

In broad terms the classical decomposition method works as follows. Seasonality is removed from the data by taking a moving average with a period of one year. A linear trend is then fitted to the deseasonalized data using regression of the deseasonalized data against time. This provides a value T_t for the trend at each time period. The seasonal component is estimated by dividing the time-series value x_t by the computed trend value to give a seasonal index for that period. The seasonal component S_t is derived by averaging the values for corresponding periods in the year: e.g. with monthly data the seasonal term for January is derived by averaging all the seasonal indexes corresponding to January. Finally the irregular term I_t is computed using equation (14) and the values of T_t and S_t previously derived. Classical decomposition is best suited where trend or seasonality, and preferably both, are marked.

Census XII

An alternative (though considerably more complex) approach to decomposition is provided by the Census XII model originally devised for the United States' Bureau of Census. This also extends the basic decomposition model of equation (14) by allowing the trend term T_t to be non-linear. The XII model involves considerably more computation than the classical decomposition model because of the relative increase in sophistication. It is mainly used by practitioners on account of the excellence of its seasonal decomposition.

Decomposition methods have been applied in the tourism forecasting area, and are often associated with the work of BarOn (1972, 1973, 1975), who uses the Census XII method (modified to allow for factors such as the effects of festival days) to forecast several time series related to the tourist industry—inward tourist visits, outward tourist visits, foreign currency earnings from tourists and the demand for bed-nights in hotels.

Box—Jenkins univariate method

The Box-Jenkins (1970) univariate forecasting method is a highly sophisticated technique and is rather more difficult to apply than the other univariate time-series methods considered. The models usually incorporate autoregressive and moving average terms; the autoregressive component implies that the forecast variable depends on its own past values, and the moving average component implies that the forecast variable depends on previous values of the error term. These autoregressive integrated moving average (ARIMA) models are very flexible—they can represent many types of stationary and non-stationary time series. Furthermore, the models contain few parameters. The Box–Jenkins model-building approach can provide relatively accurate forecasts, but it involves complex mathematical and statistical algorithms, together with subjective judgements on the part of the modeller. Experience is an essential prerequisite for improving the final models in the analysis of a time series and thus for successful application of the technique.

The Box–Jenkins method involves an iterative procedure for determining a suitable time-series model, and in describing their approach to forecasting, Box and Jenkins developed a flow diagram similar to the one shown in Figure 1.1. Initially, the forecaster postulates a general class of models applicable to his particular situation. In stage 1, the identification process, the information

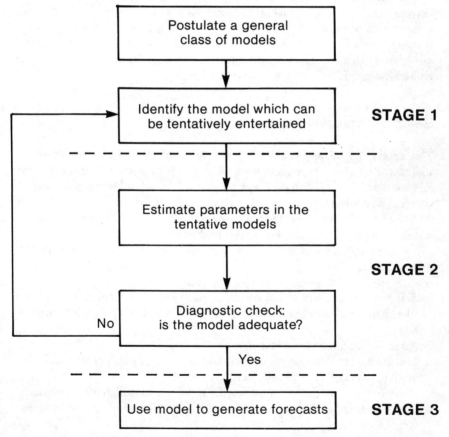

Figure 1.1 *Box—Jenkins flow diagram*
Source: Sturgess, B. T., Wilson, N., 1983, 'Forecasting advertising expenditure', *International Journal of Advertising*, 2(4): 301–16.

contained in the data on patterns of serial dependence in the forecast variable is used to discover the stochastic process which most likely represents the true data-generating mechanism (after first applying a filtering transformation which involves first differencing and seasonal differencing to render the series stationary). The parameter estimation part of stage 2 may be carried out using Gauss–Newton maximum likelihood methods, but initial approximate values of the parameters have to be input into the estimation programme together with the structure of the model. The diagnostic checks which are performed in the second part of stage 2 consist of examining the residual series of the estimated model to test for remaining serial correlation. If the residual series is not a 'white noise' process, then the approach returns to stage 1 and an alternative model is identified. When a satisfactory model has been isolated, it can be used to generate forecasts.

An example of the use of Box–Jenkins univariate methods in the tourism forecasting area is contained in a research report produced by the Canadian Government Office of Tourism (1977), in which monthly incoming tourist visit data on American travellers entering by car, plane or other transport modes and their totals are modelled and forecast. In addition, the technique is applied to quarterly data on tourism receipts/payments for travel to and from the United States and also all countries as a whole.

Multiple regression methods

The econometric approach to forecasting involves the use of regression analysis to estimate the quantitative relationship between the variable to be forecast and those variables which appear likely to influence the forecast variable. The estimation is carried out using historic data, and future values of the forecast variable are obtained by using forecasts of the influencing variables in conjunction with the estimated relationship.

The process of forecasting tourism/recreation demand by regression may be summarized as:

1. Select those variables which are expected to influence the forecast variable (the demand determinants) and specify the relationship in mathematical form.
2. Assemble data relevant to the model.
3. Use the data to estimate the quantitative effects of the influencing variables on the forecast variable in the past.
4. Carry out tests on the estimated model to see if it is sufficiently realistic.
5. If the tests show that the model is satisfactory then it can be used for forecasting.

A major advantage with econometric forecasting is that it explicitly takes into account the impact on the variable to be forecast of changes in the causal variables. Furthermore, econometric models may be used for active ('what if') forecasting, that is to assess the consequences of possible changes in the causal factors. An additional advantage with econometric forecasting is that it provides several statistical measures of the accuracy and significance of the forecasting equations. However, econometric models may be inappropriate in certain cases and are generally more expensive than non-causal models. Econometric forecasting also requires considerable user understanding in order to develop the correct relationships.

Model construction

The first stage in the econometric forecasting process is to select those variables which are likely to influence the demand for tourism/recreation. In the case of international tourism the demand function takes the general form:

$$(15) \quad Y = f(X_1, X_2, \ldots, X_k)$$

where

Y is the demand for international tourism to a given destination from a particular origin

$X_1, X_2, \ldots, X_k$ are the influencing variables and

f denotes some function.

Variables which may be included in the demand function are now considered.

Forecast variable

Tourism demand is measured in terms of the number of tourist visits from an origin country to a foreign destination country or in terms of tourist expenditures by visitors from the origin country in the destination country. As the level of foreign tourism from a given origin is expected to depend upon the origin population, the forecast variable is usually expressed in per capita form (see for example, Barry and O'Hagan, 1972; Loeb, 1982; Martin and Witt, 1987, 1988a; Papadopoulos and Witt, 1985; Smith and Toms, 1967; Witt, 1980a, 1980b, 1989; Witt and Martin, 1987a). Occasionally, however, population features as a separate explanatory variable rather than demand being expressed in per capita form (Bond and Ladman, 1972; Kliman, 1981; Paraskevopoulos, 1977).

Income

In general, income is included as an explanatory variable. Income usually enters model (15) as origin country real income per capita (corresponding to the specification of demand in per capita terms). If holiday visits or visits to friends and relatives are under consideration then the appropriate form of the variable is *personal disposable* income, but if attention is focused on business visits a more general income variable (such as national income) may be used.

Own price

Price is usually included in demand functions. For international tourism there are two elements of price—those costs incurred in reaching the destination, and those costs to be met whilst at the destination. Transport cost can be measured using representative air fares between origin and destination for air travel (Gray, 1966; Kliman, 1981; Martin and Witt, 1987, 1988a; Papadopoulos and Witt, 1985; Summary 1987; Witt, 1980a, 1980b, 1989; Witt and Martin, 1987a), and representative ferry fares and/or petrol costs for surface travel (Martin and Witt, 1987, 1988a; Quayson and Var, 1982; Witt and Martin, 1987a). Transport cost should enter model (15) in real terms in origin country currency.

It may be possible to measure the cost of tourism in the destination by a specific tourists' cost of living variable if appropriate data are available (Papadopoulos and Witt, 1985; Witt 1980a, 1980b, 1989; Witt and Martin, 1987a). Otherwise the consumer price index in a country may be used to represent tourists' cost of living, and this is the procedure adopted by most authors (see, for example, Artus, 1970; Kwack, 1972; Little, 1980; Loeb, 1982; Martin and Witt, 1988a; Uysal and Crompton, 1984). Martin and Witt (1987) have shown that the consumer price index is likely to be a reasonable proxy for the cost of tourism variable. Tourists' cost of living should be specified in real terms in origin currency for model estimation purposes. It is sometimes suggested that the exchange rate should also appear as an explanatory variable influencing international tourism demand (Gray, 1966; Martin and Witt, 1987, 1988a; Quayson and Var, 1982; Witt and Martin, 1987a). Although exchange rates are already incorporated to some extent in the other price variables, in practice people may be more aware of exchange rates than relative costs of living for tourists in the origin and destination countries, and thus pay considerable attention to this price indicator.

Substitute prices

Economic theory suggests that the prices of substitutes may be important determinants of demand. Potential tourists compare the price of a foreign holiday with the price of a domestic holiday in reaching their holiday decision (Kliman, 1981; Oliver, 1971; Papadopoulos and Witt, 1985; Witt, 1980a, 1980b, 1989; Witt and Martin, 1987a). However, they also compare the costs of holidaying in a particular foreign destination with the costs involved in visiting other foreign countries (Artus, 1970; Barry and O'Hagan, 1972; Jud and Joseph, 1974, Little, 1980; Martin and Witt, 1987, 1988a; Uysal and Crompton, 1984). Thus, substitute travel costs and substitute tourists' living costs may be important determinants of the demand for international tourism to a given destination from a particular origin. Substitute prices can be accommodated in model (15) through the inclusion of:

(a) a weighted-average substitute transport cost variable; and
(b) a weighted-average substitute tourists' cost of living variable.

The weights should reflect the relative attractiveness of the various destinations to residents of the origin under consideration, and are often based on previous market shares (for a discussion of weighting systems in international tourism demand models see Witt and Martin, 1987b).

Dummy variables

Dummy variables can be included in econometric models explaining international tourism demand to allow for the impact of 'one off' events. For example, the 1973 and 1979 oil crises are likely to have temporarily reduced international tourism demand on account of the resultant uncertainties in the world economic situation (Martin and Witt, 1987, 1988a). Tourism flows to Greece were lower than expected in 1974 because of the heightened threat of war between Greece and Turkey as a result of the Turkish invasion of Cyprus (Papadopoulos and Witt, 1985). When governments impose foreign currency restrictions on their residents, this is likely to reduce outward tourism, as was the case, for example, in the United Kingdom during the period late 1966 to late 1969 (Martin and Witt, 1987, 1988a; Witt, 1980a, 1980b). Foreign currency restrictions can also alter the distribution of foreign holidays (Witt, 1980a, 1980b, 1983). Measurement of the impact of mega-events (such as the Olympic Games) on tourism flows through the use of dummy variables has been discussed by Witt and Martin (1987d).

Trend

A trend term may be included in international tourism demand models if it is thought relevant (Artus, 1970; Edwards, 1985; Martin and Witt, 1987, 1988a; Witt and Martin, 1987a). This represents a steady change in the popularity of a destination country over the period considered as a result of changing tastes.

Promotional activity

National tourist offices often spend considerable sums in foreign countries on promoting the particular country as a tourist destination. Hence, promotional expenditure is expected to play a role in determining the level of international tourism demand and thus should feature as an explanatory variable in the demand function (15) (Barry and O'Hagan, 1972; Papadopoulos and Witt, 1985; Uysal and Crompton, 1984). The appropriate form of the variable is promotional expenditure by the destination in the origin, expressed in origin country currency and real terms.

   A major problem regarding the inclusion of promotional variables as determinants of tourism demand relates to difficulties in obtaining the relevant data. A further problem concerns the form of the relationship; the impact of advertising on tourism demand may be distributed over time, so that advertising in a given period is likely to influence not only demand in that period but also in subsequent periods, although the effect will diminish with the passage of time.

A full review and discussion of the role of marketing variables in international tourism demand models is given in Witt and Martin (1987c).

Lagged dependent variable

A lagged dependent variable is sometimes included in tourism demand functions to allow for habit persistence and supply rigidities (Martin and Witt, 1987, 1988a; Smith and Toms, 1967; Witt, 1980a, 1980b, 1989; Witt and Martin, 1987a). Once people have been on holiday to a particular country and liked it, they tend to return to that destination. Furthermore, knowledge about the destination spreads as people talk about their holidays and show photographs, thereby reducing risk for potential visitors to that country. Supply constraints may take the form of shortages of hotel accommodation and passenger transportation capacity, and these often cannot be increased rapidly. If a partial adjustment process is postulated to allow for rigidities in supply, this results in the presence of a lagged dependent variable in model (15).

The application of multiple regression analysis to **recreation** demand forecasting involves a different set of explanatory variables. For example, Steinnes and Raab (1983) investigated the determinants of angling activity at a recreational site. The influencing factors included comprise the success enjoyed by anglers at the site in the recent past as measured by the number of fish caught, weather condition variables representing temperature and precipitation, a dummy variable to allow for increased angling activity at the weekend compared with during the week and a trend variable.

Model evaluation

The mathematical form generally specified for tourism/recreation demand models is log-linear. In such cases the estimated coefficients (which show the effects of the explanatory variables on the forecast variable in the past) may be interpreted directly as elasticities.

It is necessary to evaluate the parameter estimates obtained in a regression model in terms of both sign and magnitude in order to determine whether these estimates are theoretically meaningful. Economic theory imposes restrictions on the signs and values of the parameters in demand functions, and the estimates need to be examined to see whether they satisfy these constraints. For example, foreign holidays are superior goods and thus a positive income elasticity is expected. In fact, most foreign holidays are regarded as luxuries and in such cases the magnitude of the income elasticity is expected to exceed unity. Similarly, the own-price elasticity of demand should be negative and cross-price elasticities for substitutes positive. Changes in consumer tastes may move towards or away from a particular holiday and therefore the trend variable could have a positive or negative coefficient. The promotional expenditure and lagged dependent variable coefficients are both expected to be positive. If an estimated parameter has an incorrect sign or does not satisfy the restrictions on magnitude, it should be rejected as it is theoretically implausible. In general, an unexpected parameter sign or size is the result of deficiencies in the model.

The empirical results may also be evaluated in terms of statistical measures of accuracy and significance of the forecasting equations. For example, the t test can be employed to examine the hypothesis that a particular explanatory variable coefficient is significantly different from zero or whether the estimated value may simply have been generated by chance. If the hypothesis that a coefficient is equal to zero is true, then the corresponding explanatory variable does not influence the dependent variable and should be excluded from the tourism demand function. However, when a parameter is not statistically significant (at, say, the 5 per cent level), this does not prove that there is no relationship between the explanatory and dependent variables; the insignificance of the parameter may be a result of statistical problems. Prior belief plays a vital role in the decision regarding which explanatory variables should be retained in the equation in view of the statistical evidence. If there are strong theoretical grounds for expecting a particular explanatory variable to influence the dependent variable and a 'correct' coefficient sign is estimated but the parameter is insignificant, the explanatory variable should not be eliminated from the equation, as weak support has been obtained for the hypothesis. If the 'correct' sign is estimated for a coefficient and it is statistically significant, this provides strong support for the hypothesis that the variable has an impact on the dependent variable.

Spatial models

Gravity models are spatial models and represent a particular class of multiple regression model which has been widely used in the past to forecast tourism and recreation demand. Gravity models are based on the gravity law of spatial interaction, which states (in the travel context) that the degree of interaction between two geographic areas varies directly with the degrees of concentration of persons in the two areas and inversely with the distance separating them. Whereas the demand functions considered earlier are derived from the theory of consumer behaviour, the fundamental idea underlying gravity models was originally derived by analogy with Newton's gravitational law:

(16) $F_{ij} = a\,(M_i M_j / d_{ij}^2)$

where

F_{ij} is the gravitational force between two masses M_i and M_j;
d_{ij} is the distance separating the masses and
a is a constant.

Gravity models evolved as part of the early work of social physicists who believed that social phenomena could be explained by physical laws. The most common form of travel gravity model is:

(17) $T_{ij} = a \, (P_i^{b_2} \, P_j^{b_2} / \, d_{ij}^{b_3})$

where

    T_{ij} denotes the number of trips taking place between node i and node j;
    P_i and P_j are the populations at nodes i and j respectively; and
    a, b_1, b_2, b_3 are constants.

Equation (17) is very similar in concept to equation (16). The only real dissimilarity between the two equations lies in the coefficient of distance; in the transport model (17) there is no reason for distance to perform exactly the same role as it does in Newtonian physics, so that b_3 is not restricted to equalling 2. In some applications of gravity models equation (17) is generalized so that d_{ij}, instead of being just the actual distance between nodes i and j, is considered as a general measure of impedance between them and it may be better represented by the travel time, travel cost or generalized cost (that is the travel cost plus the product of the travel time and the monetary evaluation of time).

More sophisticated variants of the gravity model (17) have been developed. For example, in recreation, Baxter and Ewing (1981) have modified the model to allow for multi-stop trips.

The gravity law of spatial interaction has been popular as a tool of spatial analysis because of its empirical regularity, but it suffers from several drawbacks. One severe problem is that as an analogy it lacks a firm theoretical foundation, and this means, moreover, that there is little theory to explain the values of the parameters in the model. When attempts have been made to strengthen the theoretical foundation of the gravity model, it has been shown that the model only applies under very restrictive conditions. For example, Wilson (1967) demonstrates that gravity models can only be valid if a homogeneous person/trip purpose category is being considered. If, therefore, the area of interest were extended to trips made by people with differing incomes, then immediately the gravity model (17) ceases to apply and a more sophisticated theory of travel demand is required. Thus, in applying this simple gravity model to the real world, the problem arises that many variables which theoretically should be present do not appear in the formulation

More complex formulations of spatial models may additionally include as explanatory variables origin income, the price level in the destination, substitute prices etc. The final form of the model may thus closely resemble the consumer theory-based demand function considered earlier, in spite of the different framework from which the model was derived. These more complicated spatial models include the intervening opportunities model (Pyers, 1966), the alternative opportunities model (Long, 1970) and models of the demand for abstract transport modes (Quandt and Baumol, 1969; Quandt and Young, 1969; Young, 1969).

Most of the recent econometric studies of tourism/recreation demand have not directly followed the spatial model approach. However, the commonly accepted multiplicative functional form of the demand function follows directly from the gravity model specification. Furthermore, the spatial model origins of certain models explaining tourism/recreation demand can be readily traced (Crampon and Tan, 1973; Witt, 1980a, 1980b; Kliman, 1981).

Box—Jenkins multivariate method

The Box–Jenkins (1970) multivariate (or transfer function) approach to forecasting is considerably more complicated than the Box–Jenkins univariate method. It is a causal forecasting method in that other variables are allowed to influence the forecast variable. As with the Box–Jenkins univariate method, the model incorporates autoregressive and moving-average terms, and complex mathematical and statistical algorithms are involved. However, the existence of more than one time series results in additional modelling problems. Again, experience is essential in order to apply the technique successfully.

Box–Jenkins multivariate models may be viewed as extensions of the multiple linear regression model. For example, if there are just two explanatory variables, then the linear regression model

(18) $Y = b_1 X_1 + b_2 X_2 + U$

where

Y is the dependent variable;
X_1, X_2 are independent variables;
U is an error term and
b_1, b_2 are parameters

may be modified as follows:

1. the terms $b_i X_i$, $i = 1, 2$ can be replaced by transfer function models which permit present and past values of X_i to influence Y;
2. the error term can be allowed to follow an ARIMA model.

The multivariate Box–Jenkins model corresponding to the regression model (18) is thus

(19) $Y = Y_1 + Y_2 + Y_n$

where

Y_1, Y_2 are the input components of Y, such that $Y_i = TF_i(X_i)$, $i = 1, 2$,
    (TF denotes transfer function), and
Y_n is the noise component, such that $Y_n = \text{ARIMA}\,(U)$.

Y is therefore the sum of components which are not directly observed, but which are determined in the process of fitting the model.

Qualitative forecasting methods

Qualitative approaches to forecasting 'depend upon the accumulated experience of individual experts or groups of people assembled together to predict the likely outcome of events. This approach is most appropriate where data are insufficient or inadequate for processing, or where changes of a previously unexperienced dimension make numerical analysis inappropriate' (Archer, 1980: 9–10).

Delphi technique

The Delphi method of forecasting aims to obtain expert opinion about the future through questionnaire surveys of a group of experts in the field, and is particularly useful for long-term forecasting. The respondents provide their estimates of the probabilities of certain specified conditions or events occurring in the future, and estimate when the events would be likely to occur. Strict anonymity is maintained to prevent dominant personalities from swaying the opinions of others. A Delphi study involves several iterative rounds, and at each stage the derived group opinion is fed back to the participants in the form of the range and distribution of responses. The panel members are requested to re-evaluate their previous replies in the light of the summary group opinion and to justify any answers which would still differ greatly from the overall group opinion. The experts are thus able to try to convince one another about their views. Eventually a group consensus emerges and it is possible to draw up a forecast. This is usually stated in terms of the *median* group responses to the various scenarios. The steps involved in executing a Delphi forecast are summarized in Figure 1.2.

The assumptions underlying the Delphi approach are first that the range of responses will decrease and converge towards the mid-range of the distribution, and second that the median response will move towards the 'correct' answer with each succeeding round of questionnaires. The distinguishing characteristics of Delphi forecasting are the aim: to generate aggregate expert opinion about the future; and the method used: iterative polling of participants with feedback of group opinion between polls.

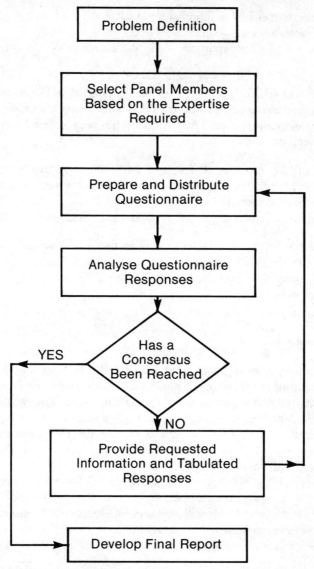

Figure 1.2 *Delphi flow diagram*
Source: Taylor, R. E., Judd, L. L., 1989.

Delphi forecasts are usually fairly reliable. As Parenté and Anderson-Parenté (1987: 130) point out, 'The characteristic phenomenon of Delphi is that the group response is typically more accurate than the average panellist's projections, and it is frequently more accurate than the most accurate panellist, if that individual could have been identified a priori'.

Seely *et al.* (1980) used the Delphi technique to forecast tourism trends in the 1980s. Among the forecasts generated by the study were the following:

1. natural resources will be rationed for tourism activities;
2. border formalities will be relaxed;
3. tourism will play an important role in the economic development of most countries.

Moeller and Shafer (1987) report the results of a Delphi study into recreation forecasting carried out in 1974, and compare the predictions with the outturn of events to date. The forecast trends seem broadly correct so far, and in general imply that:

1. action will be taken at all levels of government to face environmental pressures brought about by the increasing demands of a growing population with more time and money;
2. rational resource planning will be coupled with rigid, enforced controls.

An earlier example of a Delphi study in the recreation area is given in Dyck and Emery (1970). The object of this study was to forecast the pattern of work and leisure time over the period 1970 to 2005, and the ways in which leisure time would be spent.

Scenario writing

Scenario writing is an approach to forecasting which attempts to show how a particular future state (or set of alternative future states) could eventually occur, given the current situation as the starting point. The construction of scenarios is a method of assessing potential long-range economic, political, technical and societal developments. Scenarios describe alternative hypothetical futures, which are determined by our actions in the present (Jungermann and Thüring, 1987).

Van Doorn (1986: 36) suggests the following definition: 'A scenario gives a description of the present situation, of one or more possible and/or desired situation(s) and of one or more sequence(s) of events, which can connect the present and future situation(s).' It therefore follows that a thoroughly written scenario comprises at least three components (Van Doorn 1984b, 1986):

1. *baseline analysis*, i.e. a description of the current situation;
2. at least one *future image*, i.e. a description of a potential situation in the future;
3. for each future image, at least one *future path* which indicates how the current situation could develop into the eventual future image.

The application of scenario writing to the tourism/recreation demand forecasting area involves the description of a hypothetical sequence of events showing how demand would be likely to be influenced by particular causal processes. As Archer (1980: 10) notes, 'Attention is focused both on the variables which affect demand and on the decision points which occur, to indicate what actions can be taken to influence the level of demand at each stage and what the repercussions of such actions might be.'

BarOn (1979, 1983) provides two examples of scenario writing in the tourism area. The earlier study generates forecasts of visitor arrivals in Thailand, and the later study forecasts of visitor arrivals by air in Israel and air travel abroad by Israeli citizens. The 1983 study is more comprehensive and contains the three components suggested by Van Doorn (1984b, 1986) as being necessary for a thoroughly written scenario. A team of experts (ministers of tourism and transport, airport authority, airline officials) prepared optimistic, intermediate and pessimistic scenarios which incorporated the effect of influences such as exchange rates, source countries' economic conditions, promotional budgets, increase in charter flights, etc. These scenarios were used for short-term and medium-term forecasting (12–18 months).

Schwaninger (1989) has written a scenario for trends in tourism and leisure demand up to the period 2000 to 2010, with particular emphasis on the situation in the industrialized countries of Western Europe. He takes into account the various factors—economic, political, technological, ecological and socio-cultural—which are likely to influence this demand.

Assessment and comparison of forecasting ability

There are many studies which seek to explain the demand for tourism/recreation, and often such studies suggest that the models may be used for forecasting purposes. Furthermore, there are several studies which purport to compare the forecasting ability of different techniques. However, in general, in the tourism/recreation area, models which are constructed to explain demand are rarely used to generate outside sample forecasts which are then evaluated in terms of accuracy, and there are few comparative studies of forecasting accuracy which examine outside sample forecasting ability. As Van Doorn (1982: 164) points out, 'Despite the growing file of reports on tourism forecasting, surprisingly little attention is paid to the comparison of actual data with the corresponding forecasts.'

The assessment of forecasting ability on the basis of model fit, i.e. within sample forecasting ability, is likely to give a flattering impression of a model's ability to forecast accurately. Out-of-sample forecasting represents the situation faced by the forecaster in reality and is also a more stringent test. Thus Fildes (1985: 552) states that, 'only *empirical outside sample comparisons* will be given full weight ... it is all too easy to develop theoretically attractive models and then find data to fit them. What is more difficult is to develop models that can withstand the rigours of being tested on fresh data.'

Studies which compare the accuracy of forecasts of tourism/recreation demand generated by various techniques are now examined. Attention is restricted to those studies which focus on outside sample comparisons.

Exponential smoothing versus univariate Box—Jenkins

Geurts and Ibrahim (1975) compare the forecasting ability of univariate Box–Jenkins and exponential smoothing methods using monthly data on tourists visiting Hawaii over the period 1952–71. Their results show that the two techniques forecast equally well, with Theil's (1966) U statistic taking the values 0.102 and 0.103 for Box–Jenkins and exponential smoothing, respectively, over 24 one-period-ahead forecasts. Geurts (1982) extends the earlier study by introducing a third forecasting method into the comparison—'data modified exponential double smoothing', i.e. an exponential model using a series of data modified to take out the effect of atypical events. He obtains a U value of 0.075 for this method, and thus concludes that it provides the most accurate forecasts of the three methods.

Multivariate Box—Jenkins versus univariate Box—Jenkins

Wandner and Van Erden (1980) estimate Box–Jenkins univariate and transfer function models using monthly data on United States' arrivals in Puerto Rico. The multivariate model relates the United States' arrivals data to the insured unemployment rate in New York (the main origin area) which is taken to be a general measure of economic activity. Forecasts are generated for each month over the period July 1977 to June 1978, and mean absolute percentage error (MAPE)s calculated over six- and 12-month periods. The results show that over the period July 1977 to June 1978, and mean absolute percentage errors (MAPEs) calculated over six- and 12-month periods. The results show that respectively), but that over the longer time horizon the univariate model generates more accurate forecasts (MAPE = 5.0 per cent) than the transfer function model (MAPE = 5.4 per cent).

Econometrics versus univariate Box—Jenkins

Fritz, Brandon and Xander (1984) examine the effects of combining quarterly econometric and univariate Box–Jenkins forecasts of air arrivals in Florida. Within this study the relative forecasting accuracy of the two techniques can be compared. It is clear that the econometric model outperforms the Box–Jenkins model; in fact the mean square error of the econometric forecasts is less than half the size of that of the Box–Jenkins forecasts for one period ahead, and less than one-third for four periods ahead.

Econometrics versus trend curve analysis (TCA)

Means and Avila (1986) present forecasts of United States' outward travel split according to destination country for the years 1986–90. These forecasts are generated by the TRAM econometric model developed by Coopers and Lybrand and published by the American Express Publishing Corporation in the *World Travel Overview*. Subsequently Means and Avila (1987) analyse the performance of the TRAM model for one-year-ahead forecasts by comparing the forecast with the actual value for 1986. In addition, they evaluate the accuracy of the forecasts generated by the TRAM model relative to 1986 forecasts generated by trend curve analysis ('Growth Approach') for the Western European destinations. As well as providing the percentage error for both forecasting techniques for each of the European destinations, Means and Avila give the figures for Europe taken as a whole. The results show that the econometric forecasting method generates substantially more accurate forecasts than TCA (percentage error figures for Europe as a whole are 26.4 per cent and 42.7 per cent, respectively).

Multiple comparison 1

Van Doorn (1984c) uses data on tourist arrivals in The Netherlands over the period 1960–79 to generate forecasts using various techniques. The only forecast error statistics presented relate to summer 1980 and concern just four forecasting methods. The absolute percentage error figures for this single period (shown in brackets) give the following ranking of techniques: generalized adaptive filtering (2.3 per cent), univariate Box–Jenkins (5.0 per cent), Harrison's harmonic smoothing (16.0 per cent), and classical decomposition (19.3 per cent).

Multiple comparison 2

The most comprehensive study which examines the out-of-sample forecasting accuracy of quantitative forecasting methods applied to tourism data is published in Martin and Witt (1989). Seven forecasting methods are considered:

1. Naïve 1—the forecast for period $t + 1$ is equal to the actual number of visits in period t.
2. Naïve 2—the forecast for period $t + 1$ is equal to the actual number of visits in period t multiplied by the growth rate over the previous period.
3. **Exponential smoothing**
4. **Trend Curve Analysis**
5. **Gompertz**—an S-shaped curve fitted by non-linear methods, and often used to represent the pattern of a product life cycle.
6. **Stepwise Autoregression**—a linear regression is carried out in which the current value of the forecast variable is regressed on its historical values.
7. **Econometrics**—a full discussion of the econometric models is given in Martin and Witt (1988a).

Models are developed to forecast the following tourist flows: France to Italy, Morocco, Portugal, Spain, Switzerland and the United Kingdom; German Federal Republic (FRG) to Austria, France, Italy, Spain, Switzerland and Yugoslavia; United Kingdom to Austria, France, FRG, Greece, Italy and Spain; the United States to Canada, France, FRG, Italy, Mexico and the United Kingdom. The data used in the study are annual and for outward tourism from France and FRG cover the period 1965 to 1983; from the United States the period 1965 to 1984; and from the United Kingdom the period 1965 to 1985.

The various forecasting models are estimated over the period 1965–80 and used to forecast tourist flows in 1981 and 1982. They are then re-estimated using data for the period 1965–81 and used to forecast tourist flows in 1982 and 1983. For the United Kingdom and the United States the estimation period is then extended to 1982 and forecasts generated for 1983 and 1984, and finally, for the United Kingdom the procedure is repeated one year forward. Sets of one-year-ahead and two-years-ahead forecasts are thus generated for each origin.

The forecasting performance of the seven techniques in terms of MAPE is presented in Table 1.1. broken down by origin country and time horizon. Naïve 1, the 'no change' model, has the lowest MAPE of all the forecasting methods for each of the origin countries, France, FRG, the United Kingdom and the United States, when one-year-ahead forecasts are considered. On moving to two-years-ahead forecasts, however, autoregression performs best in each case. International tourism demand does change over time, and while a 'no change' forecast may prove adequate over a one-year time horizon, improved forecasting can generally be achieved over a two-year time horizon by taking the dynamics of a time series into account.

The relative performance of a particular forecasting method also varies considerably with the origin country being examined. For one-year-ahead forecasts the worst forecasts for France are obtained by using autoregression, for FRG by using econometrics, for the United Kingdom by using Gompertz, and for the United States by using trend curve analysis.

Econometric forecasts are not ranked particularly high overall in terms of accuracy, but the position achieved relative to the other forecasting methods varies considerably according to origin country. For example, econometrics is ranked second for the United States, third for France, fifth for the United Kingdom and seventh for the FRG for one-year-ahead forecasts.

The Gompertz curve appears to generate particularly bad forecasts; the highest ranking achieved by this forecasting method is fifth. TCA and naïve 2 are also not very accurate; TCA only appears once in the top three rankings and naïve 2 twice.

The relative accuracy of the forecasts generated by the more complex techniques compared with those generated by the naïve 1 model is particularly disturbing. In order to be useful tools, it is generally accepted that forecasting models should be able to predict better than the 'no change' model. For

Table 1.1 *Forecasting performance (MAPE) by forecasting method, origin country and forecasting horizon*

Forecasting horizon (years)	Forecasting method	Origin country			
		France	FRG	UK	USA
1	Naïve 1	9.06 (1)	5.80 (1)	12.73 (1)	11.94 (1)
	Naïve 2	12.76 (5)	10.55 (6)	15.73 (2)	14.10 (4)
	Exponential smoothing	9.38 (2)	7.29 (3)	16.72 (4)	12.95 (3)
	Gompertz	13.41 (6)	9.07 (5)	24.12 (7)	16.48 (6)
	Trend curve analysis	12.54 (4)	8.33 (4)	22.12 (6)	20.93 (7)
	Autoregression	13.45 (7)	5.96 (2)	15.81 (3)	15.03 (5)
	Econometrics	10.98 (3)	11.28 (7)	20.91 (5)	12.35 (2)
2	Naïve 1	10.08 (2)	7.59 (2)	18.24 (2)	19.43 (4)
	Naïve 2	22.13 (7)	20.77 (7)	29.42 (5)	17.34 (3)
	Exponential smoothing	10.22 (3)	12.17 (4)	23.24 (3)	20.48 (5)
	Gompertz	15.46 (5)	13.03 (5)	30.45 (7)	21.19 (6)
	Trend curve analysis	17.41 (6)	10.61 (3)	30.04 (6)	29.56 (7)
	Autoregression	10.04 (1)	6.10 (1)	16.75 (1)	10.73 (1)
	Econometrics	14.07 (4)	15.35 (6)	26.00 (4)	11.27 (2)

Note: Figures in brackets denote rankings
Source: Martin, C. A., Witt, S. F., 1989, 'Forecasting tourism demand: a comparison of the accuracy of several quantitative methods', *International Journal of Forecasting*, 5(1): 1–13.

example, Theil's (1966) inequality coefficient U compares the accuracy of forecasts generated by a particular technique with the accuracy of a naïve 1 forecast, such that $U = 1$ if the two techniques perform equally well, $U < 1$ if the chosen technique performs better than naïve 1 and $U > 1$ if the chosen technique forecasts worse than naïve 1. As Makridakis and Hibon (1979: 100) point out: 'The U-coefficient is a relative measure, it . . . allows comparisons with the naïve ($X_t = X_{t-1}$) or random walk model'.

Concluding remarks

There are many methods which can be used to forecast tourism and recreation demand, and selection of an appropriate technique will depend upon the requirements of the forecaster. For example, for short- and medium-term forecasting the various quantitative methods available can be split into causal and non-causal categories. Although 'Econometric models are not necessarily more accurate than time series (extrapolative) models' (Makridakis, 1986: 18), a major advantage of econometric models over univariate time-series models is that the former explicitly take into account the impact on the variable to be forecast of changes in the determining forces, permitting a company to link its forecasting with tactical and strategic plans for the future. Thus a company in the international tourism industry can use an econometric forecasting system to explore the consequences of alternative future policies on tourism demand ('what if' forecasting), which is not possible with non-causal models. As Makridakis (1986: 17) notes, 'the purpose of econometric models is not purely forecasting. Instead, they attempt to explain economic or business phenomena and increase our understanding of relationships between and among variables. To this direction econometric models provide unique information not available by time series methods.'

References

Archer, B. H., 1976, *Demand Forecasting in Tourism*, University of Wales Press, Bangor.

Archer, B. H., 1980, 'Forecasting demand: quantitative and intuitive techniques', *International Journal of Tourism Management*, 1 (1):5–12.

Archer, B. H., 1987, 'Demand forecasting and estimation', in Ritchie J. R. B., Goeldner, C. R. (eds), *Travel, Tourism and Hospitality Research*, Wiley, New York, pp. 77–85.

Artus, J. R., 1970, 'The effect of revaluation on the foreign travel balance of Germany', *IMF Staff Papers*, 17: 602–17.

Barnard, C. D., 1971, 'BTA's method of forecasting', in European Travel Commission, (ed.), *Papers Presented at a Seminar on Forecasting Tourist Movement*, British Tourist Authority, London.

BarOn, R. R., 1972, 'Seasonality in tourism—part 1', *International Tourism Quarterly*, Special article no. 6.

BarOn, R. R., 1973, 'Seasonality in tourism—part 2', *International Tourism Quarterly*, Special article no. 6.

BarOn, R. R., 1975, *Seasonality in tourism*, Economist Intelligence Unit, London.

BarOn, R. R., 1979, 'Forecasting tourism—theory and practice', *TTRA Tenth Annual Conference Proceedings*, University of Utah, Salt Lake City.

BarOn, R. R., 1983, 'Forecasting tourism by means of travel series over various time spans under specified scenarios', *Third International Symposium on Forecasting*.

Barry, K., O'Hagan, J., 1972, 'An econometric study of British tourist expenditure in Ireland', *Economic and Social Review*, 3(2): 143–61.

Baxter, M., Ewing, G., 1981, 'Models of recreational trip distribution', *Regional Studies*, 15(5): 327–44.

Bond, M. E., Ladman, J. R., 1972, 'International tourism and economic development: a special case for Latin America', *Mississippi Valley Journal of Business and Economics*, VII(1): 43–55.

Box, G. E. P., Jenkins G. M., 1970, *Time Series Analysis: Forecasting and Control*, Holden-Day, San Francisco.

Brown, R. G., 1963, *Smoothing, Forecasting and Prediction*, Prentice-Hall, New Jersey.

Burton, T. L., 1981, 'You can't get there from here (a personal perspective on recreation forecasting in Canada)', *Recreation Research Review*, 9(1): 38–43.

Calantone, R. J., Di Benedetto, C. A., Bojanic, D., 1987, 'A comprehensive review of the tourism forecasting literature', *Journal of Travel Research*, XXVI(2): 28–39.

Canadian Government Office of Tourism, 1977, *Methodology for Short-term Forecasts of Tourist Flows*, Canadian Government Office of Tourism, Ottawa.

Crampon, L. J., Tan, K. T., 1973, 'A model of tourism flow into the Pacific', *Tourist Review*, 28(3): 98–104.

Duke, K. E., 1981, 'Survey of travel forecasting techniques', in *Looking Ahead, 8th Annual Travel Research Seminar*, Christchurch, N.Z.; PATA, San Francisco, pp. 32–64.

Dyck, H. J., Emery G. J., 1970, *Social Futures Alberta 1970–2005*, Human Resources Research Council of Alberta, Edmonton.

Edwards A., 1985, *International Tourism Forecasts to 1995*, Economist Publications, London.

Fildes, R., 1985, 'Quantitative forecasting—the state of the art: econometric models', *Journal of the Operational Research Society*, 36(7): 549–80.

Fritz, R. G., Brandon, C., Xander, J., 1984, 'Combining time-series and econometric forecast of tourism activity', *Annals of Tourism Research*, 11(2): 219–29.

Geurts, M. D., 1982, 'Forecasting the Hawaiian tourist market', *Journal of Travel Research*, XXI(1): 18–21.

Geurts, M. D., Ibrahim, I. B., 1975, 'Comparing the Box–Jenkins approach with the exponentially smoothed forecasting model: application to Hawaii tourists', *Journal of Marketing Research*, XII (May): 182–8.

Gray, H. P., 1966, 'The demand for international travel by the United States and Canada, *International Economic Review*, 7(1): 83–92.

Gunn, C. A., 1987, 'A perspective on the purpose and nature of tourism research methods', in Ritchie, J. R. B., Goeldner, C. R. (eds), *Travel, Tourism and Hospitality Research*, Wiley, New York, pp. 3–12.

Holt, C. C., 1957, *Forecasting Seasonal and Trends by Exponentially Weighted Moving Averages*, Carnegie Institute of Technology Research Paper, Pittsburgh.

Jud, G. D., Joseph, H., 1974, 'International demand for Latin American tourism', *Growth and Change*, January: 25–31.

Jungermann, H., Thüring, M., 1987, 'The use of mental models for generating scenarios', in Wright, G., Ayton, P. (eds), *Judgemental Forecasting*, Wiley, Chichester, pp. 245–66.

Kliman, M. L., 1981, 'A quantitative analysis of Canadian overseas tourism', *Transportation Research*, 15A(6): 487–97.

Kwack, S. Y., 1972, 'Effects of income and prices on travel spending abroad, 1960 III–1967 IV', *International Economic Review*, 13(2): 245–56.

Little, J. S., 1980, 'International travel in the U.S. balance of payments', *New England Economic Review*, May/June: 42–55.

Loeb, P., 1982, 'International travel to the United States: an econometric evaluation', *Annals of Tourism Research*, 9(1): 7–20.

Long, W. H., 1970, 'The economics of air travel gravity models', *Journal of Regional Science*, 10(3): 353–63.

Makridakis, S., 1986, 'The art and science of forecasting: an assessment and future directions', *International Journal of Forecasting*, 2(1): 15–39.

Makridakis, S., Hibon, M., 1979, 'Accuracy of forecasting: an empirical investigation', *Journal of the Royal Statistical Society Series A*, 142(2): 97–125.

Martin, C. A., Witt, S. F., 1987, 'Tourism demand forecasting models: choice of appropriate variable to represent tourists' costs of living', *Tourism Management*, 8(3): 233–46.

Martin, C. A., Witt, S. F., 1988a, 'Substitute prices in models of tourism demand', *Annals of Tourism Research*, 15(2): 255–68.

Martin, C. A., Witt, S. F., 1988b, 'Forecasting performance', *Tourism Management*, 9(4): 326–9.

Martin, C. A., Witt, S. F., 1989, 'Forecasting tourism demand: a comparison of the accuracy of several quantitative methods', *International Journal of Forecasting*, 5(1): 1–13.

Means, G., Avila, R., 1986, 'Econometric analysis and forecasts of U.S. international travel: using the new TRAM model', *World Travel Overview 1986/87*: 90–107.

Means, G., Avila, R., 1987, 'An econometric analysis and forecast of U.S. travel and the 1987 TRAM model update', *World Travel Overview 1987/88*: 102–23.

Moeller, G. H., Shafer, E. L., 1987, 'The Delphi technique: a tool for long-range tourism and travel planning', in Ritchie, J. R. B., Goeldner, C. R. (eds), *Travel, Tourism and Hospitality Research*, Wiley, New York, pp. 417–24.

Oliver, F. R., 1971, 'The effectiveness of the UK travel allowance', *Applied Economics*, 3: 219–26.

Papadopoulos, S. I., Witt, S. F., 1985, 'A marketing analysis of foreign tourism in Greece', in Shaw, S., Sparks, L., Kaynak, E. (eds), *Proceedings of Second World Marketing Congress*, University of Stirling, pp. 682–93.

Paraskevopoulos, G., 1977, *An Econometric Analysis of International Tourism*, Center of Planning and Economic Research Lecture Series 31, Athens.

Parenté, F. J., Anderson-Parenté, J. K., 1987, 'Delphi inquiry systems', in Wright, G., Ayton, P. (eds), *Judgemental Forecasting*, Wiley, Chichester, pp. 129–56.

Pyers, C. E., 1966, 'Evaluation of intervening opportunities trip distribution model', *Highway Research Record*, No. 114: 71–88.

Quandt, R. E., Baumol, W. J., 1969, 'The demand for abstract transport modes: some hopes', *Journal of Regional Science*, 9(1): 159–62.

Quandt, R. E., Young, K. H., 1969, 'Cross-sectional travel demand models: estimates and tests', *Journal of Regional Science*, 9(2): 201–14.

Quayson, J., Var, T., 1982, 'A tourism demand function for the Okanagan, BC', *Tourism Management*, 3(2): 108–15.

Schwaninger, M., 1989, 'Trends in leisure and tourism for 2000 to 2010: scenario with consequences for planners', in Witt, S. F., Moutinho, L. (eds), *Tourism Marketing and Management Handbook*, Prentice-Hall, Hemel Hempstead, pp. 599–605.

Seely, R. L., Iglarsh, H. J., Edgell, D. L., 1980, 'Utilizing the Delphi technique at international conferences: a method for forecasting international tourism conditions', *Travel Research Journal*, 1: 30–5.

Sheldon, P. J., Var, T., 1985, 'Tourism forecasting: a review of empirical research', *Journal of Forecasting*, 4(2): 183–95.

Smith, A. B., Toms, J. N., 1967, *Factors Affecting Demand for International Travel to and from Australia*, Bureau of Transport Economics, Canberra.

Steinnes, D. N., Raab, R. L., 1983, 'A time series approach to forecasting angling activity at a recreational site based on past successes', *Canadian Journal of Fisheries and Aquatic Sciences*, 40(12): 2189–93.

Sturgess, B. T., Wilson, N., 1983, 'Forecasting advertising expenditure', *International Journal of Advertising*, 2(4): 301–16.

Summary, R., 1987, 'Estimation of tourism demand by multivariable regression analysis: evidence from Kenya', *Tourism Management*, 8(4): 317–22.

Taylor, R. E., Judd, L. L., 1989, 'Delphi method applied to tourism', in Witt, S., F., Moutinho, L. (eds), *Tourism Marketing and Management Handbook*, Prentice-Hall, Hemel Hempstead, pp. 95–8.

Theil, H., 1966, *Applied Economic Forecasting*, North-Holland, Amsterdam.

Tie-Sheng, W., Li-Cheng, G., 1985, 'Domestic tourism development in China: a regression analysis', *Journal of Travel Research*, XXIV(2): 13–16.

Uysal, M., Crompton J. L., 1984, 'Determinants of demand for international tourist flows to Turkey', *Tourism Management*, 5(4): 288–97.

Uysal, M., Crompton, J. L., 1985, 'An overview of approaches used to forecast tourism demand', *Journal of Travel Research*, XXIII(4): 7–15.

Van Doorn, J. W. M., 1982, 'Can futures research contribute to tourism policy?' *Tourism Management*, 3(3): 149–66.

Van Doorn, J. W. M., 1984a, 'Tourism forecasting techniques: a brief overview', *Problems of Tourism*, No. 3: 7–15.

Van Doorn, J. W. M., 1984b, 'An unexplored forecasting area in tourism: scenario writing', *Problems of Tourism*, No. 3: 63–73.

Van Doorn, J. W. M., 1984c, 'Tourism forecasting and the policymaker: criteria of usefulness', *Tourism Management*, 5(1): 24–39.

Van Doorn, J. W. M., 1986, 'Scenario writing: a method for long-term tourism forecasting', *Tourism Management*, 7(1): 33–49.

Vanhove, N., 1980, 'Forecasting in tourism', *Tourist Review*, 35(3): 2–7.

Wandner, S. A., Van Erden, J. D., 1980, 'Estimating the demand for international tourism using time series analysis', in Hawkins, D. E., Shafer, E. L., Rovelstad, J. M. (eds), *Tourism Planning and Development Issues*, George Washington University, Washington D.C., pp. 381–92.

Wilson, A. G., 1967, 'A statistical theory of spatial distribution models', *Transportation Research*, 1(3): 253–69.

Winters, P. R., 1960, 'Forecasting sales by exponentially weighted moving averages', *Management Science*, 6(3): 324–42.

Witt, S. F., 1980a, 'An abstract mode—abstraction (destination) node model of foreign holiday demand', *Applied Economics*, 12(2): 163–80.

Witt, S. F., 1980b, 'An econometric comparison of U.K. and German foreign holiday behaviour', *Managerial and Decision Economics*, 1(3): 123–31.

Witt, S. F., 1983, 'A binary choice model of foreign holiday demand', *Journal of Economic Studies*, 10(1): 46–59.

Witt, S. F., 1989, 'Cash flow forecasting in the international tourism industry', in Lee, C. F., Aggarwal, R. (eds), *Advances in Financial Planning and Forecasting, Volume III: International Dimensions*, JAI Press, Greenwich.

Witt, S. F., Martin, C. A., 1987a, 'Econometric models for forecasting international tourism demand', *Journal of Travel Research*, XXV(3): 23–30.

Witt, S. F., Martin, C. A., 1987b, 'Deriving a relative price index for inclusion in international tourism demand estimation models: comment', *Journal of Travel Research*, XXV(3): 38–40.

Witt, S. F., Martin, C. A., 1987c, 'International tourism demand models—inclusion of marketing variables', *Tourism Managment*, 8(1): 33–40.

Witt, S. F., Martin, C. A., 1987d, 'Measuring the impacts of mega-events on tourism flows', in AIEST publication vol. 28, *The Role and Impact of Mega-Events and Attractions on Regional and National Tourism Development*, AIEST, St. Gallen, pp. 213–21.

World Tourism Organization, 1978, *Handbook on Tourism Forecasting Methods*, World Tourism Organization, Madrid.

Young, K. H., 1969, 'An abstract mode approach to the demand for travel', *Transportation Research*, 3(4): 443–61.

2 Urban tourism: an imbalance in attention

G. J. Ashworth

Introduction

The growth of interest in tourism as a phenomenon for scientific study has more or less paralleled the growth of public participation in this activity in Western post-industrial societies albeit with some time-lag. Yet almost a generation's intensive study of tourism, from the viewpoints of a variety of academic disciplines, has resulted in a distinct imbalance in attention. There has been quite simply a rural bias noticeable in both the quantity of the literary output and the quality of the theorising about tourism. This is in itself remarkable because most tourists originate from cities, many seek out cities as holiday destinations and the social and economic impacts of tourism are substantial in urban areas. Thus the failure to consider tourism as a specifically urban activity imposes a serious constraint that cannot fail to impede the development of tourism as a subject of serious study.

A double neglect has occurred. Those interested in the study of tourism have tended to neglect the urban context in which much of it is set, while those interested in urban studies, itself a rapidly growing focus of academic interest, have been equally neglectful of the importance of the tourist function in cities.

Many of the researchers attracted to the study of leisure activities in what can now be considered to have been the founding years of the late 1950s and early 1960s were either land economists, like Clawson and Knetsch (1966) or the various authors of the influential American Outdoor Recreation Resources Review Commission (ORRRC, 1959–62), or geographers with a long-standing interest in land-use (see for example Patmore's (1970) influential textbook, *Land and Leisure*). It is not surprising therefore that recreation as a study became almost synonymous for a time with outdoor recreation, and thus also with rural areas where such activities were easier to identify, map and measure. Much of the underlying philosophy was implicitly conservationist and framed in terms of an inevitable and probably undesirable invasion of city dwellers into the countryside in search of spiritual renewal in a natural setting.

'It is frequently inferred by recreational studies that there exists some inherent opposition of the two environments, urban and non-urban, resulting in a strong and presumably widespread desire for residents within one to seek recreation in the other' (Stansfield, 1964: 198). Whether this was historically correct or a misinterpretation rooted in class attitudes, the result was a concentration of studies on leisure demands on rural areas and on facility planning in preparation for the 'fourth wave' (Dower, 1965) that was about to break over the countryside. Geography's most renowned theorist (Christaller, 1964), lent weight to this imbalance in one of the first spatial models of recreation which he confined firmly to the peripheries of countries and city regions. Even such spatial modelling as that of Miossec (1976) which recognized the importance of resort towns as tourist centres, nevertheless reduced them to homogeneous points within a regional system. Similarly much of the early interest in the economic effects of tourism was set at the regional rather than urban scale (see, for example, the various studies of Archer *et al.*, 1974, 1977) if only because of the availability of regional economic accounts. All too often the cities were considered only as the source of a tourist demand which spilled out over the surrounding rural areas in search of leisure facilities; Lundgren's (1974) development model of the city region is one of a number of such examples.

A new field of study with so much unexplored can be excused some selectivity. It is more difficult to explain why the numerous and longer developed investigations into urban areas have so consistently neglected the leisure function in general and tourism in particular, when almost every other aspect of the urban economy and physical morphology has received some attention. Pearce (1987: 178) understates the case: 'Given the impact which North American geographers have on urban geography in general their neglect of tourism in cities is rather surprising', and he refers to a handful of descriptive case studies of tourism in Western European cities that appeared in the 1970s in partial and unconvincing exoneration of Europe from the charge of neglect. Twenty years earlier Stansfield concluded after a long complaint over the 'non-urban bias' by the explanation, 'Apparently the relatively small output of urban recreational research may be partially attributable to past reliance on an inappropriate and inadequate methodology, which is inherently incapable of quantification' (1964: 22).

More simply, urban tourism was intrinsically more difficult to study than tourism in rural areas. In the cities tourism was less obvious because it was one of a wide variety of functions embedded in the urban economy, and with the exception of the resort towns, which significantly were excluded as an exceptional and discountable category in almost every classification of towns (following the influential example of Harris, 1943), rarely dominated large areas. On both the supply and demand sides tourism was closely linked with other urban facilities and activities. Few exclusively tourist facilities could be identified and visitors to cities had a wide variety of motives, spatial origins and patterns of behaviour. The tourism industry could not be identified in the same sense as the steel industry, tourist facilities isolated and mapped like shoe shops, nor tourist districts delimited like CBDs. It is not surprising therefore that very few urbanists had any understanding of tourism as an urban function or urban land-use. In 60 years of urban spatial modelling, tourism is ignored, rendered invisible by its very ubiquity. ·Tourism is a poor indicator of regionalization compared with many other urban functions and thus the traditional ecological structure models or urban economic location models fail to mention the tourist function.

Stansfield's 'inappropriate and inadequate methodology' is an indictment not so much of urban geographers who could not accommodate tourism within their existing frameworks of analysis, as of investigators of tourism who had, and largely still have, developed methods of approach that are unhelpful in this respect. What has occurred is that the nascent discipline of tourism developed in a systematic rather than synthetic way, spawning a variety of adjectival sub-disciplines concerned with various aspects of tourism as an activity, whereas the study of urban tourism specifically needed approaches that considered the place of tourism as one function within a multifunctional setting. The accent has been upon segregation as tourism studies have sought definitions and taxonomies of facilities, behaviour, resources and ultimately tourists themselves which has presupposed a necessary isolation of tourism supply and demand from its spatial and functional context. The very integration of tourism activities in the city, in both a functional and morphological sense, renders them particularly unsuited to such approaches. Tourism textbooks that begin with chapters searching for definitions of tourism and the tourist find it difficult to handle urban tourism, where neither the facility nor the user can be so defined, other than as an afterthought in a self-contained chapter of case studies.

This argument does not deny the value of the contributions of some researchers to tourism activities occurring in cities. Given the basic reality that most inhabitants of Western countries live and work in urbanized areas, it would be almost impossible not to include urban settings in studies of leisure behaviour. In particular in recent years those responsible for formulating urban policies have become especially interested in the impacts of tourism, whether these are viewed as desirable additions to the urban economy or undesirable intrusions on the city and its inhabitants. None of this interest, whether academic or policy-orientated, amounts to either an urban geography of tourism or a tourist urban geography, in the sense of a coherent body of techniques, concepts and methods of analysis allowing comparable studies to contribute towards some common goal of understanding either the particular role of cities within tourism or the place of tourism as an integral part of the form and function of cities. There is therefore a need for integrative approaches and this chapter will relate progress in the search for these. The choice of four broad categories of such approaches as a means of structuring some very diverse contributions necessarily imposes some constraints. The disciplinary bias is geographical in that the structuring element is a particular spatial environment, which is the consistent but by no means exclusive, concern of geography. The focus is upon tourism in the city, not upon the city as a source of recreational demands for activities located outside urban areas.

The four sets of approaches described are not offered as competing alternatives, each claiming an exclusive method of understanding the complexities of cities. The work of many researchers spans more than one approach. The ordering reflects only the chronological development of interest in the subject and contemporary work can be found falling into each approach. They do, however, provide a logical and convenient means of reviewing what has been achieved during 20 years' intellectual effort, and what remains to be done.

Facility approach

Approaches through the supply side appear to offer the advantages of visible, identifiable facilities at mapable locations. In addition, as much of the awakening interest in tourism was a reaction to actual increasing visitor demands, it is not surprising that the questions of the nature, quantity and capacity of facilities in cities would be posed early. Categorization and inventorization are preliminary stages in the development of most new areas of scientific investigation, and many attempted inventories of the tourist facilities of towns can be found especially among German (Maier, 1972) and French (Mirloup, 1984) researchers.

However the problems of the definition of the facility and thus its identification, measurement of quantity and location in space, together with the problem of comprehensiveness which afflicts all attempts at inventorization are likely to be more serious in tourism, or at least to appear at an earlier phase in the investigation, than is the case with many other urban services. As the tourist in the city is to a large extent behaving in a manner little different from a resident in the consumption of many publicly or privately provided facilities, the definition of what constitutes a tourist facility is fraught with difficulties, and from the viewpoint of the facility itself frequently irrelevant. An inventory of all urban facilities used by tourists would include most of the city's services, while the inclusion of only those facilities dominated by tourist demands would effectively exclude much of the catering, accommodation and transport sectors which are critical to the tourist experience but for which holidaymakers form a minority of the customers.

The solution adopted in many studies is the abandonment of any attempt at constructing comprehensive inventories, in favour of the selection of facilities that are appropriate to the analysis being attempted. Variables are selected which are indicative of particular aspects of tourist behaviour and which can be representative of a wide variety of other more ubiquitous or less easily identifiable facilities. The most commonly chosen are commercial accommodation facilities, some catering and entertainment facilities, especially restaurants and night clubs, tourist-oriented retailing and sight seeing attractions.

The problem of quantity follows directly from that of identification, and questions about capacity have been the subject of political debate (Lavery, 1975). The technical difficulties of answering the seemingly simple question of the tourist capacity of a city, with all the important policy implications for facility provision is aptly illustrated by de Groote's (1987) painstaking study of tourist accommodation facilities in Belgian cities. Different units of measurement (rooms, beds, 'bed spaces'), unregistered and dubiously legal, commercial accommodation provision (10–20 per cent of the total), non-commercial accommodation forms (free accommodation with acquaintances, non-commercial house exchange schemes) all conspire to frustrate a comprehensive inventory, and leave only the answers to more modest questions about the comparative position of particular cities, or the numerical balance between particular types, qualities or size of accommodation establishments. Similar attempts to measure other sorts of facilities used by tourists such as restaurants (see Smith, 1983), meet similar problems and produce non-comparable data. A recent study for example by Lerova (1987) concludes, 'at present the capacity of restaurants in the centre of Prague amounts to 100,000 seats at table, and this is far from sufficient', but the value of such a figure and how it is ascertained to be sufficient or not remains as unclear in this as in many similar urban case studies of tourist facilities.

After definition and inventory, a logical step was the locational analysis of such indicative variables. Although hotels cater for many different sorts of visitors they are one of the most visible manifestations of the urban tourist function, and being almost always in the private commercial sector, they are likely to be responsive to the same sorts of locational analysis as had previously been applied to other commercial services in the city. There are a handful of such studies of individual cities such as Madrid (Gutirrez, 1977); Christchurch, New Zealand (Pearce, 1981); Nuremberg (Vetter, 1985); Toronto (Wall *et al.*, 1985), and an attempt to present a range of case studies in comparable cities (Burtenshaw *et al.*, 1981). These remain descriptions of the locational patterns, some measurements of concentration and a range of inferences explaining the resulting patterns in terms of other urban distributions such as accessibility or local planning policy. Among the rare attempts to produce a spatial classification of hotel locations are Ritter (1985), de Groote (1987), and in more detail Ashworth and De Haan (1988), but as can be seen in Figure 2.1 these result in spatial taxonomies related to other urban distributions rather than explanatory models.

Similar studies can be found scattered through the literature using other tourist faculties such as restaurants, where Bonnain-Moerdijk (1975) claimed to have discovered a *gastronomic geography* of Paris, and others have traced the location patterns of various sorts of catering services in relation to other urban services (e.g. Gazillo, 1981) or in their spatial and functional relations to each other (e.g. Smith, 1983).

Similar, very largely descriptive, studies of the distribution of other tourist facilities in selected cases can be found for tourist shopping facilities (Werner, 1974; Dumas, 1982), night-life entertainment services (Burtenshaw *et al.*, 1981) and cultural and historical attractions (Wall and Sinnott, 1980; Moreschi, 1985). The main problem with all these studies is their partiality, in

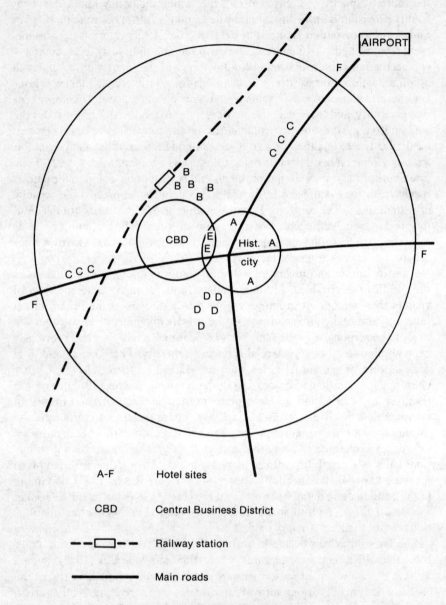

AIRPORT

A-F   Hotel sites

CBD   Central Business District

– –▭– –   Railway station

▬▬▬   Main roads

A Traditional market/city gates located.
B Railway/railway approach roads locations.
C Main access raods locations.
D Medium sized hotel on "nice" locations.
E Large modern hotels in transition zone of CBD/historic city.
F Large modern hotels in urban periphery
    on motorway and airport transport interchanges.

Figure 2.1 *Typology of urban hotel locations*

that however interesting the facility chosen for investigation, and however skilful the inventorization, spatial delimitation and description of the resulting patterns, they require an artificial separation of the facility and its users from the context in which it is enjoyed. On the demand side, any one sort of facility is only one element in the tourism package consumed, and on the supply side the tourist is only one element in the market for the service. It thus becomes very difficult to proceed further with this line of investigation into understanding tourism as an urban process without widening the method of approach so that the various facilities can be analysed in the same way that they are enjoyed, that is as a related package, and that the tourist facilities can be investigated in the functional context of the multifunctional city.

Ecological approaches

The clearly felt need for integration made *ecological* approaches more attractive even at a time when they were being widely abandoned in geography. The term had been used in urban geography since the 1920s, when such models attempted to identify distinctive intra-urban regions through a selection mix of indicative functional or formal characteristics so as to trace the relationship between such regions within the city, and thus hypothesize the processes leading to change. As biology had moved from the etymology of species to the interrelated ecology of areas, so also could tourism be considered as part of the city as a whole.

The obvious dominance of the holiday-making function within seaside resorts rendered them an early object of such studies, and Britain's pioneer development of this form of tourism, together with its tradition of historical studies of such places (see Gilbert, 1949 for an early example and Farrant, 1980 for a more recent one of the same resort), made British resorts ideal cases. Barrett's (1958) study of the spatial structure of some United Kingdom resorts must be one of the most cited dissertations in tourism, for it presented a seaside resort model within which accommodation, entertainment and commercial zones were related to each other and to the basic physical feature of the beach, and in which accessibility and centrality were used as explanatory variables (see Figure 2.2). Its very simplicity encouraged applications in many different environments and modifications of increasing complexity as more sophisticated examples were sought. Among the many variants of the structure model produced in quite different contexts were those in Britain (Lavery, 1971; De Haan and Ashworth, 1985); France (Clary, 1977; Pearce, 1978); Spain (Garcia, 1976; Mignon and Hernan, 1979); Mexico (Gormson, 1982); and Australia (Pigram, 1977).

Other types of holiday resorts were less commonly treated in this way, perhaps because they were frequently too small to produce convincing regionalizations. French and German researchers have applied the same methodology to winter sports centres (for example, Cumin, 1970) and some

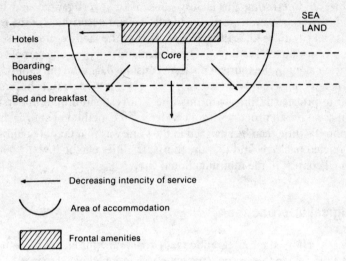

Figure 2.2 *Schematic model of an English seaside resort*
Source: *Wall 1971, after Barrett 1958.*

work exists on the structure of spas (e.g. de Haan, 1982). Cities offering a varied mix of historical or cultural attractions would seem to promise more fruitful results as they tend to be cities with both important tourist and non-tourist functions, within which the tourist resources are likely to form distinctive regions. Work on the location, concentration and functional implications of historical and architectural attractions (see for example Zywiecka, 1985; Ashworth, 1985) and on their role in visitor behaviour (Tunbridge, 1984) has been developed into a set of intra-urban structure models for tourist–historic cities (Ashworth and de Haan, 1986) and models of their development through time (Ashworth, 1987) (see Figure 2.3).

The next logical step is to consider not just the place of tourism within the individual resort but the place of resorts within regional systems. This can be done in terms of resort–market links, the links between urban and rural tourist places or more generally as the role of resorts within regional development. Much of this line of thinking has been advanced by French researchers (Miossec, 1976; Lozato, 1985) using empirical information from less-developed countries, but the specifically urban element becomes subsumed within the regional models.

All this work, however, focused upon that minority of towns where tourism was so dominant a function that they could be classified as resorts and therefore by definition exceptional places. Much less effort has been expanded on the less obvious but nevertheless ubiquitous role of tourism in non-resort towns, although the reception and entertainment of visitors is one of the most ancient purposes of towns. The resort function can be seen as a relative and not absolute condition. Among the rare exceptions to this neglect is the broadbased attempt of Yokeno (1968) to place recreational activities within the city in the framework of the classical land-use models that had been derived from concepts of land value, accessibility, transport cost and bid-rent. The results are a series of concentric zones around the theoretical city defined and labelled according to their dominant recreational purpose. The simplicity of such models, and the lack of any supporting empirical evidence, renders them of little value as urban planning blueprints but they did relate tourism to one of the main streams of urban geographical thinking. Stansfield and Rickert (1970) were even more successful in extending the concept of the Central Business District (CBD) to include their 'Recreational Business District' (RBD) variant probably because their work, which has been widely imitated, included both American case studies which applied the idea as well as a technique that allowed others to replicate the delimitation procedures elsewhere (see for example Taylor, 1975 for an application in South African towns). However the original definitions of the CBD depended upon the delimitation of exclusive land-use which is precisely what most recreational business are not. The RBD, like the Central Tourist District (CTD) described for a selection of major Western European cities by Burtenshaw *et al.* (1981), and the very similar ideas using a different terminology of Vetter (1975), is better conceived as one element in a multi-functional land-use of the central area of cities rather than a separately delimited exclusive zone.

One of the few sets of tourist facilities that have been treated within a much broader functional framework is the delimitation of inner urban entertainment districts. Although these can provide a major attraction for visitors, and in a few notable cities may be the principal motive for the visit (Wall and Sinnott, 1980), their location is generally determined by a set of urban morphological and economic processes, operating through a long history that have little to do with the tourism industry. The link between night-life areas as tourist entertainment and as a reflection of a series of urban social, economic and political circumstances is traced for a range of cities in Ashworth *et al.* (1988). In that sense this example of an aspect of urban tourism can be regarded as the most ecological, as it both combines different sorts of tourist facilities according to the purchased package of the customer, the night-out, as well as relating this aspect of the tourism industry to other urban functions within a multifunctional non-exclusive zone of the city, the entertainment district.

The very difficulties and limitations of the ecological approach are equally evident in the same example. The more multifunctional the city region, and thus the closer it accords with the urban reality, as pointed out by Vetter (1975), the harder it is to establish criteria for its delimitation. The purpose of the establishment of such urban regions is not the creation of any definitive urban mosaic in which every part can be carefully labelled, but the under-standing of urban processes. This in turn requires modelling that incorporates change. Most of the ecological models described above are essentially static, presenting descriptions of aspects of the city at one point in time, and attempts to build essentially dynamic models, not only accommodating change but

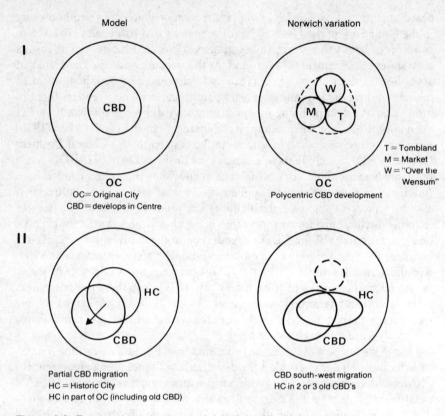

Figure 2.3 *Tourist—historic city model and the Norwich variation*

explaining it, are extremely rare. This is most likely because they are extremely difficult, and far more likely to explain the past than to predict the future as witness the handful of attempts to produce dynamic resort models such as Garcia (1976) and Butler (1980).

User approaches

Both the approaches discussed so far begin their consideration on the supply side, and although the explanation of many of the characteristics of the facilities may be sought in tourist behaviour, the visitor is peripheral to the analysis. The models introduced need peopling with users, if the way tourists use cities, and thus the impacts of this use upon the city as well as the controls the city exercises upon the tourist, are to be understood. Such an approach immediately confronts four questions:

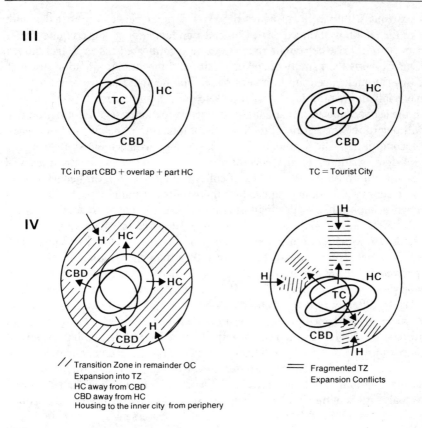

III

TC in part CBD + overlap + part HC

TC = Tourist City

IV

// Transition Zone in remainder OC
Expansion into TZ
HC away from CBD
CBD away from HC
Housing to the inner city from periphery

≡ Fragmented TZ
Expansion Conflicts

— Who visits cities?
— What do tourists do in cities?
— Why do tourists visit cities?
— How do tourists perceive cities?

The first three are strongly related, while answers to the fourth are generally used in explanation of the others. The ordering of the questions reflects both a certain historical progression in tourism research as well as an increasing inherent difficulty of research design.

Information on the various demographic, social and locational characteristics of visitors was collected in some of the earliest studies of tourist places. Tourist Boards and local authorities commissioning resort studies required such information, which was gathered by the simple expedient of asking factual questions of visitors (the negative controls which could be equally interesting, i.e. 'who does not come?' were conversely extremely difficult to obtain, needing home-based rather than site-based interviewing and rarely attempted).

Answers to the second question are intrinsically more interesting as tourist behaviour within cities provides the essential link between tourist demands and the facilities of the city as a whole. An understanding of even quite simple aspects of tourist behaviour requires quite complicated research techniques. This explains the paucity of useful studies and the strange situation in which cities can make accurate estimates of the numbers and nature of visitors but have only the vaguest idea of what they actually do in the city. It is the answers to the second question that contain the economic and social information that will determine the nature of the impacts of tourism on the city and thus are a precondition for the formulation of planning and management strategies.

A few examples of the sort of work conducted along these lines will demonstrate both the difficulties of collecting information on behaviour and the resulting limitations imposed on the results. Economic behaviour was of obvious importance to destination cities commissioning such research and a substantial and related body of studies of at least visitor spending patterns in relation to local economies exists (much of which is outlined in Vickerman, 1975). How visitors spend their time rather than their money in cities has received much less attention. A few studies have attempted to map spatial behaviour (see for example Chaudefaud's (1981) mapping of the actual routes taken by different types of visitors in Lourdes) which have tended to reveal the extreme spatial concentration of visitors and their sensitivity to variations in accessibility, features which will be important in determining both the extent of tourist impacts on the city and also the way such impacts can be managed.

Research into the last two questions involves the study of attitudes, motives and perceptions which are intrinsically more difficult to elicit than the more factual matters of the first two questions. An understanding of the expectations and reactions of the visitor to the city is nevertheless essential if any planning or management is to be undertaken by urban authorities and such understanding is already sought under the title of marketing policy by commercial operations. Despite its clear importance to all aspects of tourist behaviour the field is currently only vaguely understood and thinly researched by practitioners from a number of different disciplinary viewpoints. For convenience the three related aspects of the single process can be considered separately, not least because that is in practice how they have been approached. These are projection (the creation of ideas, information and images designed for consumption by actual or potential visitors to the city), reception (the stock of these images and the derived motives and expectations actually held by visitors) and transmission which concerns the various channels of information and perceptions between the visitor and the destination city.

Although there is an enormous and still growing level of activity in the projection of chosen images of cities as visitor destinations there has been very little systematic study of the phenomenon of city marketing at least outside marketing science (see Kotler, 1972; 1975) and even less on its specific application to tourism (see Schmoll, 1977 for an account of the mechanics of tourism promotion). The scattered literature specifically dealing with the promotion of tourist places includes Brown's (1985) historical account of marketing in some UK seaside resorts, Ashworth's (1987) attempts to classify different types of city marketing policies for tourism, and Goodall's (1988) overview of the process of destination promotion in tourist markets.

There is a substantial body of work on the formation of images of the urban environment (summarized in Pocock and Hudson, 1978) but little that has been concerned directly with images of cities as tourist destinations. There are many investigations of visitors to particular towns which include information on stated motives. Among more broadbased studies of the reactions of visitors to the characteristics of places are Relph (1976) and MaCannell (1976), the latter being especially concerned with the cognitive link between the tourist and the urban artefact.

Work on the selection and efficiency of official or unofficial channels of transmission is again largely confined to small-scale individual studies of such topics as the effectiveness of various media at the national level (see for example Crompton, 1979 or Dilley, 1986).

It is clear even from the limited selection of work mentioned above that studies of the tourist as user of the city have been richer in local detail than in comparable generalizations about visitor behaviour. Only rarely have links been drawn between perceptions, motives and actual behaviour in cities, and very few studies have considered the whole process of the projection, transmission and reception of visitor images for the same city.

The difficulty in conducting such studies is in part the familiar and practical one of data collection and in part a more profound problem of definition and conceptualization. There are many technical difficulties in collecting information on the attitudes and behaviour of tourists. In particular there is an absence of time-information, essential for the analysis of change, and data on the wider control population with which the tourist sample in any single city can be compared. Such difficulties occur at all spatial scales but are particularly apparent at the level of the individual city where there is generally an absence of the officially collected data that exists at the national and often regional levels. The conceptual problem is similar to that already encountered in studies of tourist facilities. The multifunctional city serves a multipurpose user. Attempts to produce finely drawn classifications of visitors on the basis of a single purpose for the visit is particularly unsuited to the urban tourist experience, as Jansen-Verbeke (1986) has pointed out in studies of visitor use of such near ubiquitous urban features as cafés, shops and periodic markets. Classifying visitors by the main purpose of the visit as a whole may have little relevance to motivation at the actual point of consumption. In other words from the point of view of the city and its facilities such overall categories as 'foreign tourist', 'domestic tourist', 'holiday excursionist', 'day tripper', 'conference visitor' and the like do not relate to any particular group of users of any particular set of urban facilities. Thus the study of any aspect of the behaviour of tourists in the city must come to terms with a visitor whose motives are not only mixed but change frequently during the course of the visit. Figure 2.4 shows one attempt to do this for users of the tourist–historic city.

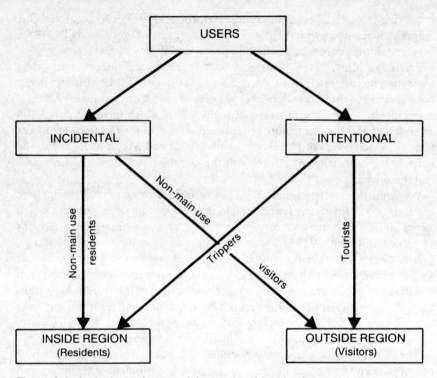

Figure 2.4 *A typology of users of the tourist—historic city*

Policy approaches

It is noticeable in general in tourism studies that the choice of themes of interest and the methods of approach have more often been determined by practical rather than theoretical considerations. The development of tourism as an academic discipline could be described as 'policy-led' in the sense that theory, the search for generalizations, conceptualizations and explanations has usually followed a research agenda that has been defined by immediate policy needs. This has been especially the case at the urban scale where tourism was recognized as an important threat or opportunity to be managed, planned or exploited by practitioners in the public or private sectors long before it was accorded similar recognition as an important focus of scientific study. Thus any review of urban tourism must acknowledge the role of a wide range of statutory bodies, variously designated in different countries, who have undertaken tourism research as part of their pursuit of particular policy aims in particular cities. The output of city government departments, local tourism development or marketing authorities, chambers of commerce and trade associations, as well as private commercial organizations, far outweighs the productivity of academic commentators. Much of this prodigious output was intended for local or even internal consumption and is therefore difficult both to obtain or to summarize, but as this has been the quantitatively dominant approach to urban tourism such a review cannot be avoided and has been attempted by some commentators. These efforts, in turn, are reviewed here and grouped for convenience into three broad categories of policies labelled **defensive, simultational** and **community**.

The extremely rapid growth in tourism in the late 1960s and early 1970s presented Western cities in particular with demands over which they had little control, and indeed of which they had little understanding. It was fair to comment that, 'Most cities do not consider it to be within their competence or authority to influence the size or direction of the tourist flow and confine their efforts to accommodating it' (Burtenshaw *et al.*, 1981: 161). It could be added that this *accommodation* was to involve as little expense or political disturbance as possible. The titles of influential publications of the period are themselves revealing. Young's (1973) popular paperback was called *Tourism: Blessing or Blight?* and the book's answer was national blessing but local blight, with the burden falling principally upon cities such as London. The content of the work of a string of witnesses throughout the period such as Hall (1970) or Lavery (1975) is usually either a discovery and definition of some new aspect of the problem of tourism in cities, defined as how to match facilities to a growing demand, or offers of solutions. As late as 1977 Eversley produced a comprehensive survey of tourism in London, the title of which expresses the mood, 'The ganglion of tourism: an unresolvable problem for London'. It is thus not surprising that the detailed urban policies, as they emerged, viewed tourism as an externally generated force acting upon cities to cause or exacerbate problems that the urban authorities themselves could only hope to contain, channel and mitigate the deleterious effects by defensive measures.

To single out the example of London, a city that experienced a dramatic growth in tourist demand in the period, a series of reports, discussion papers and plans warned of the impending threat (City of Westminster, 1972), signalled the problems of 'creeping conversion' of homes into hotels (Greater London Council (GLC, 1978) between 1961 and 1972, and produced the GLC's tourism plan (1974), which was in reality a tourism facility plan. Most planning actions were restrictive, including controls on hotel building or conversion, experiments with coach licensing for tourist sightseeing and even 'demarketing' promotion.

The onset of the economic recession and the related revival of political interest in the deteriorating economic circumstances of many Western cities, and especially their central areas, led to the widespread discovery that tourist activities were, if not a panacea, at least one of the few commercial enterprises which had a steady potential for growth, of a need for relatively large inputs of labour and an attraction to inner city locations. In 1971 the GLC had warned of 'the danger that tourism will call for precisely the sort of job opportunities we do not want' (GLC, 1971); a few years later they would be less choosy. In

Britain the English Tourist Board's influential report *Tourism and the Inner Cities* (1974) set an optimistic tone in outlining the ways in which local authorities and commercial operators could combine in using tourism as a support for local incomes, employment, services and physical infrastructure. A wide variety of **stimulational** policies resulted with a survey of progress to date appearing in English Tourist Board (ETB) (1981). The accent shifted from planning as a land-use constraint to development and marketing, and from a focus on supply to a concern with demand. The urban heritage was discovered to be a marketable product and was successfully sold in such obviously endowed cities as Bath or York, which were followed by the less obvious 'maritime heritage' of Portsmouth (Bradbeer and Moon, 1987) and the 'industrial heritage' of Manchester (Law and Tuppen, 1986). Not only was urban history and historical associations sold to tourists, but other traditional urban features such as centrality to transport networks and the very multi-functionality mentioned earlier were marketable assets in congress tourism (see Labasse, 1984, who traces the location of more than 4,000 annual international conferences, held in 39 cities, 22 of which are European); shopping tourism (Dumas, 1982); cultural or sporting festival tourism (Wall and Sinnott, 1980); and many other targeted segments of the urban tourism market.

Although Britain has been among the most successful of the West European countries in the conscious development of urban tourism especially by the marketing of heritage, parallel developments can be found elsewhere. The North American example of the use of tourism as an important element in revitalization of the inner areas of cities has been eagerly monitored (see the survey of projects reviewed in ETB, 1981; and the discussion in Murphy, 1980; and Wall and Sinnott, 1980). Notable in Europe are national concern with the urban historical and cultural heritage (see for the national-scale the example of France in Garay, 1980).

This new emphasis on the potential role of tourism as part of a package of economic stimulation measures has been reflected in new public planning initiatives in a number of countries. In Britain, Tourist Development Action Programmes (TDAPs) have been drawn up by some urban authorities for either a specific part of a city, such as *Norwich Riverside*, or for an entire urban agglomeration, such as *Portsmouth Harbour*. In The Netherlands the Tourism and Recreation Development Plans (TROPs) similarly cast the local authority as stimulator, coordinator and promoter with largely private investment realizing the facilities (Ashworth and Bergsma, 1987). Both TDAPs and TROPs are in practice inventories of existing usable urban assets, together with rudimentary market analysis and promotional ideas. Such plans are innovative in that they threaten to breach two previously more or less sacrosanct distinctions in public authorities: namely that between recreation facilities which are provided for residents on the basis of need and tourism facilities, which are the responsibility of a separate department and provided to visitors on the basis of commercial criteria; and second that between the public responsibility for infrastructure and private involvement in direct sales of services to visitors.

There is nothing particularly new about large-scale private investment in urban tourist facilities, or public–private partnerships in tourism development. What else was the traditional British seaside resort, or the nineteenth-century Continental spa, than a successful working partnership between local authority marketing and public infrastructure and private investment in accommodation, catering and entertainment facilities? It is therefore remarkable that the role of private investment decisions in shaping the patterns of urban development has gone largely unnoticed in tourism studies, especially given the growing interest in urban geography in the development process. Such neglect of the operation and impact of the international hotel chains, or the leisure conglomerates such as Ladbrokes, Rank or, in North America, the Rouse Corporation, can again be related to the tendency in urban studies to underestimate leisure, and in tourism studies to isolate tourism facilities from their wider urban context. Such private investments cannot be understood in terms of hotel beds or casino places alone but must be approached as part of multipurpose urban development projects, operating within property and investment markets. Even the new urban policy approaches outlined above with their accent upon development may in practice amount to little more than the substitution of a restricted and largely negative land-use planning approach by an equally partial vision based upon marketing, or even more restricted promotion.

Finally there is a third and distinctively different, although currently muted strand, in policy which accepts, and even welcomes, the existence of tourism in the city but which is equally concerned with its integration in the local economy and society rather than its existence as a foreign enclave. Murphy (1985) has termed this a 'community approach', and has traced such policies in a number of countries. In practice this approach is little more than a careful cost benefit analysis with the proviso that national benefits are no automatic compensation for local costs. It is a salutary reminder that tourism, *sui generis*, is neither a threat nor a panacea, and that the nature of the impacts upon the city will be largely determined by the relations between urban resources and the demands of any particular form of tourism.

Conclusions

A summary of what has inevitably been a selective review of a number of summaries of work in urban tourism can consist only of some very general answers to the two questions posed earlier: what has been achieved and what remains to be done in the search for integrated approaches to tourism in cities? It is the contention of this review that in terms of content the answers to the two questions are much the same.

The studies and policies that have been briefly examined above have all been attempts to relate the distinctive but varied set of leisure activities,

conveniently bundled together as tourism, to the complex amalgam of morphological and functional features that characterize cities. The common thread
joining together the extremely diverse material examined is this relationship
and thus attempts to understand it through integrative approaches, whether
from the standpoint of the facility, the ecological setting, the user or through
policy interventions. An assessment of past achievements and a suggestion for a
future research agenda could be encapsulated in the phrase 'more of the same',
in that these, or other interactive approaches, are essential. It is equally evident
from the work reviewed that too little integration, in another sense, has been
achieved. Many of the research studies are too individualistic in their choice of
subject matter, research design and areas of application to permit comparison
among them or generalization of wider application. This is particularly the
case with much of the policy-orientated work that is an inevitable response to
the problems and requirements of an individual city, but even with much of the
academic output in topics such as resort morphology, facility locational
modelling or visitor's spatial behaviour, where considerable expertise has been
developed and at least the beginnings of a comparable methodology and
considerable experience in data collection and processing can now be seen to
exist, there is little conscious attempt to draw from, or contribute to, a pool of
common knowledge.

To conceive of the city as a stage or setting which accommodates a
separately distinguished set of tourist demands, facilities and interactions is an
analogy which neglects the active role of urban life, resources and government
on those features of tourism. Urban tourism is thus not merely tourist activities
that occur in cities, but activities which with few modifications could equally
occur in other spatial settings. It is both a particular sort of tourism as well as an
integral, traditional and proper part of urban life. If this is so then a profitable
line of enquiry would acknowledge that different sorts of cities nurture
different sorts of tourism. A categorization of tourist motivation, behaviour,
facility demands and the like based upon the distinctive type of urban
environment is overdue. World-class multi-million cities, self-standing
provincial capitals, restructuring industrial conurbations, regional market
towns, medium and small towns with important historical or aesthetic
resources are some of the sorts of urban categories that could form the basis of
such studies.

References

Archer, B. H., 1977, 'Tourism multipliers: the state of the art', *Occasional Papers in Economics 11*, University of Wales Press, Bangor.
Archer, B. H., Shea, S., de Vane, R., 1974, *Tourism in Gwynedd: An Economic Study*, Wales Tourist Board, Cardiff.
Archer, B. H., Jones, D. R., 1977, *Tourism in Appleby, Keswick and Sedburgh*, Institute of Economic Research, University College of North Wales, Bangor.
Ashworth, G. J., 1985, 'The evaluation of urban tourist resources', in Ashworth, G. J.,

Goodall, B. (eds), *The Impact of Tourist Development on Disadvantaged Regions*, Socio-Geografisch Reeks 35, GIRUG, Groningen, pp. 37–44.

Ashworth, G. J., 1987, 'Marketing the historic city: the selling of Norwich', in R. C. Riley (ed.), *Urban Conservation: International Contrasts*, Portsmouth Polytechnic. Occasional Paper 7, pp. 51–67.

Ashworth, G. J., Bergsma, J. R., 1987, 'Policy for tourism: recent changes in The Netherlands', *Tijdschrift voor Economische en Sociale Geografie*, 78(2): 151–5.

Ashworth, G. J., de Haan, T. Z., 1988, 'Modelling the resort region: the Languedoc coast', *Field Studies 12*, GIRUG, Groningen.

Ashworth, G. J., de Haan, T. Z., 1988, 'Modelling the resort region: the Languedoc coast', *Field Studies 11*, GIRUG, Groningen.

Ashworth, G. J., White, P., Winchester, H., 1988, 'The red-light district in the West European city', *Geoforum*, 19(2): 201–12.

Barrett, J. A., 1958, 'The seaside resort towns of England and Wales', unpublished PhD dissertation, University of London.

Bonnain-Moerdyk, R., 1975, 'L'espace gastronomique', *L'Espace géographique*, 4(2): 113–26.

Bradbeer, J. B., Moon, G., 1987, 'The defence town in crisis: the paradox of the tourism strategy', in Bateman, M., Riley, R. C. (eds), *A Geography of Defence*, Croom Helm, London, pp. 82–9.

Brown, B. J. H., 1985, 'Personal perception and community speculation: a British resort in the nineteenth century', *Annals of Tourism Research*, 12(3): 355–69.

Burtenshaw, D., Bateman, M., Ashworth, G. J., 1981, *The City in West Europe*, Wiley, Chichester.

Butler, R. W., 1980, 'The concept of a tourism area cycle of evolution', *Canadian Geographer*, 24: 5–12.

Chadefaud, M., 1981, *Lourdes: un pèlerinage une ville*, Edisud, Aix en Provence.

Chenery, R., 1979, *A Comparative Study of Planning Considerations and Constraints Affecting Tourism Projects in the Principal European Capitals*, British Travel Educational Trust, London.

Christaller, W., 1964, 'Some considerations of tourism locations in Europe', *Papers, Regional Science Association*, 12: 95–105.

City of Westminster, 1972, *Hotels and Tourism*, London.

Clary, D., 1977. 'La façade littoral de Paris: le tourism sur la côte normande', *Étude géographique*, Editions Ophrys, Paris.

Clawson, M., Knetch, J. L., 1966, *Economics of Outdoor Recreation*, Johns Hopkins Press, Baltimore.

Crompton, J. L., 1979, 'An assessment of the image of Mexico as a vacation destination', *Journal of Travel Research*, 17(4): 18–23.

Cumin, G., 1970, 'Les stations intégrées', *Urbanisme*, 116: 50–3.

Dilley, R. S., 1986, 'Tourist brochures and tourist images', *Canadian Geographer*, 30: 59–65.

Dower, M., 1965, *The Challenge of Leisure*, Civic Trust, London.

Dumas, D., 1982, 'Le commerce de détail dans une grande station touristique balnéaire Espagnole: Benidorm', *Annales de géographie*, 506: 480–9.

English Tourist Board, 1974, *Tourism and the Inner City*, London.

English Tourist Board, 1981, *Planning for Tourism in England*, London.

Eversley, D., 1977, 'The ganglion of tourism: an unresolvable problem for London, *London Journal*, 3(2): 186–211.

Farrant, S., 1980, 'Georgian Brighton 1740–1820', *Occasional Papers 13*, University of Sussex, Brighton.

Garcia, M. V., 1976, 'Social production and consumption of tourist space: outline of methods applied to the study of the Bay of Palma, Majorca', in *ECE Planning and Development of the Tourist Industry in the ECE Region*, United Nations, New York, pp. 83–94.

Garay, M., 1980, 'Le Tourisme culturel en France', *Notes et études documentaires*, Direction de documentation Française, Paris.

Gazillo, S., 1981, 'The evolution of restaurants and bars in Vieux Québec since 1900', *Cahiers de Géographie du Québec*, 25(64): 101–18.

Gilbert, E. W., 1949, 'The growth of Brighton', *Geographical Journal*, 114: 30–52.

Goodall, B., 1988, 'How tourists choose their holidays: an analytical framework', in Goodall, B., Ashworth, G. J. (eds), *Marketing in the Tourism Industry: The Promotion of Destination Regions*, Croom Helm, London.

Gormson, E., 1982, 'Tourism as a development factor in tropical countries—a case study of Cancun, Mexico', *Applied Geography and Development*, 19: 46–63.

Greater London Council, 1971, *Tourism and Hotels in London*, London.

Greater London Council, 1974, *Tourism in London: a Plan*, London.

Greater London Council, 1978, *Tourism A Paper for Discussion*, London.

Groote, P. de, 1987, *De Belgische hotelsector: een economisch-geographische analyse*, Universitaire Pers, Leuven.

Gutirrez, R. S., 1977, 'Localizacion actual de la hosteleria Madrilena', *Bol. de la Real Sociadad Geografica*, 2: 347–57.

Haan, T. Z. de, 1982, 'Kuuroord: een onderzoek naar groei en functioneren van de Kurort Bad Bevensen', *Field Studies 5*, GIRUG, Groningen.

Haan, T. Z. de, Ashworth, G. J. 1985, 'Modelling the seaside resort: Great Yarmouth (UK)', *Field Studies 7*, GIRUG, Groningen.

Hall, P., 1970, 'A horizon of hotels', *New Society*, 12 March: 445.

Harris, C. D., 1943, 'A functional classification of cities in the United States', *Geographical Review*, 33: 86–9.

Jansen-Verbeke, M., 1986, 'Inner city tourism: resources, tourists, promoters', *Annals of Tourism Research*, 13: 79–100.

Kotler, P., 1975, *Marketing for Non-profit Organizations*, Prentice-Hall, Englewood Cliffs.

Kotler, P., 1972, 'A generic concept of marketing', *Journal of Marketing*, 90: 46–54.

Labasse, J., 1984, 'Les congres activités tertiaire de villes priviliges', *Annales de Géographie*, 520: 687–703.

Lavery, P. (ed), 1971, *Recreational Geography*, David and Charles, Newton Abbot.

Lavery, P., 1975, 'Is the supply of accommodation outstripping the growth of tourism?' *Area*, 7(6): 289–96.

Law, C. M., Tuppen, J. N., 1986, *Urban Tourism Project: Final Report*, Department of Geography, University of Salford/Greater Manchester Council, Manchester.

Lerova, I., 1987, 'The conservation and introduction of shops and industries in Prague', *Proceedings, Conference*, International Federation of Housing and Planning, Seville, pp. 77–87.

Lozato, J. P., 1985, *Géographie du Tourisme*, Masson, Paris.

Lundgren, J. O. J., 1974, 'On access to recreational lands in dynamic metropolitan hinterlands', *Tourist Review*, 29(4): 124–31.

Maier, J., 1972, 'München als Fremdenverkehrsstadt', *Mitt. der Geog Ges. München* , 57: 51–91.

MaCannell, D., 1976, *The Tourist: A New Theory of the Leisure Class*, Macmillan, London.

Mignon, C., Hernen, F., 1979, 'La Costa del Sol et son arrière pays', in Bernal, A. M. (ed.), *Tourisme et dévelopment régional en Andalousie*, Editions de Boccard, Paris.

Miossec, J. M., 1976, 'Un modèle de l'espace touristique', *L'Espace géographique*, 6: 41–8.

Mirloup, J., 1984, 'Tourisme et loisirs en milieu urbain et periurbain en France', *Annales de géographie*, 520: 704–18.

Moreschi, E. C., 1985, 'Le Tourisme à Padove', in Vetter, F. (ed.), *Big City Tourism*, Reimer Verlag, Berlin.

Murphy, P. E., 1980, 'Tourism management using land-use planning and landscape design: the Victoria experience', *Canadian Geographer*, 24: 60–71.

Murphy, P. E., 1985, *Tourism: A Community Approach*, Methuen, London.

Outdoor Recreation Resources Review Commission (1959–62), 26 reports, Washington D.C.

Patmore, J. A., 1970, *Land and Leisure*, David and Charles, Newton Abbott.

Pearce, D. G., 1978, 'Form and function of French resorts', *Annals of Tourism Research*, 5: 142–56.

Pearce, D. G., 1981, 'L'Espace touristique de la grande ville: éléments de synthèse et application à Christchurch, *L'Espace géographique*, 10(3): 207–13.

Pearce, D. G., 1987, 'Motel location and choice in Christchurch', *New Zealand Geographer*, 43(1): 10–17.

Pigram, J. J., 1977, 'Beach resort morphology', *Habitat International*, 2: 525–41.

Pocock, D., Hudson, R., 1978, *Images of the Urban Environment*, Macmillan, London.

Relph, E., 1976, *Place and Placelessness*, Pion, London.

Ritter, W., 1985, 'Hotel location in big cities', in Vetter F. (ed.), *Big City Tourism*, Reimer Verlag, Berlin, pp. 353–64.

Schmoll, G. A., 1977, *Tourism Promotion*, Tourism International Press, London.

Smith, S. L. H., 1983, 'Restaurants and dining out: geography of a tourism business', *Annals of Tourism Research*, 10: 515–49.

Stansfield, C. A., 1964, 'A note on the urban–nonurban imbalance in American recreational research', *Tourist Review*, 19(4)/20(1): 196–200, 21–3.

Stansfield, C. A., Rickert E. J., 1970, 'The recreational business district', *Journal of Leisure Research*, 2(4): 213–25.

Taylor, V., 1975, 'The recreational business district: a component of the East London urban morphology', *South African Geographer*, 5(2): 139–44.

Tunbridge, J. E., 1984, 'Whose heritage to conserve? cross cultural reflections on political dominance and urban heritage conservation', *Canadian Geographer*, 26(2): 171–80.

Vetter, F., 1975, 'Present changes in West German big city tourism', *Occasional paper 4*, Trent University, Peterborough.

Vetter, F. (ed.), 1985. *Big City Tourism*, Reimer Verlag, Berlin.

Vickerman, R. W., 1975, *The Economics of Leisure and Recreation*, Macmillan, London.

Wall, G., Dudycha, D., Hutchinson, J., 1985, 'Point pattern analysis of accommodation in Toronto', *Annals of Tourism Research*, 12(4): 603–18.

Wall, G., Sinnott, J., 1980, 'Urban recreational and cultural facilities', *Canadian Geographer*, 24: 50–9.

Werner, E., 1974, 'Die fremdenverkehrsgebiete des Westlichen Hampshire-Beckens', *Regensburg Geografisches Schriften 4*, p. 191.

Yokeno, N., 1968, 'La localisation de l'industrie touristique: application de l'analyse de Thunen-Weber', *Cahiers du Tourism Série C*, 9: 1–18.

Young, G., 1973, *Tourism: Blessing or Blight?* Penguin, Harmondsworth.

Zywiecka, D., 1985, 'Historical values of tourism', in Vetter, F. (ed.), *Big City Tourism*, Reimer Verlag, Berlin.

3 The statistical measurement of tourism

J. Latham

Introduction

Tourism is a complex process comprising many parts and interconnections, involving not only the visitor and his movements but also the destination and host community. It is not surprising therefore that it is increasingly being seen as an important area of study in its own right with some debate as to whether it can be considered as a scientific discipline with its own theoretical development and methodologies (Dann, Nash and Pearce, 1988). For discussions of the conceptual framework of tourism and its evolution as a discipline, see Leiper (1979), Medlik (1988) and Goeldner (1988).

The realm of measurement is particularly important in this context. 'An important part of the maturing process for any science is the development or adaptation of consistent and well-tested measurement techniques and methodologies which are well-suited to the types of problems encountered in practice' (Ritchie, 1975). Without a reliable historical and ongoing quantitative account of tourism, its development as an area of study would be severely hampered.

The statistical measurement of tourism is a relatively recent activity—its historical development is described in some detail by Burkart and Medlik (1981). Tourism statistics are typically measurements of arrivals, trips, tourist nights and expenditure, and these often appear in total or split into categories such as business and leisure travel. They are normally estimates, often based on sample surveys with grossing-up procedures, and are liable to large errors. Much of the methodology used to compile tourism statistics centres on standard social survey work involving questionnaires, interviewers, observers etc. and is well documented. Nevertheless, within a general framework of research methodology that is applicable in numerous areas of study, the statistical measurement of tourism does have its own peculiarities.

Problems arise because of the very nature of the populations under study. Tourists are by definition highly mobile individuals, thus making it difficult to ensure in any sampling procedures representative or probabilistic samples. Further, a mobile subject can be difficult to isolate for a period of time and the interviewing of tourists often takes place in unfamiliar surroundings, sometimes in locations where there are crowds or a high level of noise. There are other variable influences such as the weather: when interviews are conducted out of doors for example, periods of heavy rain can reduce response rates as well as affect the quality of information gained.

Even if the theoretical problems of sampling and its practical aspects can be overcome, serious doubts can still be cast on the reliability of tourism data. It is recognized that intentions studies (where measurement is taken before travel) are likely to produce information that is at variance with the reality that occurs at a later date. Data collected during travel represent a mixture of actual and intended behaviour, and post-travel measures involve problems of identifying and locating respondents as well as those associated with individuals finding difficulty in accurate recall. There are, therefore, methodological problems that may be present in survey research in general, but which are particularly acute in the measurement of tourism. For a fuller account of the unique nature of travel and tourism research, see McIntosh and Goeldner (1986).

It is the aim of this chapter to describe the current position and review the progress made in recent years in the collection and organization of tourism statistics; a discussion of methodological issues is included. For convenience, international tourism statistics and domestic tourism statistics are treated separately, although it is recognized that international and domestic tourist movements may be considered as different aspects of the same activity, with the result that there is much commonality.

Statistics of international tourism

Sources

In 1987 the number of international tourist arrivals worldwide was estimated to be 355 million, generating US$150 billion in international tourist receipts (BTA/ETB, 1988). These figures are the sum of estimates for regions which are themselves totals for individual countries. Such impressive values are in fact one point in an increasing trend and it is forecast that, by 1990, international tourist arrivals will approach 400 million (Shackleford, 1987a). Individual countries produce their own statistics; the two main compilations of international tourism statistics, both published annually, are

1. the World Tourism Organisation (WTO) *Yearbook of Tourism Statistics*, which has been published since 1947 under the titles *International Travel Statistics*; *World Travel Statistics*; *World Travel and Tourism Statistics* and its present title.
2. the Organisation for Economic Co-operation and Development (OECD) *Tourism Policy and International Tourism in OECD Member Countries*, sometimes referred to as the 'Blue Book'.

The Yearbook of Tourism Statistics (two volumes) provides a summary of the most important tourism statistics for about 150 countries and territories, and can be supplemented by the WTO's *Compendium of Tourism Statistics* (since 1985 published annually), a pocket-book designed to provide a condensed and quick reference guide on the major tourism statistical indicators. The OECD 'Blue Book' is more restrictive in the sense that its coverage is for 25 countries only, although these do include the main generating and receiving countries. As its name suggests, it is not merely a statistical compilation and is much concerned with an examination of government policy and planning and of the obstacles to international tourism. There are, however, areas in the 'Blue Book' which act to expand on the WTO publication. For a fuller analysis of sources, see Withyman (1985); Travis (1986).

Why measure international tourism?

Governments are keen to evaluate the dimensions and assess the significance of international tourism in terms of movements into and out of their own countries mainly to determine its effect on their balance of payments. There have been few countries in recent years without balance-of-payments' problems and in many cases tourism, as an invisible export, has been seen as a means of supporting a current account that might otherwise have been heavily in the red. It is for this reason that countries measure inward tourism more enthusiastically than outgoing tourism!

Outward visitors seem to attract less attention from the polsters and the enumerators. Of course, one country's outward visitor is another country's (perhaps several countries) inward visitor, and a much more welcome sort of visitor, too, being both a source of revenue and an emblem of the destination country's appeal in the international market. This has meant that governments have tended to be generally more keen to measure inward than outward tourism, or at any rate, having done so, to publish the results. [Withyman, 1985]

Governments' interest in tourism statistics is not merely in terms of the effect of tourism on balance of payments. Trends in movements can be monitored and information collected for official records. Statistics are used for planning purposes—a main aim of the WTO's *Yearbook of Tourism Statistics* is to present a comprehensive compendium of comparable data for the analysis of tourism development at world, regional and national levels. The marketing arm of government is also likely to make use of information collected, such as origins of international visitors. Tourism organizations at regional and local levels also make use of international tourism statistics as they seek information on which to base development programmes and marketing activities.

Finally, although commercial organizations within the tourism industry that use international tourism statistics are in a minority, nevertheless there are many for whom information provided can be of help, again mainly in the areas of planning and marketing. For example, an incoming tour operator needs to be aware of current trends so that programmes can be adjusted accordingly.

Shackleford (1980) considers that the collection of tourism statistics as an element of state responsibility to be both necessary and desirable, beyond economic and commercial considerations. Although most states do take this responsibility, the collection and analysis of detailed statistics requires commitment in terms of resources. It is only when the benefits, both economic and otherwise, are recognized that there will be a desire to compile statistical information in line with international standards.

What is measured?

Having outlined in broad terms some of the reasons for measuring international tourism, it is necessary to match what is measured against the purpose of measurement. An initial problem is the lack of comparability of data, not only in terms of the measures themselves (for example, visitor days or visitor nights) but also in terms of the procedures and methodology used (for example, different sampling procedures). This makes comparison between countries difficult although the OECD and WTO in particular attempt to make clear any obvious differences in data collection procedures and group countries accordingly. Further the WTO has organized various activities in the last ten years and has published much material with the aim of reducing differences in practice and terminology (WTO, 1981a, 1981b, 1983a, 1983b, 1983c, 1984, 1985a, 1985b).

Frechtling (1976), following an examination of the approaches taken by national and international bodies including the WTO, concluded that the travel industry was converging on definitions of trip, travel and traveller. He also identified three principles which need to be observed in the formation of definitions and terminology:

i. definitions should be discrete and unambiguous;
ii. definitions should facilitate measurement as much as is consistent with other objectives; and
iii. definitions should follow established usage as much as possible.

Clearly these principles are sound, though it should be noted that in 'normal' usage the term 'tourism' itself would refer to pleasure travel and exclude business travel. This is not in line with what has become accepted as standard as it is usual to include, as a tourist, a person travelling not only for pleasure but also on business, visiting friends and relatives and for other personal business such as shopping. Nevertheless, 'Americans display some aversion to the word tourism and prefer to talk about travel' (Medlik, 1988).

Traveller type is in fact central to the discussion. The official traveller hierarchy commended by the United Nations Conference on International Travel and Tourism held in Rome in 1963 has been adopted as the international standard. Figure 3.1 is a diagrammatic representation of the classification and shows the division of all international travellers into visitors (those to be included in tourism statistics) and others (such as immigrants). Burkart and Medlik (1981) provide concise definitions based on the UN recommendations:

A **visitor** is a person visiting a country other than that in which he has his usual place of residence, for any reason other than following an occupation remunerated from within the country visited.

A **tourist** is a temporary visitor staying at least 24 hours in the country visited and the purpose of whose journey can be classified as either leisure or business.

An **excursionist** is a temporary visitor staying less than 24 hours in the country visited (including travellers on cruises).

It is interesting to compare this classification of travellers with one given by Chadwick (1987)—see Figure 3.2. Note the different relative positioning of the terms **visitor** and **traveller**. Chadwick places to one side types of traveller generally regarded as being outside 'the area of interest', although these are included in some travel surveys. BarOn (1984) lists the basic standard definitions and terminology of the WTO and UN Statistical Office, and Ngoh (1985) examines problems relating to definitions and methodology in measuring international tourism, and different attempts made towards their resolution. Schadlbauer (1984) presents a case for alternative definitions of tourists because of the increasing number of second homes in tourist areas.

There are three main categories of statistics: of volume, of expenditure and statistics relating to the profile of the tourist and his trip.

Volume statistics

The most obvious measure of volume is that of the total number of international tourist arrivals/departures in a given time period. Such a measure relates to trips and not individuals in the sense that, for example, a businessman who makes ten trips in a year is counted ten times. A disadvantage of using this particular measure is that it does not take account of the length of stay, which is important to most suppliers of the tourism product such as accommodation establishments, though not for passenger transport carriers. A more satisfactory measure of volume for some purposes is that of total tourist nights as it is a measure of overall demand, but also acts as a measure of the likely impact on a destination in physical terms. It can be calculated as the product of tourist arrivals/departures and average length of stay. The implied equation here is exact, though of course errors in the values of the two terms of the product combine in the normal way.

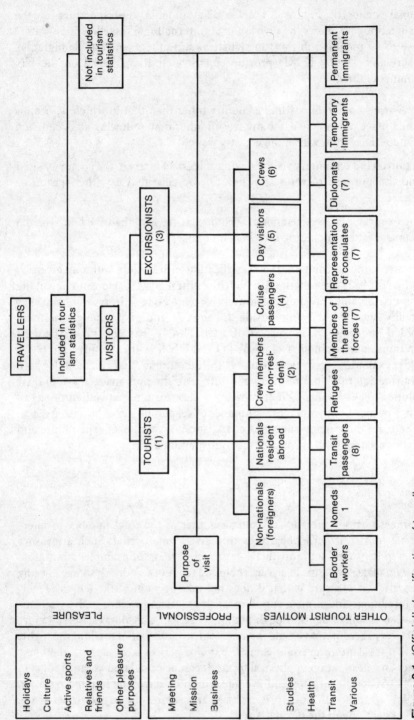

Figure 3.1 *'Official' classification of travellers*
Source: World Tourism Organisation.

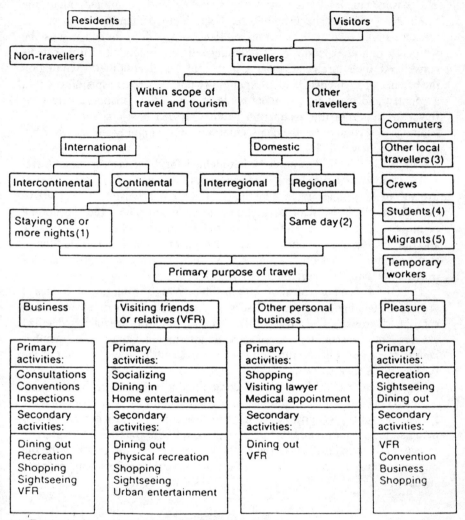

(1) 'Tourists' in international technical definitions.
(2) 'Excursionists' in international technical definitions.
(3) Travellers whose trips are shorter than those which qualify for travel and tourism, e.g. under 50 miles (80 km) from home.
(4) Students travelling between home and school only—other travel of students is within scope of travel and tourism.
(5) All persons moving to a new place of residence including all one way travellers such as emigrants, immigrants, refugees, domestic migrants and nomads.

Figure 3.2 *Classification of travellers*
Source: Chadwick (1987).

Expenditure statistics

The basic statistics of monetary flows are naturally compiled under the headings of income and expenditure. Total visitor expenditure is a simple measure of the economic value of tourism to a nation, though it must be tempered by the expenditure of outgoing tourists. Incoming visitors can be considered to be purchasing exports in view of the effect of their spending on the balance of payments. Tourist expenditure normally covers spending within a country and excludes payments made to passenger transport carriers for travel to and from the destination country. It can be classified under the headings of accommodation, meals, entertainment, shopping and travel within the host country.

The WTO (1985b) has published guidelines for the measurement of travel and tourism expenditure in the form of a comprehensive analysis of the items of expenditure as well as practical methods for obtaining statistics. The objective of their methods is to make available to member states, the developing countries in particular, operational tools to facilitate the collection, processing and publication of data, thus leading to greater precision in the evaluation of the economic impact of tourism. The WTO's *Yearbook of Tourism Statistics* provides statistics of international tourism receipts and expenditure.

The OECD is an organization with the objectives of promoting high rates of growth in member countries and sees tourism expenditure as an important catalyst of growth. The OECD 'Blue Book' therefore provides a detailed coverage of the economic importance of international tourism in member countries, in terms of receipts and expenditure, and the travel account in the balance of payments.

The difficulties involved in collecting reliable expenditure figures from tourists, coupled with the absence of a strictly enforced and all-embracing system of exchange control, have led to the accuracy of expenditure figures being seriously questioned (White and Walker, 1982; Baretje, 1982). Baretje considers there to be a bias in the methods used towards underestimating the number of tourists which leads to the measure of tourist receipts being prone to substantial error.

Profile statistics

Statistics relating to the profile of the tourist typically include details of age, sex, occupation, income, nationality or country of residence and group type. The profile of the visit or trip covers origin, destination, timing of visit, purpose of visit, mode of transport, type of accommodation, details of activities engaged in and places visited and whether the visit is part of a tour or is independently organized. Chadwick (1987) gives a description of trip characteristics used in North America.

Mode of transport for international tourism refers to the transport used to enter the country visited. It is interesting to note that a tourist who enters a country by plane and then hires a car may appear to be an arrival by road. The usual classifications of transport are air, sea, rail and road. *Type of accommodation* used covers a wide range of possibilities with much variation by country.

Methods used

In view of the difficulties involved in measuring the movement of people and associated variables, it is not possible to produce exact values. Most statistics of tourism are in reality estimates. Even though there are controls at boundaries between countries and currency controls and restrictions, these do not work to provide accurate relevant information.

Volume statistics can be the result of counting procedures either at entry/ exit points or at accommodation establishments using registration forms. These are supplemented by records kept by passenger transport carriers. In addition household and destination surveys will elicit information on international travel even though they are not intended solely for this purpose.

The procedures used at frontiers are often not satisfactory in that they do not always have tourism purposes in mind but are for administrative controls. Further, counting at entry/exit points does not provide an effective measure if no information is available on length of stay, as explained above. Counting using accommodation establishments gives only partial coverage—for example it may not be possible to estimate the volume associated with tourists who stay in the homes of friends or relatives.

Expenditure statistics can be derived indirectly using foreign currency estimates from bank records or from providers of tourist services and facilities supplying estimates of receipts. Increasingly information is obtained directly from a sample of tourists who are asked to provide details of their expenditure on leaving or, in the case of outgoing tourists, on return.

Some examples
(a) Canada

International travel statistical methodologies in Canada have been patterned upon the preponderance of travel between Canada and the United States (Baille, 1985). Taylor (1987) describes some of the research initiatives in Canada as a response to a review of data needs and availability. Canada's international market is divided into four groups:

1. U.S.A.
2. Countries such as the United Kingdom, West Germany and Mexico which have consistently produced a large visitor volume and have shown high growth rates.

3. Countries such as Switzerland, Sweden and Venezuela that have produced fewer visitors than those of the above category, but have shown consistent recent growth.
4. Countries that appear to have potential for providing incoming tourists to Canada.

A comprehensive research programme covering the overseas markets has been undertaken with different research activities conducted on a regular and planned basis in the overseas markets, the methods used being: voluntary completion of questionnaires by visitors to Canada; questions on national omnibus surveys in the countries in categories 2, 3, and 4 above (every two years); and personal interviews with residents of countries in category 2 above (every four or five years). Further details of Canadian tourism statistics can be found in Baille (1985), Taylor (1986 and 1987), Campbell (1986) and Wilk (1986).

(b) *The United Kingdom*

The UK has one single survey, the International Passenger Survey (IPS) which measures both incoming and outgoing international tourism flows in a consistent manner. It started in 1961 by covering only major routes but has since developed so that all the ports of exit/entry are covered. The survey is based on a stratified random sample of passengers entering and leaving the UK, sampling being carried out separately for air and sea. For further details of the sample design, see Griffiths and Elliot (1988).

The aims of the IPS are:

1. to collect data for the travel account (which acts to compare expenditure by overseas visitors to the UK with expenditure overseas by visitors from the UK) of the balance of payments;
2. to provide detailed information on foreign visitors to the UK, and on outgoing visitors travelling overseas;
3. to provide data on international migration;
4. to provide information on routes used by passengers as an aid to aviation and shipping authorities.

(c) *Developing countries*

Following a survey of 'tourism experts', Theuns (1984) concluded that there is a serious lack of reliable and uniform statistical information in developing countries. The World Tourism Conference in Manila (WTO, 1980) commented on the frequent duplication of tourist market information and called on the WTO 'to continue its efforts to facilitate the exchange of technical tourist information, specifically by considering the possibility of establishing a worldwide tourist information system'. Such an effort would keep expenditure on market research by developing countries to a minimum, since most are mainly interested in the profiles of small segments of the populations of the industrialized countries. It is possible for a number of developing countries to group together for research within the generating countries in a similar way to that undertaken by bodies such as the European Travel Commission (Shackleford, 1987b). Before market research is instigated, Shackleford recommends that relevant information be obtained from tourists visiting the country and suggests that departure surveys are particularly worthwhile.

Statistics of domestic tourism

Why measure domestic tourism?

The main difference between domestic and international tourism from the statistical point of view is that with the latter a frontier has to be crossed—this provides the easy opportunity to observe and record such a movement. Demand for accommodation and other services and facilities by domestic tourists may complement or compete with that by tourists from abroad. It is therefore desirable to analyse the two types of demand together, though in practice this is not as yet normally the case owing to the higher priority given to the collection of international tourism statistics and the greater difficulties of measuring domestic tourism.

Domestic tourism worldwide is in terms of volume much more important than international tourism. Generally figures underestimate true domestic movements, as visits to friends and relatives, the use of forms of accommodation other than hotels (for example, second homes, camp and caravan sites) and travel by large segments of a population from towns to the countryside are not for the most part included. The WTO (1984) reported that 'there are relatively few countries that collect domestic travel and tourism statistics. Moreover some countries rely exclusively on the traditional hotel sector, thereby leaving out of account the many travellers staying in supplementary accommodation establishments or with friends and relatives.' A full coverage of domestic tourism clearly requires the use of methods of collection other than the traditional use of hotel records, which may nevertheless still provide valuable information.

The WTO (1981a) identifies four main uses of domestic tourism statistics.

1. To measure the contribution of tourism to the overall economy. The authorities responsible for tourism wish to know its contribution to the Gross Domestic Product. Because of the complex nature of the tourism sector, there are enormous problems involved in this calculation— nevertheless estimates are produced.
2. For promotion and marketing policies. Increasingly countries are aware

of the need to encourage nationals to spend holidays within their country rather than abroad and develop campaigns to this end.

3. **To assist area development policies.** Many governments assume responsibility for the geographical distribution of domestic tourism with the dual aim of ensuring a better quality of the environment in the principal tourism areas, and to promote under-developed areas and relieve congested areas.

4. **To aid social policies.** A small but increasing number of authorities provide aid for the underprivileged either directly for holidays or in the form of subsidies for the construction and operation of socially orientated tourist reception plants (see OECD, 1987 for current developments). Because of the financial implications, a statistical knowledge of holiday-taking habits and trends by nationals is required for the formation of policies.

In addition to the above, use is made of domestic tourism statistics by regional and local tourist organizations in order to market and develop their own destinations; and by individual businesses within the tourist industry.

Definitions

Domestic tourism refers to trips undertaken by residents of a country within the national territory of that country. On closer examination, definitions do vary considerably:

(i) **purpose of visit**—all countries using this concept define a domestic tourist as one who travels for a purpose other than the exercise of a remunerated activity.

(ii) **the length of trip and/or distance travelled**—certain definitions state that the traveller should, for example, be involved in an overnight stay and/or travel a prescribed minimum distance.

(iii) **type of accommodation**—for practical reasons, some countries restrict the concept of domestic tourism to cover only those persons using commercial accommodation facilities.

The WTO (1983c) recommends the following definition of domestic visitors:

... the term 'domestic visitor' describes any person, regardless of nationality, resident in a country and who travels to a place in the same country for not more than one year and whose main purpose of visit is other than following an occupation remunerated from within the place visited.

This definition covers domestic tourists, where an overnight stay is involved, and domestic excursionists where the stay in the place visited is less than 24 hours and no overnight stay is involved.

What is measured?

Burkart and Medlik (1981) consider there to be two needs present for the measurement of domestic tourism: first to obtain the volume, value and characteristics of tourism of the population of the country; and second to obtain the same information related to individual destinations within the country.

The WTO (1981a) examines the concepts and classification of domestic tourism statistics in depth. It considers the minimum requirements to be:

domestic tourism arrivals and nights classified by
— the month concerned;
— the type and class of accommodation establishment;
— the location of the accommodation establishment; and
overall expenditure on domestic tourism.

Certain other variables such as length of stay, occupancy rate and average expenditure may be derived from these basic statistics. Data supplementary to such basic minimum requirements are in fact gathered by many countries and information concerning the socio-economic characteristics (age, sex, social group), mode of transport and purpose of visit is clearly of use in promoting domestic tourism. It should be remembered that resources in many of the developing countries are often limited and restrict data collection.

Methods used

As with international tourism statistics, statistics of domestic tourism are in reality estimates, subject to various forms of error and are produced with differing levels of accuracy. In recent years methods other than those based on the use of hotel records have been developed and involve eliciting information from the tourists themselves via sample surveys. The main methods are detailed below.

Household surveys are suitable for recording the tourism of large numbers of people, and a resident of a country, whether he travels within the country or abroad, can be contacted in his home. They are based on a knowledge of the profile of the resident population and provide a balanced view of domestic tourism for pleasure purposes. Further, in theory, they allow international comparisons to be made.

An example of the use of a household survey in Canada is given by Taylor (1987). The mainstay of Canada's tourism industry is domestic travel and there was a management stipulation that studies be carried out to measure the value, volume and characteristics of Canadian domestic tourism by the most cost-efficient method possible, and in conjunction with the central statistical agency, Statistics Canada. Statistics Canada runs a monthly household survey and government departments can purchase supplementary questions in units of 10,000 households. From 1978 Tourism Canada decided to provide four quarterly surveys of one unit each and covering travel in the preceding three months; other government departments or individual provinces could purchase further units if more reliable results were required for a particular purpose. Since 1982 the survey has been conducted twice a year, instead of four times, as a result of the evidence of stability of travel patterns prior to this date.

Most countries nowadays conduct national travel surveys and cover domestic travel and travel made by their residents to foreign destinations. In addition to providing profiles of those who travel, they interestingly provide information relating to those who do not. A national holiday survey is one which concentrates solely on holiday tourism, normally dealing with the previous year's holidays although in some cases interviewing takes place at regular intervals throughout a year in order to minimize recall problems. Less common is the all-tourism survey which provides a more comprehensive profile and an example of which is the United States National Travel Survey.

National holiday surveys are normally household enquiries. Medlik (1984) provides a source of reference for national holiday surveys in Western Europe and gives basic information about each survey, its scope and method and key indicators about holiday levels in some individual countries. Particular attention is paid to Britain, France and West Germany, the main generators of holiday travel in Western Europe.

Although trends can be monitored within a country on an annual basis, it is dangerous to make firm comparisons between countries because of the differing definitions and methodologies used. In 1967 the OECD Tourism Committee published details of common data that it recommended be obtained through national holiday surveys undertaken by its members (see, for example, the OECD 'Blue Book', 1979). Relatively little multilateral effort has been apparent to stimulate uniformity of statistics in the measurement of dometic holidays since this publication.

Destination surveys are normally limited to areas with high levels of tourist activity and can provide information outside the scope of a household survey on the volume, value and characteristics of tourism to individual destinations within a country, such as a region or a resort. Information is drawn from surveys of accommodation establishments (using registration forms) and sample surveys of visitors at the destination, and can build on details from a national travel survey which might provide data for trips to the regions of a country.

Enroute surveys, or surveys of travellers during the course of their journey, are similar to frontier surveys in the sense that a strategic point is selected for interviewing. The way the survey is conducted depends on the transport used. Its main advantages are that all forms of tourism can be covered and many interviews can be conducted in a day. However the representativeness of the sample is in doubt, making errors difficult to estimate because of an incomplete knowledge of traffic movement within a country. A further potential problem, as in most survey work, concerns non-response, particularly if the respondent is asked to complete the questionnaire in his own time and then to post it. Enroute survey response rates are optimized by selecting the respondent at a propitious point in his trip and collecting the information *in situ*—response rates of over 90 per cent are then possible (Hurst, 1987). Hurst reviews the use of enroute survey methods and provides guidance in assessing their value with regard to cost per interview, sampling error and control.

In addition, **surveys of the suppliers of tourism** services can be undertaken in order to elicit information such as occupancy rates, numbers of overnight stays, visitor numbers. In North America, for example, the airlines have been required through the Civil Aeronautics Board in the USA and the Canadian Transport Commission to produce origin and destination data from samples of used flight coupons from passengers on scheduled flights (Chadwick, 1987).

An example

There are four surveys covering domestic tourism in the United Kingdom, the results of which together provide a comprehensive statistical analysis. Figure 3.3 provides details of their history, coverage and survey design.

Methodological issues

Some different methods

Over the last ten years, the WTO (1979, 1981a, 1981b, 1983a, 1983b, 1984a, 1985a, 1985b) has produced several methodological publications relating to the collection, analysis and presentation of tourism statistics—for example, WTO (1985a) analyses in detail the methods employed by different countries. This chapter has briefly described, in the context of international and domestic tourism, the main methods in use.

Perdue and Botkin (1988) explain two general types of survey which tend to dominate state-supported tourism research in the United States. Inquiry conversion surveys are conducted in order to evaluate advertising campaigns and involve surveying a sample of individuals who request state travel information packets. The methodology is explained more fully by Ballman *et al*. (1984) and Hunt and Dalton (1983). Second, visitor surveys are used to monitor changes and trends in a state's tourism industry and involve surveying a sample of state visitors: Perdue (1985a, 1986) and Balden and Associates (1978) deal with this methodology. Perdue and Botkin examine the similarities and differences of the two methods and suggest that the methodologies provide different estimates of both visitor characteristics and travel behaviour. They

Survey	British Tourism Survey—Monthly (BTSM).	British Tourism Survey—Yearly (BTSY).	National Survey of Tourism in Scotland (NSTS).	Northern Ireland Holiday Survey (NIHS).
Commencing	1972 as British Home Tourism Survey. Annual and monthly reporting. Became BTSM in 1985. Monthly, annual and trend reports (6 per annum).	1951 as British National Travel Survey. Annual since 1960. Became BTSY in 1985. Annual reporting.	1984 with annual and monthly reporting.	1972 with annual reporting.
Coverage	All tourism by GB residents of 1+ nights at home and abroad.	All holidays by GB residents of 4+ nights at home and 1+ nights abroad. GB includes Isle of Man and Channel Islands.	All tourism by GB residents of 1+ nights to Scotland.	NI holidays of 4+ and 1–3 nights at home and abroad (outside NI). Trips for other purposes also collected.
Design	2,000 random in-home interviews of adults 16+ undertaken each month. Trip recall period is the previous two months.	3,500 random in-home interviews of adults 16+ undertaken in November/ December. Boosted by a further 5,280 interviews to raise the sample of abroad holidays to around 2,000. Trip recall period is the last 12 months.	Quota of 2,000 in-home interviews of adults 15+ drawn each month from randomly selected Parliamentary Constituencies. The sample is boosted by a further 500 Scottish households. Trip recall period is previous three months.	2,000 quota in-home interviews of adults 16+ undertaken in November/ December. Trip recall period is the last 12 months.

Figure 3.3 *Surveys covering domestic tourism in the United Kingdom*
Source: UK Domestic Tourism Statistics Review Group (1988)

conclude that inquiry conversion surveys are inappropriate surrogates for visitor surveys.

Diary questionnaires can be used in surveys of visitors to an area. The methodology involves giving visitors a questionnaire to be completed during their visit and returned by post after they leave. Although data collected may be superior to those produced by visitor surveys, its low response rate is normally considered a major limitation (Perdue, 1985b).

Unobtrusive observation of visitors and their behaviour is a relatively inexpensive and reliable method of collecting data about visitors in a variety of settings. Mullins and Heywood (1984) describe methods of observation and detail procedures to aid in the gathering of data.

A relatively cost-efficient method of acquiring detailed tourist flow information, called the front-end (FE) method, is described by Gartner and Hunt (1988). It has been developed, tested and utilized at the Institute of Outdoor Recreation and Tourism, Utah State University, and is shown to reduce non-response and recall bias to negligible levels.

By far the most common method of data collection is the personal interview. Hartmann (1988) however argues the case for combining and integrating different field methods and techniques. He describes research on the European trips of young Canadian and American tourists which used a mix of interview, observation and counting procedures. The information gained by the different methods allowed a degree of cross-checking of findings and 'new aspects and unknown dimensions of the tourists' habits emerged from the joint results'. Certainly there are opportunities to improve on methodologies used in the statistical measurement of tourism and the efficient integration of different methodologies is one way forward.

Some technical points

Cannon (1987) explains the basic concepts of sampling and sample design within the context of tourism studies. He explains simple random sampling, systematic sampling, stratified random sampling, cluster sampling and quota sampling, together with their advantages and disadvantages. In large surveys, methods are normally combined and sampling details of travel surveys in North America are given. Cannon also explains, with examples, the meaning of sampling and non-sampling errors. Aaker and Day (1986) provide a more detailed descriptive account of the different sources of error that may be present at the different stages of the research process. Griffiths and Elliot (1988) provide a comprehensive analysis of sampling errors on the United Kingdom's International Passenger Survey.

Butcher and Elliot (undated) describe the importance of standard errors during analysis:

The standard error of an estimate from a sample survey is a measure of the reliability of the estimate in that it indicates how close the estimate is likely to be to the population value. Survey analysts therefore need to be able to obtain standard errors for their surveys in order to interpret the results. For many surveys in the past, standard errors, if they have been calculated at all, have assumed a simple random design rather than the complex multi-stage designs that are usual for national interview surveys.

Little attention has been given to error analysis within the reporting of tourism statistics and it is rare to see an indication of error bounds associated with estimates. The usefulness of point estimates is doubtful without a knowledge of their precision, and trends may be misinterpreted without an understanding of the potential errors involved. The interpretation of results often depends on their reliability and so it is desirable that some reference is made to the sources and size of errors within the main body of a report. Further 'it is important that large-scale descriptive surveys which are likely to provide the main source of reference data on a subject for some time to come should provide a more comprehensive discussion of sources of error, including sampling error, than should smaller analytical surveys' (Butcher and Elliot, undated).

Butcher and Elliot, in addition to presenting mathematical formulae, based on work by Kish and Hess (1959), for calculating standard errors that take account of complex sample designs, also describe how their values can and have been used in the analysis of some surveys. A recent report on domestic tourism statistics within the United Kingdom prepared by the Domestic Tourism Statistics Review Group in 1988 examines 'a wide range of matters governing the successful sampling of tourism activity in the United Kingdom population' and identifies the unacceptable size of the BTSM (British Tourism Survey Monthly) sampling errors for Wales, Scotland and the English regions as a priority issue.

Sampling visitors to large geographical areas with relatively open access is a complex mathematical problem, often magnified by an inability to stop visitors at entry or exit points. Perdue (1986) examines potential sampling bias associated with duplicate listing in a sample frame obtained by distributing diary questionnaires to visitors. Such bias may affect visitor survey results concerning both visitor and trip characteristics and it is necessary to apply appropriate correction procedures.

Data relating to group composition are collected in most surveys of visitors, both at frontiers and within a tourist region. There are important methodo-logical and statistical problems associated with size of group. Latham (1988) explains bias that may be present in a survey due to group size for different sampling procedures. Heady (1985) examines procedures which use sampling based on:

(i) time—interviewing the first person to leave after a predetermined number of minutes; and
(ii) convenience—interviewing the first person to leave after the previous interview is completed.

He develops a model of visitor flow for these procedures which is tested on data from three visitor surveys and succeeds in predicting distortions in figures on group size. Unless adjustments are made, any procedure that assigns different probabilities of selection to individuals according to the size of group to which they belong will lead to biased survey results. Bias will not only be present in the distributions of group size, but also in any result that involves a variable which is dependent on group size. In some surveys, an individual is asked to complete a return for an entire group and often bias is created because the spokesperson is not a representative of the group. Holland *et al.* (1986) suggest that group type may be an important factor to consider and that studies based on large proportions of family groups are more liable to this bias.

The future

In recent years there have been moves towards a greater coverage of tourism statistics, together with the use of more sophisticated research techniques by the developed countries. There is concern about the reliability of estimates and analyses show that error bounds are not always within acceptable limits. There has been convergence in the area of definition although research designs do vary considerably, often of necessity, even in the collection of similar data on domestic as well as international tourism. The near future is likely to see refinements of methodologies used in many countries, together with attempts to ensure comparability of data on domestic as well as international tourism. For example, during 1988 the statistical office of the European Community has put forward draft proposals concerning the harmonization of European tourism statistics.

Modern technology is such that a global tourism database, perhaps under the auspices of the WTO, would be set up to meet information needs of countries all over the world. Certainly, in the case of the developing countries with their greater resource constraints in collecting statistics, this would be of great benefit, supplementing data that could be collected at a more reasonable cost, say, in the form of a destination survey.

References

Aaker, D. A., Day, G. S., 1986, *Marketing Research*, John Wiley, New York.

Baille, J. G., 1985, 'The evolution of Canadian international travel documentation', *Annals of Tourism Research*, 12(4): 563–79.

Balden and Associates, 1978, *Identifying Traveler Markets: Research Methodologies*, contract report to the United States Travel Service, US Department of Commerce, Washington DC.

Ballman, G., Burke, J., Korte, D., Blank, U., 1984, 'Towards higher quality conversion studies: refining the numbers game', *Journal of Travel Research*, 22(4): 28–33.

Baretje, R., 1982, 'Tourism's external account and the balance of payments', *Annals of Tourism Research*, 9(1): 57–67.

BarOn, R. R. V., 1984, 'Tourism terminology and standard definitions', *Tourist Review*, 39(1): 2–4.

British Tourist Authority/English Tourist Board, 1988, *Tourism Intelligence Quarterly*, 10(1), BTA/ETB, London.

Burkart, A. J., Medlik, S., 1981, *Tourism—Past, Present and Future*, Heinemann, London.

Butcher, B., Elliot, D., undated, *A Sampling Errors Manual*, OPCS, London.

Campbell, K., 1986, 'National task force on tourism data: progress report', in *International events: The Real Tourism Impact, Proceedings of the Canada Chapter Travel and Tourism Association Annual Conference*, Edmonton Alberta, October 1985, Edmonton, Alberta, Canada, pp. 67–75.

Cannon, J. C., 1987, 'Issues in sampling and sample design—a managerial perspective', in Ritchie, J. R. B., Goeldner, C. R. (eds), *Travel, Tourism and Hospitality Research: A Handbook for Managers and Researchers*, John Wiley & Sons, Inc., New York, pp. 101–16.

Chadwick, R. A., 1987, 'Concepts, definitions and measures used in travel and tourism research', in Ritchie, J. R. B., Goeldner, C. R. (eds), *Travel, Tourism and Hospitality Research: A Handbook for Managers and Researchers*, John Wiley & Sons, Inc., New York, pp. 47–62.

Dann, G., Nash, D., Pearce, P., 1988, 'Methodology in tourism research', *Annals of Tourism Research* , 15(1): 1–28.

Frechtling, D. C., 1976, 'Proposed standard definitions and classifications for travel research', *Marketing Travel and Tourism, Seventh Annual Conference Proceedings*, The Travel Research Association, Boca Raton, pp. 59–74.

Gartner, W., Hunt, J. D., 1988, 'A method to collect detailed tourist flow information', *Annals of Tourism Research*, 15(1): 159–72.

Goeldner, C. R., 1988, 'The evolution of the discipline of tourism', paper presented to Teaching tourism into the 1990s, international conference for tourism educators, University of Surrey, Guildford, July 1988, proceedings to appear.

Griffiths, D., Elliot, D., 1988, *Sampling Errors on the International Passenger Survey*, New Methodology Series, OPCS, London.

Hartmann, R., 1988, 'Combining field methods in tourism research', *Annals of Tourism Research*, 15(1): 88–105.

Heady, P., 1985, 'A note on some sampling methods for visitor surveys', *Survey Methodology Bulletin*, 17: 10–17.

Holland, S. M., Fedler, A. J., and Ditton, R. B., 1986, 'The group representative bias: another look', *Leisure Sciences*, 8(1): 79–91.

Hunt, J., Dalton, M., 1983, 'Comparing mail and telephone for conducting coupon conversion studies', *Journal of Travel Research*, 21(3): 16–18.

Hurst, F., 1987, 'Enroute surveys', in Ritchie, J. R. B., Goeldner, C. R. (eds), *Travel, Tourism and Hospitality Research: A Handbook for Managers and Researchers*, John Wiley & Sons, Inc., New York, pp. 401–16.

Kish, L., Hess, I., 1959, 'On variance of ratios and their differences in multi-stage samples', *Journal of the American Statistical Association*, 54: 416–46.

Latham, J., 1988, 'The analysis of group size in visitor surveys', *Tourist Review*, 43(2): 5–9.

Leiper, N., 1979, 'The framework of tourism', *Annals of Tourism Research* , 6(4): 390–407.

McIntosh, R. W., Goeldner, C. R., 1986, *Tourism Principles, Practices, Philosophies*, John Wiley & Sons, New York.

Medlik, S., 1984, *Europeans on Holiday*, Horwath and Horwath (UK) Ltd, London.

Medlik, S., 1988, 'What is tourism?', paper presented to Teaching tourism into the 1990s, international conference for tourism educators, University of Surrey, Guildford, July 1988, proceedings to appear.

Mullins, G. W., Heywood, J. L., 1984, 'Unobtrusive observation'. A visitor survey technique', *Ohio Agricultural Research Development Circular*, Ohio Agricultural Development Center, No. 280, Columbus, Ohio.

Ngoh, T. S., 1985, 'Guidelines for the harmonisation of international tourism statistics among PATA Member Countries', in The Battle for Market Share: Strategies in Research and Marketing, Travel and Tourism Research Association, Sixteenth Annual Conference, California, June 1985, Salt Lake City, Bureau of Economic and Business Research, Graduate School of Business, University of Utah, pp. 291–306.

Organisation for Economic Cooperation and Development, Annual, Tourism Policy and International Tourism in OECD Member Countries, OECD, Paris.

Perdue, R. R., 1985a, 'Segmenting state travel information inquirers by timing of the destination decision and previous experience', *Journal of Travel Research*, 23(3): 6–11.

Perdue, R. R., 1985b, 'The 1983 Nebraska visitor survey: achieving a high response rate with a diary questionnaire', *Journal of Travel Research*, 24(2): 23–6.

Perdue, R. R., 1986, 'Duplicate listing sampling bias in visitor surveys', *Annals of Tourism Research*, 13(2): 261–87.

Perdue, R. R., Botkin, M. R., 1988, 'Visitor survey versus conversion study', *Annals of Tourism Research*, 15(1): 76–87.

Ritchie, J. R. B., 1975, 'Some critical aspects of measurement theory and practice in travel research', in McIntosh, R. W., Goeldner, C. R., 1986, *Tourism Principles, Practices, Philosophies*, pp. 437–451, John Wiley & Sons, Inc., New York.

Schadlbauer, F. G., 1984, 'Neue Tendenzen in der Frage der Definition des Fremdenverkehrs', in Hormeister, B., Steinecke, A., Darmstadt, G. F. R. (eds), *Geographie des Freizeit und Fremdenverkehrs*, Wissenschaftliche Buchgesellschaft, pp. 63–7.

Shackleford, P., 1980, 'Keeping tabs on tourism: a manager's guide to statistics', *International Journal of Tourism Management*, 1(3): 148–57.

Shackleford, P., 1987a, 'Global tourism trends', *Tourism Management*, 18(2): 98–101.

Shackleford, P., 1987b, 'Research needs of developing countries', in Ritchie J. R. B., Goeldner C. R. (eds), *Travel, Tourism and Hospitality Research: A Handbook for Managers and Researchers*, John Wiley & Sons, Inc., New York, pp. 141–52.

Taylor, G. D., 1986, 'Canada's mega travel research', in *Technology and Tourism: a Growing Partnership, Travel and Tourism Research Association, Seventeenth Annual Conference*, Memphis, Tennessee, June 1986, Salt Lake City, Utah, USA; Bureau of Economic and Business Research, Graduate School of Business, University of Utah, pp. 169–71.

Taylor, G. D., 1987, 'Research in national tourist organisations', in Ritchie J. R. B., Goeldner C. R. (eds), *Travel, Tourism and Hospitality Research: A Handbook for Managers and Researchers*, John Wiley & Sons, New York, pp. 117–28.

Theuns, H. L., 1984, 'Tourism research priorities; a survey of expert opinions with special reference to developing countries', *Les Cahiers du Tourisme, no 96*, Centre des Hautes Etudes Touristiques, Aix-en-Provence.

Travis, A. S., 1986, 'Statistics for tourism', in Midgley, C. M. (ed.), *Statistics for Sport and*

Leisure, SPRIG Seminar no. 1, University of Birmingham, May 1986, Sport and Recreation Information Group, London, pp. 47–51.

White, K. J., Walker, M. B., 1982, 'Trouble in the travel account', *Annals of Tourism Research*, 9(1): 37–56.

Wilk, M. B., 'National task force on tourism data', 1986, in *Technology and Tourism: A Growing Partnership*. Travel and Tourism Research Association, Seventeenth Annual Conference, Memphis Tennessee, June 1986, Salt Lake City, Utah, USA; Bureau of Economic and Business Research, Graduate School of Business, University of Utah, pp. 173–5.

Withyman, W., 1985, 'The ins and outs of international travel and tourism data', *International Tourism Quarterly*, Special report no. 55.

World Tourism Organisation, annual, *Yearbook of Tourism Statistics* (2 volumes), WTO, Madrid.

World Tourism Organisation, annual, *Compendium of Tourism Statistics*, WTO, Madrid.

World Tourism Organisation, 1979, *Survey of Surveys and Research in the Field of Tourism*, WTO, Madrid.

World Tourism Organisation, 1980, *Manila Declaration on World Tourism*, WTO, Madrid.

World Tourism Organisation, 1981a, *Technical Handbook on the Collection and Presentation of Domestic and International Tourism Statistics*, WTO, Madrid.

World Tourism Organisation, 1981b, *Guidelines for the Collection and Presentation of Domestic Tourism Statistics*, WTO, Madrid.

World Tourism Organisation, 1983a, *Methodologies for Carrying Out Sample Surveys on Tourism*, WTO, Madrid.

World Tourism Organisation, 1983b, *Techniques for Preparing and Disseminating Tourism Statistics*, WTO, Madrid.

World Tourism Organisation, 1983c, *Definitions Concerning Tourism Statistics*, WTO, Madrid.

World Tourism Organisation, 1984a, *Domestic Tourism Statistics*, WTO, Madrid.

World Tourism Organisation, 1984b, *Survey of Surveys and Research in the Field of Tourism*, WTO, Madrid.

World Tourism Organisation, 1985a, *Methodological Supplement to World Travel and Tourism Statistics*, WTO, Madrid.

World Tourism Organisation, 1985b, *Measurement of Travel and Tourism Expenditure*, WTO, Madrid.

4 Tourism marketing—its emergence and establishment
D. C. Gilbert

The theoretical basis of the marketing of tourism

A survey of the tourism marketing literature—which attempts to construct a holistic approach of the subject area—indicates the application of a structural approach. The majority of authors have organized their work around the evolution of marketing from a definitional level to a prescriptive management process level. Here, the subject area is seen as being philosophically grounded in an initial definition which logically leads to particular concepts and ultimately a marketing orientation. The structure is circular as the definition has to emanate out of the practice and knowledge built up by the application of marketing in industrial management situations (Middleton, 1988; Holloway and Plant, 1988; Schmoll, 1977 and to a lesser extent Burkart and Medlik, 1981; Wahab *et al.*, 1976).

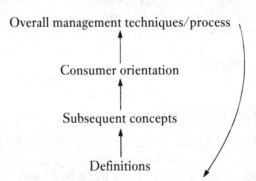

THE STRUCTURED MARKETING APPROACH

Overall management techniques/process

↑

Consumer orientation

↑

Subsequent concepts

↑

Definitions

The definition has evolved out of the
process of marketing management

The main marketing definitions adopted are quoted from the work of Kotler, Krippendorf or the British Institute of Marketing. Kotler is generally held to be the major exponent of general marketing theory and therefore, in all applications of marketing, his work has become the most widely referenced. Kotler (1988) defines marketing as: 'a social and managerial process by which individuals and groups obtain what they need and want through creating and exchanging products and value with others'. In 1984 the British Institute of Marketing defined marketing as: 'the management process responsible for identifying, anticipating and satisfying customers' requirements profitably'. Certain points regarding these definitions are significant. They both stress marketing as a management process. The Institute of Marketing clarifies that assessment of consumer demand through the identification and anticipation of customer requirements (i.e. research and analysis) is part of this process.

The definitions lead to the notion of the *marketing concept*. The marketing concept holds that the key to achieving organizational goals depends upon determining the needs and wants of target markets and delivering the desired satisfactions more effectively and efficiently than competitors (Kotler, 1984). The various tourism-marketing authors have utilized a variety of definitions and meanings but they all have a consistent element emphasizing the concept that companies should focus on consumers and be aware of their needs. This relates to the central idea of marketing which represents an emphasis on *consumer orientation*. This stresses the need for companies to be outward looking and to develop and produce those products and services for which demand has been identified. This is opposed to production-orientation or operations-orientation where companies remain inefficient because the consumer is not the focus of their planning and products are provided which do not maximize demand.

As outlined, the final level of the structural approach of marketing is the development of management techniques such as strategic planning, control of the marketing mix (product, price, promotion and place) and marketing research. The management process has been developed taking into consideration the theoretical basis which emanates from a consumer-orientated perspective. Marketing within tourism becomes the application of the marketing process to the specific characteristics which apply to the tourism industry and its products.

The adoption of marketing

The nature of the tourism industry is one where custom and tradition are particularly strong. This is not surprising, given that many other similar service industry sectors exhibit an emphasis on traditional service. It is this author's belief that the present adoption of marketing in tourism has taken place within a conflict between traditionalism and the need for change to take place.

The tourism industry has been characterized by custom and procedure which at times has lagged behind the need for change. Holloway and Plant (1988) illustrate the traditional role taken by British industry. They relate that there has been a tendency in tourism to believe that the best way of 'learning the business' is to recruit staff straight from school and 'train them up'. They argue that this system has led to a lack of innovation and skilled market analysis as well as restraint in the development of modern marketing techniques.

Schmoll (1977) in parallel to this, points out that many of the changes brought about in the tourism industry came from those who had been initially trained or had worked outside the industry. This was not easy as there was a mistrust of highly qualified or formally trained marketing people in many companies.

The forces which lead to consumer orientation

In order to examine why companies adopt marketing, it is necessary to understand both the internal and external forces which bring this about. If we consider first the internal factors, we have to be aware of the dynamic nature of any organization. Companies are more than just collections of individuals. Companies are social systems in miniature with norms, values and status groups which are controlled by means of rewards and punishments. The business system can be viewed as an organism with the sole purpose of survival and proliferation. Following this argument, when a system is threatened, it will take functional steps to improve the situation. To illustrate this, we can refer to Baker (1987) who utilizes the case of a simple organism whose cells divide and grow exponentially. If the cells are placed in a test tube containing nutrients, they will reach a ceiling point of growth and then either try to mutate (diversify) or settle into equilibrium (stagnation).

In a similar way in the case of threat, marketing departments become essential, especially in the planning of tactical action. On the other hand, in times of shortage—such as war and post-war periods—production systems can dominate because there are few demand problems. Within periods of over-supply, mass production and market saturation, marketing assumes a key role in the system. This is even more important in the case of tourism products, which are high risk, perishable products: an airline seat, hotel bed, or meal not sold is lost forever. Burkart and Medlik (1981) identified that marketing assumed a new significance in the 1970s. They argued that this was linked to over-production within the airline and hotel industry and also the rapid growth of inclusive tours to Europe. In the 1960s and 1970s, in the United Kingdom, many tourism industry companies set up marketing departments because of the high risk nature of the product they were selling. Unfortunately, many of these departments did not function properly and companies became disillusioned with the results. Much of the problem lay in the inability to understand what a marketing department should do, and how marketing should be integrated throughout the company. These arguments are clearly elucidated in the following paragraph which describes how British Airways took until the mid-1980s to discover the role of marketing.

Consumer orientation for British Airways

British Airways offers a recent case example of success due to the adoption of a marketing orientation for the company. Although British Airways had announced a massive loss in 1981–2 of £544m it created an operating surplus of £272m in the financial year 1983–4. This represented one of the fastest and largest changes in fortunes ever achieved by a major commercial concern. The industry was becoming more healthy and British Airways had sold off some aircraft but the success of the company was mainly due to a marketing orientation led by Sir Colin Marshall. The company reported (*Marketing*, 10 May 1985) that 'until re-organisation British Airways had not been truly marketing led. Even though it had a Marketing department, it had been operations led. The key change was to ensure operations delivered what the Marketing department requested due to an identification of consumer needs.' The overall success was explained as attributable to three main thrusts: satisfying customer requirements; becoming more people orientated; and the creation of overall long-term strategies.

The importance of technology

In understanding marketing fully, we have to establish the pressures and forces which have, and will, mould tourism's future. Much of the change we have witnessed in the last decade is due to the advance of electronics. According to Heller (1984) the electronic age has performed three feats at once in the camera market: it has lowered manufacturing costs; raised reliability; and led to innovation.

Tourism has felt the impact of electronics in the form of centralized reservation systems for hotels, airlines, tour operators, car hire etc which has led in turn to more effective and cost-efficient distribution systems. There is the availability of Prestel or teletext services for the home consumer, or the travel trade, which can deliver a whole range of information and services. Videotex technology has been adopted by the majority of travel agencies in the United Kingdom because the interactive qualities allow the instant confirmation of reservations without the need to provide further paperwork or time-consuming transactions. Applied computer technology has probably created the biggest impact on tourism. Computer-aided design for both cars and aircraft has given rise to more fuel-efficient transport while computer applications for marketing research enable information to be gathered and analysed more effectively. The larger companies have introduced marketing information systems with models and statistical techniques which enable managers to forecast more accurately and control the marketing effort more effectively. For the consumer, home electronics have led to a range of labour-saving devices which allow more leisure time.

It is this author's experience that the management function has changed in companies which have been responsive to new technology and emerging consumer needs. Within the Marketing department, progress has been shown in the development of both main line marketing management functions as well as planning functions. Marketing planning sections have been set up in Marketing departments with the responsibility for implementing marketing information sytems, which enable more effective pricing patterns due to analysis of competitors' price offers. These departments are given the responsibility for forecasting or late offer decision making. The progress has occurred due to the ability to harness computer power to information systems. Reservations for airlines, tour operators and hotels are computerized and this lends itself easily to different modelling inputs. However, it may be argued that the industry has concentrated on utilizing technology to save costs and set low prices. For example, tour operators have developed a fixation on the price sensitive nature of demand patterns, perhaps to the detriment of creating campaigns which encourage brand loyalty or develop added value. The next era of 'on line' computer systems should have yield management or expert system programmes which will give decision support to marketers. This will aid in the maximisation of profit by only allowing inventory to be offered at the optimum price. Because the tourist market is volatile, short run profitability and cash flow become focal points for marketing strategy. Such low horizon planning is a serious deterrent to improvement in product planning or long term image building of a brand. The high risk nature of the tourism industry should not blind management to the importance of price over service.

The service aspects of tourism

The majority of textbooks related to tourism marketing, stress the importance of tourism as a service product (Middleton, 1988; Holloway and Plant, 1988; Buttle, 1986; Foster, 1985; Schmoll, 1977). A service product is normally described in terms of the characteristics of intangibility, perishability and inseparability, following from the earlier work of Stanton (1978), Sasser (1978), and Shostock (1977). However, Middleton (1983) also added to the debate in arguing for the term *fast-moving consumer services*. Whereas the characteristics associated with a service product are discussed in the literature, some authors fail to develop theories of customer service provision, or different marketing mix strategies which would obtain more to services than goods marketing. In relation to this point, there have been particular theorists who have taken more of a services management stance and have consequently emphasized the service encounter. Within tourism we are selling both the combination of a product and service but the emphasis is on service. Davidson (1978) has noted that the service industry manager is only as important as the delivery of friendly, polite and well-trained customer contacts. Collier (1983–4) has reinforced this by stating that in the service business, you cannot make happy guests with unhappy employees. Albrecht and Zenke (1985) suggest that when service encounters go unsupervised, the quality of service regresses to mediocrity.

The rediscovery of customer care

Service has been rediscovered by many organizations in tourism as the main factor of customer satisfaction. Government Tourist Boards have made videos in order to encourage customer care and heighten the awareness of personal hygiene and presentation. British Rail and British Airways have invested millions of pounds into training schemes to improve customer service interactions. However, customer service training is not always handled correctly and may not achieve Gronroos' (1981) objective for internal marketing which is the development of 'motivated' and 'customer conscious' personnel who will secure increases in productivity. British rail advertised the fact that it was 'getting there' in terms of service, prior to finding out whether there had been any perceptual improvement in service provision on behalf of the commuter. Whereas progress may have been made in the emphasis placed on training staff to deliver a better service, it is not training which brings about the most effective means of customer service provision. It is the corporate culture of the organization which passes on the norms and values of customer interaction procedures and, therefore, we may see more emphasis in the future on inward marketing to change or reinforce corporate culture, rather than short-term training schemes which lead to higher expectations from the public (who then feel dissatisfied if the reality of the product consumption experience is too low). Davidson's (1978) solution is to remove employees if they do not measure up to the service task but this approach has been attacked by organizational theorists who suggest such an approach has not been successful. In order to improve overall service levels we may have to focus on those individuals in an organization who are capable of influencing the performance level of interpersonal situations. Following this argument, individuals who could become culture-carriers would be rewarded for exhibiting positive patterns of behaviour and values within the organization.

Theoretical aspects of service provision

We may want to identify the aspects of service which are important to the consumer. Bitner *et al.* (1985) have developed the use of critical incident analysis to assess the service encounter. In their research, respondents specify incidents in which *good* or *poor* service was delivered. The respondent has to be sure in stating the way the incident was critical to the outcome of the activity. By utilizing Gronroos' (1985) typology of technical versus functional service quality dimensions, the authors discovered that 77 per cent of the service encounters mentioned as either satisfactory or unsatisfactory pertained to the functional aspects of service. The negative functional aspects related to rudeness, indifferent treatment, unprofessional behaviour or lack of apologies for system breakdowns. On the other hand, the positive aspects of service delivery included apologies, helping with children etc. Technical quality negatives involved lost baggage, poor food, lateness of flights etc.

Owing to the importance of the aspect of service within the overall tourist product experience, tourism organizations, as service providers, may want to study the techniques of those industry leaders who have adopted the strategy of adopting a service culture. Disney, Marriott Hotels and McDonalds seem to be leading the way in the late 1980s.

Strategic planning

Marketing management which plans for the optimum use of an organization's resources would seem to be fundamental for success. There is an obvious need for strategic planning. Walt Disney Productions correctly identified they were in the entertainment business. They adopted a marketing strategy which emphasized resources should be released for theme parks, television pro- grammes and motion pictures directed at family markets with six to twelve year olds (*Business Week*, 31 July 1978). However, Disney management having recognized the decline in the younger age market and the emerging emphasis on education linked with leisure, looked for new market opportunities. This led to the development of the Epcot centre in Florida on what had previously been cheap low-lying swamp and agricultural land. Successful marketing management is always concerned with analysing emerging needs and demographic trends. There is always the need to develop a sustainable competitive advantage for tourism attractions and products. Butlins in the United Kingdom had ignored the fact that consumer holiday needs had become more sophisticated during the 1980s. They are now embarking on a multi-million refurbishment programme of their sites to improve the experi- ence of their product offer and to enable them to offer a year-round programme.

The role of research

The new developments in tourism such as the Jorvik Centre, Alton Towers and Center Parcs are all based upon providing consumers with products which satisfy their needs. This has placed a heavy reliance on market research activity. There is a developing belief in research as an important aid to feedback and decision-making. The corollary of this is that systematic marketing research is both the front and catalyst of any marketing decision- making. However, some authors (Samuels, 1973; Capstick and Riley, 1977) attack the weakness of the availability of relevant information regarding service provision in the tourism and recreation industry. Some authors even point to the irrelevance of research to applied decision-making processes (Rossi *et al.*, 1978; Dimaggio and Useem, 1980; Driver and Knopf, 1981). Moreover, we may place some of the blame for this weakness on the manager who fails to specify objectives clearly or who lacks the logical rigour necessary to define specific research needs. Beaman (1978) has identified that appropriate research has not been carried out because of the weakness of those involved in early tourism research work. We should also remember that research is only the means by which to reduce uncertainty. As Luck (1970) stresses: 'Research is the handmaiden of competent management, but never its substitute.'

Within companies, there is now the adoption of research systems which can provide part of a structured decision-making support process. These systems are either **Decision Support Systems** (DSS) which can provide clerical or database analysis systems (Keen and Scott-Morton, 1978) or **Management Information Systems** (MIS) which produce routine information in an automated process.

Hotel marketing

Much of the hotel industry is sales-orientated according to Buttle (1986). He observes that since hotels are immobile and structural alterations costly, they can neither be moved to locations where demand is higher nor are they readily converted to new uses such as offices, flats or retail outlets without consider-able expense. He therefore concludes that hotel marketers have been required to demonstrate sales skills. In contrast to this, physical developments have occurred recently where some hotel groups have developed the concept of segmentation through the provision of executive floors, business centres, rooms for non-smokers or female executives and improved speed and comfort of checking in or out of the hotel. Buttle's argument may be valid in relation to the smaller hotels which, to follow Schmoll (1977) suffers, as does the whole tourism industry, from being characterized by a large number of small- and medium-sized enterprises which have found it difficult to invest in specialist marketing staff. This author's experience in research into the strategy formula-tion of medium and large hotels would seem to indicate it is only some of the larger hotel groups which are truly marketing orientated. However, given the pressures of the market-place and the arguments expressed earlier, regarding marketing adoption, changes in hotel marketing would seem to be imminent. The following paragraphs outline the main changes which have occurred recently in the hotel industry.

Budget hotel development—a market gap

The demand for hotel accommodation in the United States has grown approxi-mately in line with the overall growth in the economy but has not kept up with the growth shown in many sectors of the tourism market (Goeglein, 1986). There are early signs that hotel demand patterns may be changing. There is a great deal of activity in the budget sector of the market where new, good quality standard accommodation is being offered. Strategically, the hotel as a product in the United Kingdom has always been viewed as requiring constant upgrading and refurbishment. Hotel management have equated status of their role in comparison to the star rating of the hotel. In terms of product positioning this has led to a constant desire to upgrade the star-rating of hotels. At the same time, new hotel development for many years has been targeted towards the top end of the market. These factors combined to create a gap in the market for good quality two-star accommodation. This gap was identified not by the marketing departments of British companies but mainly by the French companies who are now developing what has been termed the *budget hotel* in the British accommodation market. This description seems inadequate as the association of the word 'budget' is that of poor quality. This category of hotels is reported to have high demand patterns in the United States where Marriott and Holiday Inns are developing low-price, no-frills chains.

The development of specialist hotel products

A major change in hotel marketing has been the development of short-break or mini-break holidays to fill low occupancy periods. These holidays, once known as *bargain breaks*, are now a common package offer supplied in the hotel market. However, nowadays, there is a vast variety of forms and promotions linked to these products.

Marketing is all about identifying opportunities which arise from emerging consumer needs. The modern weekend break has developed into many different forms, from activity to education leisure, since its inception by Grand Metropolitan back in the mid-1960s. The Grand Met holidays were marketed successfully under the brand name 'Stardust' holidays and offered a weekend in London with rail travel included in the package. These holidays were promoted at rail stations and priced to be attractive to average wage earners in regional areas. Planning these holidays in the 1960s perhaps marked the initial departure from a mere sales department to a marketing orientation of satisfying consumer needs at prices which offered good value for money.

The initial packages for 'bargain breaks' were planned on the basis of discounting the under-utilized weekend bed supply of hotels in urban locations. The emphasis now is to package different experiences. This has led to an expansion of the product into midweek periods and created a highly developed market for mini-breaks based around themes of interest or activities. For many hotels who have realized that the market is not solely price based there have been successful partnerships between regional tourist boards, who can help with the addition of local features of heritage products. Marketing initiatives shown by those who realize the potential of the short-break market have led to the evolution of an important segment of the domestic tourism market.

Government and tourism marketing

Governments have considered tourism a business which is essential to economies because of the direct effects on employment, the balance of payments and society in terms of educational and cultural benefits. Tourism is characterized by the fragmentation of supply, the complementarity of tourist services and the predominance of small enterprises. As Schmoll (1977) has pointed out, it is not surprising that official organizations—whether local, regional, national or international—have important functions and responsibilities in relation to tourism marketing. Lickorish (1987) has written that central government must create the right conditions for growth. Governments have, therefore, been involved in the provision of help and guidance to the industry in setting up boards which include departments with tourism marketing expertise. The boards have attempted to improve the industry's marketing expertise by providing a range of booklets, pamphlets and guidelines which help explain marketing functions and give ideas for the solution of problems. An example of this is a regular British Tourist Authority (BTA) publication featuring ways of improving low-season demand.

More recently as world economies have suffered, there has been even greater emphasis on creating employment through both domestic and international tourism demand, especially in areas where alternative economic development is not a cost-effective alternative. A sign of change in the United Kingdom's support of tourism projects is the indication by tourism minister David Trippier (1987) that grants for tourism ventures will be made more available for the larger projects. This is because it is the larger projects which are seen to bring the most benefit in terms of job creation.

Intervention by public bodies is essential for product development

Lickorish (1987) has pointed out that whereas governments do not market direct to the customer, local government has a more direct role to play. He suggests it has to intervene to ensure that the destination's infrastructure develops. He argues this should preferably be in partnership with operators or providers of amenities because it is essential that the local government should play a part rather than simply setting the rules. Bradford, an industrial city in the United Kingdom, is a prime example of how public- and private-sector enterprise and marketing can create success for tourism. In 1985, 25,000 tourists were attracted to the city through the development of specific products and packages. This exploitation of the tourist potential for the city was initially due to the commercial backing of the city which allocated £100,000 for the project.

Local authorities are becoming increasingly important in relation to the attraction created by shopping environments in combination with leisure facilities. As local authorities have a great deal of planning control over central shopping areas, they can act as catalysts in providing focal points to help inner city revitalization. Covent Garden in the United Kingdom, Baltimore's inner harbour in the United States and the West Edmonton Mall in Canada are all examples of projects which have created a synergy between shopping and pleasure and ultimately provided a stronger 'sense of place'.

The importance of image of place

Significant steps are being taken in the United Kingdom to market regional areas in order to disperse tourists from London. One way to do this is to create a stronger image for regional locations. The improvement of an area's image brought about by marketing can also enhance a community's pride in its area. The improvement and marketing of British cities such as Bradford, Liverpool, Cardiff and Bristol have brought about a resurgence of pride in heritage and place. A major objective of the 'I love N.Y.' marketing promotion was to improve individual citizen pride for New York City as well as to create wider awareness for the city throughout the world.

The emphasis placed upon the creation of images is due to particular tourism products being very similar to each other in what they offer. For example, one airline flight is very similar to another flight. This has led to a greater emphasis on creating an improved or better image for individual tourist products. Schmoll (1977) takes the standpoint that it is evident if a tourist's experience is mainly subjective in nature then ideas or expectations associated with a product and how these correspond to reality, or are transformed, will have a significant bearing on both the choices made by potential tourists and the satisfactions and benefits they gain. Lawson and Baud-Bovy (1977) have written of image as the expression of all objective knowledge, impressions, prejudice, imaginations and emotional thoughts associated with place or product. The importance of images is that they form part of our decision-making process and influence the choices we make. This has been more fully understood and consequently the creation of image-utilizing PR, advertising and sales literature has become an important aspect of tourism marketing. However, some tourism products are created with multi-images because of the number of different segments to which they will be sold. Each segment has a different marketing mix targeted to it. In this way, places such as cities can be marketed to many different customers for different uses.

Product quality control

Governments have also attempted to control and improve standards of product quality. Award schemes such as the 'Dragon Award' in Wales for caravan parks and annual awards such as the BTA's 'come to Britain' trophy award are all planned to encourage excellence in product formulation. The English Tourist Board has also expanded its classification scheme to all types of establishment from hotels to guest houses by utilizing up to five 'crown' symbols per unit.

Conclusion

The emergence of effective marketing is a multi-faceted phenomenon. One key judgement is whether a company has recognized the need to be consumer orientated and subsequently created the environment and company structure to fulfil the resulting philosophy this entails. For a company to judge whether it has established marketing as an integrated guiding function, the following activities should have been formalized.

Senior executives in the company have to support the concept of consumer orientation. The British Airways' experience is but one example of success due to this. The orientation leads to a belief in the systematic collection of research material from various internal and external sources so as to identify emerging trends and needs of the consumer. Companies should also devise a system of planning. An integrated approach should be adopted where strategies, policies and programmes are formulated as a focus for the whole company's future effort in the market-place. This will be itemized in a marketing plan which will guide the long-term objectives and activities of each unit in the company.

This chapter has presented examples from the hotel market and government tourist boards to illustrate the focus which the tourism industry places on the market-place. The more tourism as an industry understands its markets the stronger its position will be to identify and harness change, rather than simply to follow in the wake of others.

References

Albrecht, K., Zenke, R., 1985, *Service America*, Dow Jones-Irwin, Illinois.

Baker, M. J., 1987, 'One more time—what is marketing', *The Marketing Book*, Institute of Marketing, Heinemann, London.

Bartos, R., 1982, 'Women in travel', *Journal of Travel Research*, 20(4): 3–9.

Beaman, J., 1978, 'Leisure research and its lack of relevance to planning management and policy formulation: a problem of major proportions', *Recreation Research Review*, 6(3): 18–25.

Bitner, M., Nyquist, J., and Booms, B., 1985, 'The critical incident as a technique for analyzing the service encounter', in Bloch, T., *et al.*, *Services Marketing in a Changing Environment*, American Marketing Association, Chicago, pp. 48–51.

Bruce, M., 1987, 'New technology and the future of tourism', *Tourism Management*, 8(2): 115–22.

Burdenski, H., 1986, 'Tourism, America's hottest industry', *Tourism Services Marketing Conference*, 11: 3–12.

Burkart, A. J., Medlik, S., 1981, *Tourism, Past, Present and Future*, Heinemann, London.

Buttle, F., 1986, *Hotel and Food Service Marketing*, Holt, Rinehart and Winston, London.

Capstick, M., Riley, S., 1973, 'Problems of implementing tourism policy to achieve optimum economic impact', Tourism as a tool for regional development, *Edinburgh Leisure Studies Association Conference*.

Collier, D. A., 1983–4, 'Managing a service firm: a different management game', *National Productivity Review*, Winter: 36–45.

Davidson, D. S., 1978, 'How to succeed in a service industry: turn the organisation chart upsidedown', *Management Review*, April: 14–16.

Dimaggio, P., Useem, M., 1980, 'Small scale policy research in the arts', *Policy Analysis*, 6(2): 171–91.

Driver, B. L., Knopf, R. C., 1981, 'Some thoughts on the quality of outdoor recreation, research and other constraints on its application: social research in national parks and wilderness areas', Atlanta, USDT National Park Service, South East Region Office, pp. 85–99.

Economist Intelligence Unit, 1981, *Forecasts to 1990*, Special Report, No. 93.

Edgell, D., 1987, 'Managing the research function for effective policy formulation and decision making', in Ritchie, J. R. B., *et al.* (eds), *Travel, Tourism and Hospitality Research*, Wiley, New York, pp. 35–43.

Foster, D., 1985, *Travel and Tourism Management*, Macmillan Education Ltd., London.

Frechtling, D. C., 1987, 'Five issues in tourism marketing in the 1990s', *Tourism Management*, 8(2): 177–8.

Goeglein, R. J., 1986, 'The technology and tourism: a growing partnership', *TTRA 17th Conference Proceedings*.

Gronroos, C., 1985, 'Internal marketing—an integral part of marketing theory', in Donnelly, J. and George, W. (eds), *Marketing of Services*, American Marketing Association, Chicago, pp. 236–8.

Gurney, J., 1984, 'Tourism and Local Authorities: firming up for the future', *Hospitality*, 50: 2–4.

Hartley, C., 1987, 'Video dreamland', *Audio Visual Communications*, June: 41.

Heller, R., 1984, *The Naked Market*, Sidgwick and Jackson, London.

Holloway, J. C., Plant, R. V., 1988, *Marketing for Tourism*, Pitman, London.

Keen, P. F., Scott-Morton, M. S., 1978, *Decision Support Systems: An Organizational Perspective*, Addison Wesley, Reading (Mass.).

Kotler, P., 1988, *Marketing Management*, Prentice Hall, Englewood Cliffs, New Jersey.

Lawson, F., Baud-Bovy, M., 1977, *Tourism and Recreational Development*, London, Architectural Press, London.

Lickorish, L., 1987, 'Trends in industrialized countries', *Tourism Management*, 8(2): 92–5.

Long, M., 1987, 'The 1987 Seers catalogue', *Omni*, January: 37–40.

Luck, D. J., Wales, H. G., Taylor, D. A., Rubin, R. S., 1970, *Marketing Research*, 3rd edition, Prentice Hall, Englewood Cliffs, New Jersey.

Middleton, V. T. C., 1988, *Marketing in Travel and Tourism*, Heinemann, Oxford.

Middleton, V. T. C., 1983, 'Product marketing—goods and services compared', *Quarterly Review of Marketing*, 8(4): 1–10.

Murphy, P. E., 1985, *Tourism: A Community Approach*, Methuen, New York.

Rochester, P., 1986, 'The unreal thing', *Omni*, 3 Dec.

Rossi, O. M., Wright, J. P., and Wright, S. R., 1978, 'The theory and practice of applied social research', *Evaluation Quarterly*, 2(2): 171–91.

Samuels, J. A., 1973, 'Research to help plan the future of a seaside resort', *The Marketing of Tourism and Other Services: Proceedings of the 12th Marketing Theory Seminar*, University of Lancaster, Lancaster.

Sasser, W. E., 1978, *Management of Services Operations*, Alleyn and Baron, Boston, Mass.

Schmoll, G. A., 1977, *Tourism Promotion*, Tourism International Press, London.

Shostack, G. L., 1977, 'Breaking free from product marketing', *Journal of Marketing*, April: 73–80.

Slattery, P., Roper, A., and Boer, A., 'Hotel consortia: their activities, structure and growth', *Service Industries Journal*, 5(2): 193–9.

Stanton, W. J., 1981, *Fundamentals of Marketing*, 6th ed., McGraw Hill, New York.

Trippier, D., 1987, 'Tourism in the 1990s—UK government view', *Tourism Management*, 8(2): 79–82.

Wahab, S., Crampon, L. J., and Rothfield, L. M., 1976, *Tourism Marketing*, Tourism International Press, London.

Watkins, T., 1986, *The Economics of the Brand*, McGraw Hill, London.

5 Competitive strategies for a 'new tourism'
A. Poon

Introduction

International tourism is undergoing rapid metamorphosis—a transformation toward a new industry *best practice* or *common sense*. This new common sense holds a number of important implications for companies in the tourist industry. It also holds important consequences for developing countries, such as Caribbean islands, that are growing increasingly dependent on the tourist dollar.

This chapter examines the way in which the international tourist industry is being transformed into a new industry best practice of flexibility, segmentation and diagonal integration. The implications of this new best practice for companies within the tourist industry as well as for Caribbean-type economies are considered.

International tourism in metamorphosis

The radical transformation of the international tourist industry can best be illustrated by what this author describes as old tourism and new tourism. *Old tourism* is the tourism of the 1950s, 1960s and 1970s. It is characterized by mass, standardized and rigidly packaged holidays, hotels and tourists. *New tourism* is the tourism of the future. It is characterized by flexibility, segmentation and more authentic tourism experiences. It is also marked by a thrust toward the diagonally integrated organization and management of the tourist industry.

Old tourism

Old tourism was not only mass, but it was also standardized and rigidly packaged. It is argued, for example, that 'the quintessence to today's mass tourist industry is that everything is standardized' (Turner and Ash, 1975: 111). This view is supported by the sociological/anthropological school (Noronha, 1977), observing the increasing trend toward cultural 'commercialization', 'culture by the pound' (Greenwood, 1978), 'staged authenticity'

(MacCannell, 1973), and the 'recurrent tendency toward simplification, increase in volume, standardization and eventual mass production (of tourism) on an assembly line basis' (Graburn, 1979, cited in McKean, 1978: 103).

Mass, Standardized and *Rigidly Packaged* (MSRP) tourism was created and nurtured by a number of favourable post-war developments (Poon, 1987). These included: the arrival of the jet aircraft in 1958; promotional fares such as the Advance Purchase Excursion (APEX) fare; cheap oil; Keynesian-inspired economic growth; paid holidays; sun-lust tourists; the entry of multinational corporations; vertical and horizontal integration; and the ubiquitous franchise. With respect to franchises, and the multinational hotel chains which perpetuated them, it is argued that their growth resulted in 'stultifying homogenization of products and communities. They destroy a sense of community by mass producing environments that minimize personal contacts' (Luxenberg, 1985: 10). By 1972, the World Tourism Organization (WTO) concluded that:

... the changes that have already taken place and the future investment plans and programmes of numerous travel enterprises leave no doubt that the travel sector will, in the main, be structured on the basis of *large units* backed by strong financial interests and on the selling of *standardized packaged deals at low rates to a large clientele*. [WTO, 1972: 39, emphasis added].

New tourism

Today, there are already signs that the tourist industry is beginning to take on a different shape. International tourism is responding to, and internalizing a number of signals—socially, culturally, technologically, ecologically, economically and institutionally—that emanate from the world environment. One is already witnessing a transformation toward a new tourism, a tourism based upon a new 'common sense' or 'best practice' of *Flexibility*, *Segmentation* and *Diagonal Integration* (FSDI). This new best practice of FSDI is created by a number of factors including the diffusion of a system of new information technologies (SIT) in the tourist industry; deregulation of the airline industry and financial services; the negative impact of mass tourism on host countries; the movement away from sun-lust to sun-plus tourists; environmental pressures; technology competition; and changing consumer tastes, leisure time, work patterns and income distribution (Poon, 1987).

The factors which are engineering the metamorphosis of the tourist industry can be seen in Figure 5.1. One can observe from the figure that it is the factors which facilitated the creation of mass tourism that are themselves being changed. With these changes come the transformation of the entire industry best practice.

From Figure 5.1 it can be seen that the economics of new tourism is very different from the old—profitability no longer rests solely on economies of scale and the exploitation of mass undifferentiated markets. Economies of

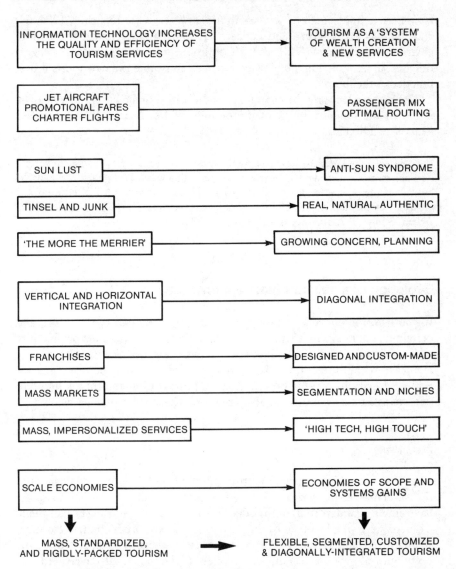

Figure 5.1 *International Tourism in metamorphosis*

scope, systems gains, segmented markets, designed and customized holidays
are becoming more and more important for profitability and competitiveness
in tourism. Traditional managerial and organizational practices of vertical and
horizontal integration are also giving way to *diagonal* integration. Tourists
themselves are moving away from 'tinsel and junk' (Coates, 1986: 77–8) to
more real, natural and authentic experiences. There is also a movement away

movement away from (handwritten)

from mass, impersonalized services to *high tech, high touch* (Naisbitt, 1984: 64) and there is greater care and concern for and conservation of the natural environment (Krippendorf, 1986). Flexibility, segmentation, diagonal integration and more authentic holiday experiences constitute the new tourism best practice of the future.

The best evidence for the emergence of this new tourism best practice can be found in the industry itself. In the opinion of Jim Harris, British Airways Marketing Director:

We have seen the *end of mass marketing* in the travel business . . . we are going to have to be much more sophisticated in the way we *segment* our market. Technology is expensive, but it provides scope for *flexibility*; the trick will be to move with the technological changes but maintain the flexibility to *move with the market*. [*Travel Trade Gazette, UK & Ireland*, 3 July 1987: 21, emphasis added]

Evolution of a new tourism best practice

In tourism, the concept of best practice refers to the set of principles and ingrained common sense which guide the everyday practices for profitability and competitiveness of the industry. A new best practice can be readily identified within the new tourism. Four elements of a new best practice are evident: **flexibility, segmentation, diagonal integration** and the evolution of tourism as a total **system of wealth-creation**. These are explained below.

Segmentation

The mass market in tourism is splitting apart. One of the profound changes in the travel market-place comes from the tourists themselves. Tourists no longer have single, standardized and rigidly packaged wants. They never had them. Tourists were simply forced by the economics of mass production, to consume standardized and rigidly packaged holidays *en masse*. Today, however, the economics of new tourism allows suppliers to deal more effectively with the increasing complexity and diversity of consumer requirements. New technologies, coupled with diagonal integration, are making it possible to produce flexible and segmented vacations, which are *cost-competitive* with mass, standardized holidays (Poon, 1987).

It is interesting to observe, in addition, that segmentation in today's travel environment is unique, unprecedented and infinitely more complex. In the past, it was common practice to segment the holiday market along traditional uni-dimensional lines of sex, age and income. Today, one has to be much more sophisticated when markets are segmented. Specifically, *cluster segments* of the vacation market must be catered for—that is, segments based on clusters of multi-optioned needs and consumer characteristics. This means that the choice is not between sun *or* fun holidays; young *or* old; male *or* female; but rather, creative holiday combinations which incorporate a *cluster* of market requirements. For example, vacations must be provided which cater to Double Income No Kids (DINKS) couples, from the sunbelt region of the United States who seek sun *plus* windsurfing, *plus* bird watching *plus* fresh air *plus* Trinidad Carnival. Similarly, vacations tailored to the over-50s couples, who seek sun *plus* sailing *plus* educational tours *plus* walking *plus* healthy foods, etc. The key challenge for travel suppliers is to understand the components and composition of these cluster segments and to determine in which clusters an organization can gain a competitive advantage.

Flexibility

Flexibility, as a core element of the new tourism best practice, is reflected at three levels: flexibility in the organization, production and distribution of travel; flexibility in the choice, booking, purchase and payment of holidays; and flexibility in the consumption and enjoyment of the holiday experience. These aspects are all interlinked. Information technology plays a major role in facilitating flexibility in the travel market-place. This is clearly evident in the case of time-share vacations.

Time share, as its name implies, refers to the purchase of vacation time at a specified tourist resort. It amounts, for example, to owning time (usually one week) covering one room in a resort, for a number of years (spanning the life of the unit). The very concept of time share is inflexible. It could mean, for example, that a retired couple would be limited to spending their vacation in the same room, in the same resort, in the same country for the rest of their lives. But information technologies have come to the rescue: it is now possible to facilitate the *exchange of time and venue* among time-sharing vacationers. For example, assuming that the correct matches can be made, it is possible for a couple who own a week in a villa in Spain to exchange this for a different week—at destinations from Tobago to Timbuktu. Information technologies have thus increased the flexibility, choice and variety with which time-share vacations can be produced, marketed and consumed.

Flexibility is also evident in the development of *computerized reservation systems* (CRS) which allow travel agents to look, book and sell in one call; in *teleconferencing* which allows meetings and conferences to take place from remote locations; in *smart cards* which can be used to purchase airline tickets outside normal working hours and outside travel agencies; *satellite printers* which automatically deliver airline tickets to corporate offices. Flexibility is also evident in the proliferation of all-inclusive/club vacations which emphasize more informal and flexible ways in which to spend free time. Flexibility will increasingly be a key element of profitability and competitiveness in tourism.

Diagonal integration

Diagonal integration is created by new information technologies (computer and communications). It is the process whereby service firms move into new and different activities, with tremendous **synergies, systems gains** and **scope economies** to be derived from such integration (Poon, 1988b). Synergies are benefits which accrue to the management, operation and organization of inter-related activities, where each activity is capable of generating benefits that mutually reinforce each other. Each activity adds value to the other, thereby making the whole output greater than the sum of the discrete parts. Systems gains refer to the benefits of economies derived from creating and engineering linkages among design, production, marketing organization and management. Examples of systems gains are networked activities, where each activity (or sub-division within an organization) can share a common data base or pool of knowledge. Economies of scope refer to the lower costs associated with the joint provision of more than one product or service, rather than producing each separately (Willig, 1979). With economies of scope, the joint production of two goods by one enterprise is less costly than the combined costs of two firms producing either goods 1 or goods 2. Assuming that scope economies existed in the provision of car rentals and hotel bed nights, for example, it would mean that the cost of adding the provision of car rentals to hotel bed nights would be cheaper than producing car rentals alone.

The essence of diagonal integration is that $2 + 2 = 5$. The economics of diagonal integration will lead the increasing cross-fertilization of many un-conventional services, with tremendous implications for travel suppliers. In tourism, therefore, it will no longer be best practice to produce single and un-related items of tourism output. It is increasingly common sense to produce clusters of interrelated services (which may not all be tourism-specific) which are integrated into a total system of wealth creation.

Tourism as a total system of wealth creation

One corollary of diagonal integration is that tourism is becoming a total system of wealth creation. In other words, wealth in tourism is created and value-added through the diagonal and synergistic integration of a number of activities into a total system. Within this total system of wealth creation, a computer and communications infrastructure provides the critical foundation from which a number of services can be spawned.

The fundamental backbone of this system of wealth creation is intelligence and information—i.e. the intelligent transaction in and manipulation of information. Information as well as its intelligent manipulation is of vital importance to the tourist industry in understanding, manipulating and profitably satisfying the tourism market. The economics governing this system of wealth creation is very powerful. This can be seen both from the demand and supply imperatives of the system.

On the supply side, investment in a telecommunications infrastructure results in diminishing marginal costs with increasing utilization. A computerized reservation system (CRS), for example, can market a number of travel services including airline and hotel reservations, flower and champagne services, cruises, car rental, etc. The beauty of these CRS, however, is that once an initial investment is made in a computer and communications infrastructure, a number of services can be added at little or no marginal costs to the provider. Since the users (travel agents) and other suppliers (co-hosts) pay market prices, rather than marginal cost prices, profitability to the suppliers (hosts) of the system is very great.

On the demand side, the wealth-creating potential of the tourism system lies in the character of demand for its output—i.e. the *combinational* and *lifetime* character of demand for tourism and other related services. Travel is not consumed like washing machines, where relatively few purchases fix the need. Rather, it is purchased over one's lifetime. Travel, moreover, is not purchased by itself. It is usually purchased in combination with a number of other services such as travellers cheques, credit, insurance, investment services, ground tours, etc. The profitability potential of producing and marketing a well-appointed cluster of services which are effectively demanded by a targeted group of consumers is tremendous. Indeed, the economics of producing a whole range of services to a targeted market is different from providing the same item to a supermarket of clients.

Information technology—a vital pillar of the new tourism

In tourism, it is not a computer *or* a telephone *or* videotext that is being diffused, but a whole system of these technologies, based upon microelectronics (see Figure 5.2). The System of Information Technologies (SIT) comprises computers, computerized reservation systems, digital telephone networks, videos, videotext (viewdata in the United States), interactive videotext, teleconferencing, management information systems, energy management, and electronic locking systems. Moreover, this system of technologies is not being used by airlines or hotels or travel agents, but by *all* of them (Poon, 1988d).

The diffusion of the system of information technologies in tourism will increase the efficiency, quality and flexibility with which travel services are supplied. It has already led to the generation of new services (teleconferencing, interactive videotext, video brochures, etc). Technology will have the greatest impact on the marketing and distribution of travel but will leave relatively untouched the human-intensive areas of guest–host relations and supplier–consumer relationships (Poon, 1988d). Information technologies applied to the tourism system will increase the efficiency and quality of services provided and lead to new combinations of tourism services. All this will be achieved without changing the manifest human *high touch* content of travel (Poon, 1988d).

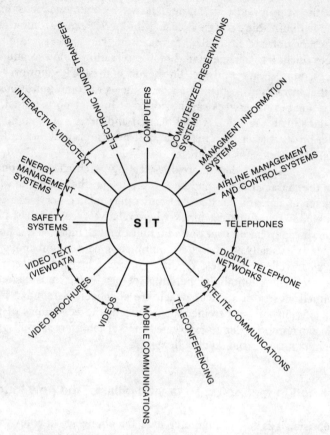

Figure 5.2 *The system of information technologies in tourism*

It is the systematic use of the system of information technologies by all tourism suppliers, together with its profound impact on the travel industry, which creates the foundation for a new tourism best practice and a *total system of wealth creation*.

Implications of the new tourism common sense

Competitors come from outside the industry

One of the implications of the diagonally integrating practices of companies and the evolution of tourism as a total system of wealth creation is that a firm's competitors will increasingly come from outside the tourism industry. This means that a firm's competitive advantages can be eroded not by obvious, readily identifiable competitors within its own market segment or industry, but from the entry of firms from completely unpredictable places (e.g. banks, telecommunication suppliers or real estate agents). This is clearly evident in the United Kingdom's travel market, for example, where banks (Midland Bank bought Thomas Cook, the second largest travel agency chain) and tele-communications providers (British Telecom's Prestel) have entered the travel market. The competitive threat of these suppliers that come from outside the traditional boundaries of the travel industry is potentially very great because firms from outside bring different experiences, resources, client bases and competitive strengths to the travel industry. In responding to increased competition from the outside, two complementary avenues are open to travel suppliers—industry monitoring and **cross-fertilization** of travel services.

In the first option, systems of information provision, intelligence gathering, research and development and market monitoring are necessary. Firms must be continuously on the look-out for changes and new developments, not just in their own market segment or industry, but from the entire tourism system. Information about markets and competitors must be intelligently utilized to render and reinforce competitive advantage.

Cross-fertilization of services also provides an important opportunity for survival and competitiveness in the travel industry. In other words, just as other suppliers are entering the travel industry, travel suppliers must creatively enter other areas. This practice of cross-fertilization is already being adopted by travel suppliers as they attempt to respond creatively and competitively to an increasingly dynamic, complex and changing travel environment. British West Indian Airways (BWIA), the national airline of Trinidad and Tobago, for example, is responding to a deregulated travel environment by diagonally integrating into venture services, offering a number of high value-added, computer-related services to the domestic market. In 1987, Hogg Robinson, a travel agency chain in the United Kingdom responded to the increasing entry of other firms to the travel market by moving into estate agency and financial services (*Travel Trade Gazette UK*, 1987, 1).

Innovation holds the key to survival and competitiveness

Survival within the transformed and continuously changing travel industry means that innovation is needed in order to survive. In today's tourism market-place, a firm has virtually to run in order to stand still. Innovation is the essence of being creative and bringing new ideas and tourism services to the market-place. Innovation must, however, be interpreted in the true Schumpeterian sense—encompassing innovations in goods, services, markets, methods of production, organizations, and sources of raw material (Schumpeter, 1965). It is necessary, therefore, to be totally innovative—not just in the marketing or vacation concepts, but also in the organization, product blending, packaging, management of tourism (Poon, 1988c). A stand-alone or de-linked innovation is not likely to be as potent as a cluster of innovations related to different spheres of a firm's operation.

Innovation must not only be total; it must also be continuous. Indeed a company cannot hope to produce a single innovation and expect it to provide sustainable competitive advantages. The innovation itself has to be sustainable. With innovation, however, sustainability usually implies more innovation. Competitiveness, then warrants the origination and sustenance of continuous clusters of innovation. A detailed comparative analysis of the Jamaican SuperClub hotel chain and the Benetton clothing concern in Italy revealed unambiguously that the ability of these organizations to evolve continuous clusters of innovation were vital ingredients in the success of both enterprises (Poon, 1988a).

Get closer to the consumer

The complexity and unpredictability of tourists, coupled with the increasing diversity of their needs, mean that producers will have to get even closer to their customers. This closeness will be necessary in order to understand consumer demand, monitor its pattern and satisfy it competitively and at a profit.

A profound understanding of complex requirements, expectations and desires of consumers as well as their time and budget constraints is vital. Creating a travel option simply because it is sophisticated, or because the technology is available, or because the firm has some unused capacity simply will not work. Any innovation, new idea or concept must be grounded in the market-place. It has to reflect the effective needs and requirements of consumers. It also has to be properly marketed in order to reach the target group. In this regard, choice of advertising mode and media is also basic.

Match the firm's skills and resources with the market-place

While it is important to understand the travel market, to be creative and to utilize new information technologies, these activities constitute only half of the tourism profitability and competitiveness equation. The other half of the equation is related to the actual endowments of the firm, and how suited they are to the new requirements of the travel market-place. In other words, a firm may be very creative in thinking about a new service for the travel market; a proven demand for the service may exist; and the technology and software may be available to bring the new service to the market. However, the venture could fail because there has to be a good match between the competitive strengths and resources of the enterprise and the requirements of the new travel services. New travel services as well as cross-fertilizations must be spawned from resources and competitive strengths already developed and acquired by a firm (e.g. reputation, information, intelligence, vision, financial assets, software, skilled manpower). It is very easy to run into dis-economies of capital, skills and resources if an optimal match does not exist between the market-place and the capabilities of a firm.

This is a very important point which should not be overlooked. Since the tourism system and its ancillary services are so complex and interrelated, just about any activity within the system can be perceived as related to any other (for example, hotels and theme parks; theme parks and cruise ships). Moreover, information technologies can easily make it possible to link just about any activity—from hotels to portfolio management—into a total system of wealth creation. However, this will not necessarily lead to market success.

The difficulty lies in the fact that for any given firm, this cross-fertilization (diagonally integrating) process can be severely limited by the availability of human intelligence, skills, finance and other resources (political connections, contacts and information), some, all, or none of which a firm may possess. This seems to be the case with the Mariott hotel chain, for example, which succeeded in diversifying into restaurants and hotels but 'largely failed in gourmet restaurants, theme parks, cruise ships and wholesale travel agencies' (Porter, 1987: 56). Understanding the market, therefore, only constitutes half of the tourism profitability equation. The second half relates to harnessing the skills, resources and competitive strengths of the firm (augmenting them where necessary) to satisfy the market.

Summary

International tourism is in metamorphosis and a new tourism is emerging—a tourism that promises flexibility, segmentation and diagonal integration; a tourism driven by information technologies and changing consumer requirements; a tourism which will produce an entire system of wealth creation. This new tourism has a number of profound implications for survival and competitiveness in tourism: competitors will increasingly come from outside the tourist industry; suppliers must get closer to the consumer; and firms have to match their skills and resources with the market-place. Innovation holds the key to future survival and competitiveness in the dynamic and radically changing tourism environment.

References

Bush, M., 1984, 'The age of market segmentation: new opportunities in today's market place', a special presentation at the American Society of Travel Agents' World Travel Congress, Las Vegas, Nevada, November.

Coates, J., 1986, 'The next 30 years in travel', paper presented at the US Travel Data Center, *1985–86 Outlook for Travel and Tourism*, US Travel Data Center, Washington, pp. 75–84.

Greenwood, D. J., 1978, 'Culture by the pound: an anthropological perspective on tourism as cultural commoditisation', in V. L. Smith (ed.), *Hosts and Guests: The Anthropology of Tourism*, Basil Blackwell, London, pp. 129–38.

Krippendorf, J., 1986, 'Tourism in the system of industrial society', *Annals of Tourism Research*, 313(4): 393–414.

Luxenberg, S., 1985, *Roadside Empires: How the Chains Franchised America*, Viking, New York.

MacCannell, D., 1973, 'Staged authenticity: Arrangements of social space in tourist settings', *American Journal of Sociology*, 79: 589–603.

McKean, P. F., 1978, 'Towards a theoretical analysis of tourism: economic dualism and cultural involution in Bali', in V. L. Smith (ed.), *Hosts and Guests: The Anthropology of Tourism*, Basil Blackwell, London, pp. 93–107.

Naisbitt, J., 1984, *Megatrends: Ten New Directions Transforming Our Lives*, Macdonald, London.

Noronha, R., 1977, 'Social and cultural dimensions of tourism: a review of the literature in English', *IBRD Draft Working Papers*, May, International Bank for Reconstruction and Development, Washington DC.

Poon, A., 1987, 'Information technology and innovation in international tourism— implications for the Caribbean tourism industry', unpublished Doctoral Thesis, Science Policy Research Unit, University of Sussex, Brighton.

Poon, A., 1988a, 'Flexible specialization and small size—The Case of Caribbean tourism', Science Policy Research Unit, *DRC Discussion papers No. 57*, February, *World Development* (forthcoming).

Poon, A., 1988b, 'Diagonal integration—a commonsense for tourism and services', paper presented to the Fourth Annual Seminar on the Service Economy hosted by PROGRES Research Program on the Service Economy, Geneva, 30, 31 May and 1 June 1988.

Poon, A., 1988c, 'The future of Caribbean tourism—a matter of innovation', *Tourism Management*, 9(3).

Poon, A., 1988d, 'Information technology and tourism—ideal bedfellows?' *Annals of Tourism Research* 15(4).

Poon, A., 1989 (forthcoming), *Tourism, Technology and Competitive Advantage— International and Caribbean Perspectives*, (forthcoming).

Porter, M., 1987, 'From competitive advantage to corporate strategy', *Harvard Business Review*, May/June: 43–59.

Porter, M., 1985, 'Technology and competitive advantage', *Journal of Business Strategy*, Winter: 60–78.

Schumpeter, J. A., 1965, *The Theory of Economic Development: An Enquiry into Profit, Credit, Interest and the Business Cycle*, Oxford University Press, Oxford, 4th printing.

Travel Trade Gazette, 1987, 'Agents must diversify to survive', *TTG UK and Ireland*, 29 January.

Travel Trade Gazette, 1986, 'Grasp the technology nettle', *TTG UK and Ireland*, 3 July.

Travel Trade Gazette, 1987, 'Travicom fights US competition', *TTG UK and Ireland*, 3 July.

Turner, L., Ash, J., 1975, *The Golden Hordes: International Tourism and the Pleasure Periphery*, Constable, London.

Willig, R. D., 1979, 'Multiproduct technology and market structure', *American Economic Review*, Papers and Proceedings, May: 346–51.

World Tourism Organization, 1972, 'Economic review of world tourism: a study of the economic impact of tourism on national economies and international trade', *Travel Research Journal*, Madrid.

6 Tourism—the environmental dimension

M. Romeril

Introduction

The early years of mass tourism blossomed with the promise of new employment opportunities and economic growth. However the popularity with the expanding tourist sector of beach (sun, sea and sand) holidays carried with it the seeds of future problems because coastlines are mostly extremely fragile and sensitive environments. Along some sections of the Mediterranean coast, hotel buildings and associated developments which catered for those heady days of early mass tourism are now recognized as typifying the worst excesses of unbridled tourism development and despoilation. As the choice of holiday destinations has widened (for example, winter sports in Alpine regions) so the spread of mass tourism has generated further inimical environmental change.

Physical damage to the environment is not, however, the only consequence of the rapid spread and growth of tourism. Socio-cultural changes, though less tangible and paralleled by similar non-tourism induced effects, have in some cases been just as profound as physical impacts (Greenwood, 1976; Archer, 1978). Against all such negative impacts must be set the undoubted economic benefits and the creation of employment opportunities. Tourism can also generate a renaissance of traditional arts and crafts activities. Furthermore tourist-generated revenue is often channelled back into conservation efforts where tangible related benefits are evident as is the case with many of the large African National Parks (Sindiyo and Pertet, 1984). Such positive benefits can accrue also through the attraction of restored ancient monuments and buildings.

The growing concern for conservation and the health of our environment over the last two decades or so has not passed unnoticed in the tourism sector. While this awareness has touched all sectors of the public, the increased concern of those involved in tourism is no doubt due, in part, to the growing appreciation that environmental degradation can have very direct and undesirable consequences for the industry itself as despoiled destinations become less and less attractive to more and more discerning tourists. It has become clear that if the natural attractions (resources) of popular destinations are damaged or destroyed, a major reason for the area's popularity disappears.

Early international environmental initiatives emanated mainly from traditional conservation-oriented organizations with perhaps little specific reference to tourism, or indeed, to development of any kind; for example, the International Convention for the Prevention of Pollution of the Sea by Oil (1954) and the 'Ramsar' Convention on Wetlands of International Importance (1971). However the Stockholm United Nations Human Environment Conference of 1972 provided a major impetus to attempts to integrate the conservation of natural resources within broader economic and social strategies. The publication of the *World Conservation Strategy* (1980) and the *Report of the Brandt Commission* (1980) were further notable milestones. The Strategy's central theme of 'the sustainable utilisation of resources' was echoed by the latter's (socio-economic) study which stated *inter alia*, that '. . . the care of the natural environment is an essential aspect of development'.

Although the development of environmental tourism policy has lagged behind other environmental policy areas (Farrell, 1987), attempts to link conservation and tourism were being forged in the 1970s, for example the Copenhagen Conference (1973) organized jointly by Europa Nostra and the European Travel Commission. Then, in 1980, the Manila Declaration on World Tourism clearly reflected the mood of other global initiatives. It stated that '. . . the satisfaction of tourism requirements must not be prejudicial to the social and economic interests of the population in tourist areas, to the environment and above all, to natural resources, which are the fundamental attractions of tourism, and historical and cultural sites'.

The Declaration significantly broadened the environmental concern from its more common preoccupation with the physical environment and landscape. It recognized the need to weave tourist growth and development into the fabric and structure of local societies and their cultural heritage. If these initiatives are seen as events constituting a honeymoon period between environmental forces and tourism organizations, then the marriage was surely the formalizing of inter-agency coordination between the World Tourism Organization (WTO) and the United Nations Environment Programme (UNEP) in 1982. The Joint Accord agreed by these two influential and respected organizations placed a clear obligation on countries and development agencies to give environmental factors a high priority in tourism planning. UNEP's involvement reflects an earlier commitment to broaden the scope of environmental initiatives to encompass tourism as evidenced by its Regional Seas Programme, initially launched in 1975 for the Mediterranean, and now covering 11 regions, and which now includes a very significant tourism element.

Environmental impacts

The range of environmental impacts is extensive but they are generally categorized under three main headings: physical, biological and socio-economic (which includes cultural). However it is inevitable that impacts in one category do not occur in isolation but interrelate and overlap with one another. This is true also for positive and negative impacts. It makes the assessment of the net effect even more difficult since tangible economic impacts have to be evaluated alongside unquantifiable physical and biological effects. For comprehensive accounts of the full range of environmental impacts readers are referred to the publications of Haulot (1974), Cohen (1978), OECD (1980), Pearce (1981), Mathieson and Wall (1982), UNEP/WTO (1983), and UNEP (1984).

Saturation tourism, often the result of seasonality-induced peak inflows of tourists, leads to obvious manifestations of pollution and undesirable environmental change. The resort infrastructure becomes overloaded causing water shortages and sewage disposal problems. Sewage pollution, with its attendant ecological and health implications, is a major problem at many older Mediterranean tourist resorts (FAO, 1972; Tangi, 1977). Moreover the negative impact affects tourism itself since if the pollution is extreme, bathing may be banned from the affected beach. Overcrowding and congestion, especially that of traffic, is another obvious manifestation of saturation tourism. Mathieson and Wall (1982), quoting examples of traffic congestion, identify the phenomenon as a particularly serious consequence of resort development. High tourist traffic has been identified as the cause also of air pollution (lead and carbon monoxide) in mountain pass roads serving ski resorts (Council of Europe, 1978). Indeed, with the great boom in winter ski holidays, popular mountain resorts are experiencing many problems and pressures similar to beach resorts subject to mass tourism (Council of Europe, 1978; Brugger and Messerli, 1984).

Landscape impacts are often considerable and significant. Inappropriately designed and sited accommodation, built usually to cater for the peak levels of tourism, scar the landscape and constitute 'architectural pollution' (Pearce, 1978). Controls to limit the height of buildings and their proximity to the beach are increasingly being introduced. In mountain areas, the proliferation of tourist accommodation, ski lifts, cable cars, power lines and access roads can cause extensive negative visual impacts. _Sunny Beach—Bulgaria_

Demands on a critical resource such as water create direct and indirect impacts. A new reservoir may need to be constructed in an ecologically sensitive area or on high quality agricultural land if that is the only convenient location with a suitable topography. Indirectly, reduced water flows below the impoundment affect the ecology of the watercourse, and impair the ability of the water adequately to dilute polluting discharges, pointing up the vital need of watershed management (Rodriguez, 1987).

People 'foot pressure' is probably the best documented phenomenon of recreational activities which has been observed all over the world. Impact targets range from man-made structures (for example the Parthenon, Greece) and natural 'hard' features (for example Ayres Rock, Australia) to vulnerable ecosystems such as dunes and, in the marine context, coral reefs. In the terrestrial context the concern is twofold. Initially causing loss of vegetation, and therefore habitat, excessive trampling eventually leads to increased erosion, soil loss and gullying.

Even in wilderness areas where tourist density is usually low, many negative effects can occur (Rivers, 1974). Thus specific predator/prey relationships may be disrupted, wildlife killed, feeding and breeding habits adversely affected and migratory patterns upset. An especially worrying aspect of wilderness areas is the extensive souvenir trade in shells, corals and other animal artifacts (Rogers, 1981). Such items are increasingly sold globally regardless of their country of origin (Wells, 1981).

The changing pattern of more recent publications on tourism/environment issues reflects the wider and growing awareness, interest and concern (not necessarily in that order) of current problems. These can range from purely scientific concern for flora to a real risk of loss of human life. Thus botanists are anxious that the floral integrity of the Teide National Park in Tenerife (Canary Islands) is at risk from alien seeds carried (unwittingly) on the shoes and person of over a million tourists who visit the Park each year (Dickson *et al*., 1987). At the other extreme is the increasing alarm in Alpine regions that deforestation programmes, mainly servicing winter sports tourism, are a major cause of mudslides, floods and avalanches (Simons, 1988). The consequences are very real. The series of mudslides and floods in the North and South Tyrol, in the space of three weeks in July 1987, left more than 60 people dead, 7,000 homeless and 50 towns, villages and holiday centres wrecked. Moreover the restoration costs often fall mainly to local ratepayers who may not have been the main beneficiaries of the tourism-generated revenues.

The choice of these two examples in no way implies a specific priority or place on the spectrum of environmental impacts. However they do provide a useful reminder of the range of disciplines and research areas required to make an input into the formulation of environmental tourism policy. Farrell and McLellan (1987) make very pointed comments on the difficulties inherent in such diversity. They talk of '. . . social scientists groping with the intricacies of ecosystem research . . .' and of '. . . natural scientists long immersed in ecological concepts becoming aware that the natural principles gained from their disciplines have limited utility applied to human beings . . .'. Furthermore the integration of the 'academia' with the practitioners, both environmental and tourist, can be a further handicap to be overcome.

Even in the area of non-mass tourism, increasing numbers of visitors are travelling to ever more remote destinations. Sometimes this is merely to search for a relaxing haven that is still uncrowded, but increasingly tourists are seeking the wilderness experience of remote areas well away from so-called 'creature comforts'. The paradise islands of the Maldives, for example, provide the ever-popular sun, sea and sand holiday in uncrowded conditions. The islands gain considerable economic benefit from tourism but, despite a caring and very well planned strategy, are not totally without negative environmental impacts (Romeril, 1986).

In the wilderness context, the Himalayas provide an illuminating example of the potential consequences of tourism growth in an area environmentally and socially fragile (Singh and Kaur, 1985). Like coastal regions, mountains are fragile ecosystems and their carrying capacity is often low. Socially, in an area such as the Himalayas, it is vital to avoid an excessively exploitive emergence from the traditional subsistence economy. However, even with very low-density tourism, common negative impacts occur and it is salutory to note that the authorities in Nepal now insist that extra sherpas must accompany every Everest expedition to carry back discarded equipment, etc.—an unusual example of the ubiquitous litter problem (Cullen, 1986).

On the positive side, mention has already been made of the impetus tourism provides for the revival of art and crafts, and of the manner in which tourist revenues provide the means, often the only one, of maintaining historic buildings and ancient monuments. The continued existence of National Parks, and the creation of new ones, is often quoted as one of tourism's major positive conservation impacts and this is certainly true of many of Africa's large parks. In the marine environment, examples of harnessing visitor interest to encourage conservation efforts are evident in New Zealand (Ballantine and Gordon, 1979) and Indonesia (Salm, 1985).

The way forward

The last two examples quoted in the previous paragraph point up the potential for the successful promotion of tourism in a manner sympathetic to environmental objectives and of considerable mutual benefit. The potential for such a symbiotic relationship between environmental conservation and tourism was highlighted in 1976 by Budowski and emphasized especially by Romeril (1985) in a special edition of the *International Journal of Environmental Studies* devoted as it was to the theme of 'mutual dependence'. In the latter publication it was argued that tourism's strong dependence on quality natural resources makes the goal of their enduring and sustainable use an economic necessity as much as a desired ideal. Even more recently the value of such a mutual dependence or symbiosis received further support with respect to some Caribbean wetlands (Bacon, 1987).

The key to such policies lies not only in the increased environmental awareness but in the development of appropriate strategies and methodologies. This is far from easy in such diverse fields as tourism and environment where integration requires interdisciplinary and multidisciplinary approaches between two components which are, themselves, often without unity (Pigram, 1980). The broad review of Farrell and McLellan, of the philosophical and logistical problems, has been mentioned already. Pearce (1985) highlights the more specific shortfalls of research into the environmental impact of tourism and the role such research may play in tourist development. Handicapped itself by the wide spectrum of generally complex interrelationships and impacts, the appropriate research is further disadvantaged by being fed only slowly into the decision-making process.

This lack of appropriate research and data is very evident in one of the most

commonly quoted concepts relevant to environmental impacts and tourism—
that of carrying capacity. The concept of a threshold level of tourist activity
beyond which overcrowding, congestion and deleterious environmental
impacts will occur is an attractive one and not difficult to perceive in theory.
However the reality is far more difficult to rationalize and quantify since no
single typology of tourism, nor of environment, exists. Thus despite a long
history of use in relation to outdoor recreation, especially in the United States,
its value in the tourism context remains less clear (Wager, 1974; Wall, 1982;
O'Reilly, 1986). Nevertheless, as Wall points out in his critical appraisal of the
concept, if its use encourages tourism planners and managers to give greater
consideration to environmental matters, to the qualities of the experiences
available to both hosts and guests and to specify their goals and objectives, then
it will have served a useful purpose.

The concept itself attracts a plethora of definitions. Mitchell (1979)
discusses the concept under two headings: biophysical and behavioural;
Pearce and Kirk (1986) identify three types: environmental, physical (facilities)
and perceptual/social; and Shelby and Heberlein (1987) define four types:
ecological, physical (space), facility and social capacities. The last authors
propose a generic definition, 'that carrying capacity is the level of use beyond
which impacts exceed levels specified by evaluative standards'. This identifies
a value for one management parameter, use level, and assumes a fixed and
known relationship between use levels and impacts. The capacity can be varied
if other management parameters alter the relationship, if management
objectives are changed or if user values change radically.

The literature on carrying capacity tends to reflect the emphasis on
recreational capacities and, especially, the behavioural component. Mitchell
(1979) provides a particularly useful review. More recent publications draw
upon the considerable knowledge and experience gained in North American
National Parks (Lindsay, 1986; Shelby and Heberlein, 1987).

Shelby and Heberlein's book, useful as it is, does not cover the broad
spectrum of capacities as one might expect from its title. Ecological capacity is
soon dismissed and there are those who would question the authors' claim that
'in many settings social capacity is likely to be the limiting factor'. It focuses
very much on the behavioural component—capacity levels which relate to a
tourist's experience of crowding and overall satisfaction. As that experience
will depend very much on the tourist's perception and expectation of what
constitutes crowding and satisfaction, the difficulties in establishing consistent
capacity levels are self evident.

The Great Barrier Reef, Australia, provides an interesting example of this
phenomenon. There, the so-called wilderness diver appears to feel over-
crowded when there are more than two small boats or 20 divers at a single reef
whereas, at the other end of the scale, 500 tourists all contained within a single
high-speed catamaran and taken to moored pontoons on the reef appear also to
gain a satisfying 'wilderness' experience and do not seem disturbed by each
other's presence (Kenchington, 1983). In another context it is perhaps ironic

that a major complaint about visitor intrusion into wilderness areas such as the large African National Parks may come from other tourists to whom the attraction of these parks lies as much in the absence of humans as in the presence of animals (Hutchinson, 1975).

Physical and facility capacities are probably the most used by tourist planners. Beach capacities, for example numbers of people per square metre of beach, provide one measure which can be used as a planning tool (Lawson and Boyd-Bovey, 1977). In this instance the developer or manager will fix capacities at levels which will reflect the desired ambience of the resort. A whole range of other measurement criteria, for example bed spaces, equipment ratios, population (host/tourist) ratios may be used to fix capacities and a useful review is provided by WTO (1984).

Handicapped as it is by the fact that any area of significant size will have an infinite variety of habitats, plants and animals, ecological evaluation is probably the least developed aspect of the carrying capacity concept. Lindsay (1986) poses the questions: how many tourists does it take to kill a particular species of grass? or how much development renders a wetland no longer productive of wildfowl? The relationship between trampling and vegetation cover provides the most frequently used expression of biological carrying capacity. Generally, excessive trampling leads to adverse effects ranging widely from total loss of vegetation cover to physiological and morphological changes. The nature of the trampling impact will be critical and at alpine resorts there is the need to evaluate the winter versus the summer use of the mountain slopes. Clearly the carrying capacity will vary depending on the type of impact and the biological system. A general range of studies has been widely reviewed (Goldsmith, 1974; Liddle, 1975; Wall and Wright, 1977; Ittner, et al., 1979; and Mitchell, 1979).

Despite its limitations, carrying capacity evaluations can function as an operational concept for the planning exercise which is now considered necessary to avoid the negative effects which inevitably follow tourist saturation. However, other pragmatic approaches are being developed. Sorensen, et al. (1984) provide a comprehensive review of strategies for coastal resource management. The strategies emphasize the integrative approach where tourism is one of a number of land-use options. Although especially relevant to coastal resources, the strategies are not necessarily coast specific.

New methodologies are also evolving. A computerized approach to a procedural theory of planning, called SIRO-PLAN, has been developed in Australia where it has been applied across a range of inland and coastal areas including the Great Barrier Reef (Cocks, et al., 1983). Coastal Zone Management Planning (CZMP) is another technique proving of actual practical value (IUCN, 1986). The technique uses policies, plans and protected area designations as tools to facilitate the protection and management of sensitive and/or valuable coastal environments. A CZMP completed recently in the Sultanate of Oman offers an example of this type of approach (Salm and Dobbin, 1987).

Such developments offer hope for operational guidelines that decision-makers can use with enthusiasm and confidence. Farrell and McLellan (1987) list many papers covering examples over a range of special environments: recreational parks, alpine regions, small islands, tropical islands, coral reefs, lakes and inland waters. Yet the tenor of their paper clearly points up the many inadequacies of research and knowledge that remain. They call for a more systematic approach to the carrying out of research and the collating of the knowledge generated. Contextual interdisciplinary and multidisciplinary approaches are considered of prime importance. This integration is given a special focus by Murphy (1985) who, in proposing a community approach, emphasizes the local perspective—the need to encourage local initiative, local benefits and a tourism in harmony with the local environment and its people. He stresses the value of ecological dimension in tourism planning. Thus while their emphases may vary, Murphy and Farrell and McLellan are agreed on the paramount need to provide linkages to all aspects of the total human environment. Such a holistic approach, built on a symbiosis between tourism and the social and physical environment, surely provides the way forward.

Two difficulties seem to remain. Inbuilt suspicions still tend to maintain a polarization between the environmental lobby and the tourist industry. The conservationist is seen as a negative force, resisting any change, and the tourist developer is seen as an uncaring opportunist. Such extremes will always exist but many fall into neither category. However, so much often depends on the compatability and accord between the personnel, organizations and/or governments involved. The tragedy is that despite the many joint initiatives, conferences, workshops and publications, polarization to a lesser or greater extent remains and progress towards environmentally sound tourism planning remains slow. One waits for actions which will confirm **real** intent, or as Farrell and McLellan (1987) stress, 'one longs for specificity and directly applicable utility in the local area'.

The second difficulty relates to the disparate nature of research efforts. While not in itself a reason for the polarization identified in the previous paragraph, it does little to increase the mutual trust and co-operation needed foster a constructive and fruitful liaison between environmental and tourism practitioners. Many academic tourism courses have grown in recent years to take on board the expansion due to new technology and changing tourism practices yet, in general, they remain weak with respect to the environmental dimension, both in teaching and research. This should not remain so since it is likely that, in the next decade or so, concern for the environment (and its care) will dominate global issues while, at the same time, tourism (encompassing all leisure and recreation activity) is likely to become a major social influence for man. Thus a marriage of interests and goals is surely of more than passing significance. A healthy environmental integrity means the possibility of successful tourism, which, when managed properly, becomes a resource in its own right (Farrell and McLellan, 1987).

Such concern amongst environmentalists and tourism practitioners, and the very real gains in understanding and awareness of tourism/environment issues do represent significant progress. However that progress must be viewed against the backdrop of expediency and financial gain that still motivates too many involved in the industry. Two examples serve to illustrate this continuing dichotomy. The present rapid expansion of tourism in Turkey has been matched this year by heavy marketing in Britain and many holiday reviews of its attractions have appeared in the media of that country. While all have spoken highly of its tourist attractions, the articles have, almost without fail, carried a sting in their tail. Whether it was the tabloid press or up-market glossy magazines, nearly all the travel correspondents had a closing paragraph with one very clear warning. To quote one—'Turkey is the place for now; go there before it goes the way of the rest!' The symbiotic ideal of Budowski and Romeril will remain a distant goal while such detrimental change is still seen by so many, who know the industry so well, as the only inevitable outcome of the development of an emerging tourist industry.

On the other hand, the course of developing tourism in the Falkland Islands offers hope of change for the better. Thus Fielder Green Associates, the marketing consultants with the responsibility for developing tourism in those Islands have shown an especially enlightened approach in including, in their brief, the necessity to undertake after five years an environmental impact assessment. This will ensure that any negative effects, admittedly not anticipated by the careful marketing approach, will be monitored early enough to react in a manner which will ensure their reversal. The goal is to maintain a viable and profitable tourism industry without detriment to the environment.

References

Archer, B. H., 1978, 'Domestic tourism as a development factor', *Annals of Tourism Research*, 5: 126–41.

Bacon, P. R., 1987, 'Use of wetlands for tourism in the insular Caribbean', *Annals of Tourism Research*, 14: 104–17.

Ballantine, W. J., Gordon, D. P., 1979, 'New Zealand's first marine nature reserve, Cape Rodney to Okakari Point, Leigh', *Biological Conservation*, 15: 273–80.

Brandt Commission, *North–South, A Programme for Survival*, 1980, Pan, London.

Brugger, E. A., Messerli, P. (eds), 1984, *The Transformation of the Swiss Mountain Regions*, Verlag Paul Haupt, Bern.

Budowski, G., 1976, 'Tourism and environmental conservation: conflict, coexistence or symbiosis', *Environmental Conservation*, 3(1): 27–31.

Cocks, K. D., Ive, J. R., Davis, J. R., and Baird, I. A., 1983, 'The SIRO-PLAN land-use planning method', *Environment and Planning B, Planning and Design*, 10: 331–45.

Cohen, E., 1978, 'The impact of tourism on the physical environment', *Annals of Tourism Research*, 5: 215–37.

Council of Europe, 1978, *Proceedings on the Seminar on Pressure and Regional Planning Problems in Mountain Regions, Particularly in the Alps Grindelwald (Switzerland)*, Council of Europe, Strasbourg.

Cullen, R., 1986, 'Himalayan mountaineering expedition garbage', *Environmental Conservation*, 13(4): 293–7.

Dickson, J. H., Rodriguez, J. C. and Machada, A., 1987, 'Invading plants at high altitudes on Tenerife especially in Teide National Park', *Botanical Journal of the Linnean Society*, 95: 155–79.

Europa Nostra and European Travel Commission, 1973, *Tourism and Conservation— Working Together*, ETC, Dublin.

Farrell, B. H., McLellan, R. W., 1987, 'Tourism and physical environment research', *Annals of Tourism Research*, 14: 1–16.

FAO, 1972, *The State of Marine Pollution in the Mediterranean and Legislative Controls*, Studies and Reviews Report, No. 51.

Goldsmith, F. B., 1974, 'Ecological effects of visitors in the countryside', in Warren, A., and Goldsmith, F. B., *Conservation in Practice*, Wiley, London, pp. 201–15.

Greenwood, D., 1976, 'Tourism as an agent of change', *Annals of Tourism Research*, 3: 128–42.

Haulot, A., 1974, *Tourisme et environnement; la recherche d'un equilibre*, Marabout Monde Moderne, Verviers, Belgium.

Hutchinson, A., 1975, 'Elephant survival: two schools of thought', *Wildlife*, 17: 104–7.

IUCN, 1980, *World Conservation Strategy: Living Resource Conservation for Sustainable Development*, IUCN, Gland, Switzerland.

IUCN, 1986, *Oman Coastal Zone Management Plan: Greater Capital Area*, IUCN, Gland, Switzerland.

Ittner, R., Potter, D. R., Agee, J. K., and Anschell, S. (eds), 1979, *Recreational Impact on Wildlands, Conference Proceedings*, US Forest Service No: R-6-001—1979.

Kenchington, R. A., 1983, 'The development of methods for selection and monitoring of tourist operations and sites', *Marine and Coastal Processes in the Pacific, Ecological Aspects of Coastal Zone Management*, UNESCO, Jakarta, pp. 4–16.

Lawson, F., Boyd-Bovy, M., 1977, *Tourism and Recreation Development—A Handbook on Evaluating Tourism Resources*, Architectural Press, London.

Liddle, M. J., 1975, 'A selective review of the ecological effects of human trampling on natural ecosystems', *Biological Conservation*, 7: 17–36.

Lindsay, J. J., 1986, 'Carrying capacity for tourism development in national parks of the United States', *UNEP Industry and Environment*, 9(1): 17–20.

Mathieson, A., Wall, G., 1982, *Tourism: Economic, Physical and Social Impacts*, Longman, New York.

Mitchell, B., 1979, *Geography and Resource Analysis*, Longman, New York, pp. 176–200.

Murphy, P., 1985, *Tourism—A Community Approach*, Methuen, New York.

OECD, 1980, *The Impact of Tourism on the Environment*, OECD, Paris.

O'Reilly, A. M., 1986, 'Tourism carrying capacity; concept and issues', *Tourism Management*, 7(4): 254–8.

Pearce, D., 1985, 'Tourism and environmental research: a review', *International Journal of Environmental Studies*, 25(4): 247–55.

Pearce, D., 1978, 'Form and function in French resorts', *Annals of Tourism Research*, 6: 245–72.

Pearce, D., 1981, *Tourist Development*, Longman, New York.

Pearce, D., Kirk, R. M., 1986, 'Carrying capacities for coastal tourism', *UNEP Industry and Environment*, 9(1): 3–7.

Pigram, J. J., 1980, 'Environmental implications of tourism development', *Annals of Tourism Research*, 7: 554–83.

Rivers, P., 1974, 'Tourist troubles', *New Society*, 23(539): 250.

Rodriguez, S., 1987, 'Impact of ski industry on the River Hondo watershed', *Annals of Tourism Research*, 14: 88–103.

Rogers, C., 1981, 'Caribbean—coral reefs under threat', *New Scientist*, 5 Nov: 382–7.

Romeril, M., 1985, 'Tourism and the environment—towards a symbiotic relationship', *International Journal of Environmental Studies*, 25(4): 215–18.

Romeril, M., 1986 (ed.), *Proceedings of Workshop on Environmental Assessment of Tourism Development*, Department of Tourism, Male, Republic of Maldives.

Salm, R. V., 1985, 'Integrating marine conservation and tourism', *International Journal of Environmental Studies*, 25(4): 229–38.

Salm, R. V., Dobbin, J. A., 1987, *A Coastal Zone Management Strategy for the Sultanate of Oman, Proceedings of Coastal Zone '87'*, WW Division, ASCE, Seattle, pp. 97–106.

Shelby, B., Heberlein, T. A., 1987, *Carrying Capacity in Recreation Settings*, Oregon State University Press, Oregon.

Simons, P., 1988, 'Après ski le déluge', *New Scientist*, 14 Jan.: 49–52.

Sindiyo, D. M., Pertet, F. N., 1984, 'Tourism and its impact on wildlife in Kenya', *UNEP Industry and Environment*, 7(1): 14–19.

Singh, T. V., Kaur, J., 1985, 'In search of holistic tourism in the Himalays', in Singh, T. V., Kaur, J. (eds), *Integrated Mountain Development*, Himalayan Books (The English Book Store), New Delhi.

Sorensen, J. C., McCreary, S. T., and Hershman, M. J., 1984, *Institutional Arrangements for Management of Coastal Resources*, Renewable Resources Information Series Coastal Management Publication No. 1, National Parks Service, US Department of the Interior.

Tangi, M., 1977, 'Tourism and the environment', *Ambio*, 6: 336–41.

UNEP/WTO, 1983, *Proceedings of Workshop on Environmental Aspects of Tourism*, joint publication of UNEP, Paris, and WTO, Madrid.

UNEP, 1984, 'Tourism and the environment', *UNEP Industry and Environment*—species edition, 7.

Wager, J. A., 1974, 'Recreational carrying capacity reconsidered', *Journal of Forestry*, 72: 274–8.

Wall, G., 1982, 'Cycles and capacity—incipient theory or conceptual contradiction', *Tourism Management*, 3(3): 188–92.

Wall, G., and Wright, C., 1977, *The Environmental Impact of Outdoor Recreation*, Publication Series No. 11, Department of Geography, University of Waterloo, Waterloo.

Wells, S. M., 1981, *International Trade in Ornamental Corals and Shells*, Proceedings of 4th International Coral Reef Symposium, Manila, pp. 323–9.

WTO, 1980, *Manila Declaration*, WTO World Tourism Conference, Manila.

WTO, 1984, 'Tourist carrying capacity', *UNEP Industry and Environment*, 7(1): 30–6.

7 Tourism in the South Pacific islands

J. Fletcher and H. Snee

The potential for tourism growth in East Asia and the Pacific is enormous, with many destinations recording the highest growth rates in the world. In 1950 the East Asia and Pacific region was accountable for less than 1 per cent of the world's international tourist arrivals; by 1960 this figure had only risen to 1 per cent. The following decade witnessed increasing tourism activity and in 1970 the region accounted for 3 per cent of the world's tourist arrivals; by 1980 this figure had risen to 7 per cent and by 1986 it was 8.8 per cent and the countries enjoyed well over 10 per cent of the world's total international tourism receipts.

The majority of tourism activity in the East Asia and Pacific region takes place in countries such as China (22.819 million visitor arrivals);[1] Malaysia (over 5 million); Hong Kong (3.7 million); Singapore (3.2 million); Thailand (2.8 million) and Japan (2.1 million), whereas all of the South Pacific islands combined account for less than 0.2 per cent of the world's international tourist arrivals.

There is also great diversity in the levels of tourism activity within the Pacific islands themselves, ranging from the mass tourist destinations of the mid-Pacific such as Guam, Hawaii and Saipan to those islands such as Yap, Western Samoa, the Republic of Palau and the Solomon Islands where tourism is very much in its embryonic stage. To emphasize this point, it should be noted that the three islands of Guam, Hawaii and Saipan cater for the needs of approximately six million tourists per annum which is some 12 times greater than all of the South Pacific islands combined.

There are a number of factors which can explain the relatively slow development of tourism activity in many of the South Pacific islands. First, their historical background has not been conducive to the early development of tourism activity—many of the islands have been colonial islands and only in the past 30 years have they achieved some level of political independence.

Second, most of the islands are relatively small in size and population with poor communication facilities with the larger, more economically developed land masses of the region. This tends to preserve and strengthen the cultural bonding of the island and creates social resistance to the development of an industry where the consumers of the tourism export must consume the product within the geographical boundaries of the exporting country. There have been two symposia on the socio-cultural impacts of tourism on Pacific islands (Farrell, 1977 and Finney and Watson, 1977) and Mathieson and Wall (1982) refer to the 'numerous unwanted social and cultural side-effects as a result of the rapid growth of the (tourism) industry'. Other studies, such as the ones by Urbanowicz (1977a, 1977b) and Koea (1977) have also emphasized the strains on the social framework in countries such as Tonga.

Third, and most important, the South Pacific islands are physically far removed from the major tourist generating countries of Europe and North America. The vast distances which the tourist must cover to reach the South Pacific destinations makes such visits relatively expensive and outside the budget of most sun, sand and sea tourists—the mass market. Therefore, tourism in the region has tended to focus on either the special-interest traveller (Second World War specialists, scuba divers, flora and fauna specialists, etc), those in search of an exclusive vacation or intra-regional tourism which, because of poor economic growth, tends to be a limited market. Conversely, islands such as Hawaii owe a significant part of their tourism development to their close proximity to a major tourist-generating country (see Gray, 1974; and Turner, 1976).

Fourth, most of the islands are at a very early stage of economic development and do not possess the infrastructure necessary to cater for the needs of mass tourism. Communications by air are often infrequent, road communications are poor, health facilities tend to be inadequate, shopping facilities are rudimentary and potable water and sewage disposal services are not capable of catering for the demands of mass tourism.

Finally, because the islands are in the early stages of economic development, the perceived rewards from tourism activity are not as evident as they are in more developed economies. If tourism development begins with the construction of one or two large hotels, they tend to be foreign-owned so profits leak out of the economy, managerial staff tend to be imported resulting in part of the wages and salaries leaking out of the economy, the construction materials tend to be imported and many of the tourist consumables tend to be imported.

All of these factors lead to a high-import content associated with tourism and, consequently, a low multiplier value. Of course, different types of tourist establishments are likely to have different propensities to import (Lundberg, 1972), but, in general, tourism activity in small, developing island economies is associated with a high-import content. The benefits of tourism tend to be small whereas the costs in terms of government services, society, culture and environment seem to be disproportionately high. The import content of tourism activity in the South Pacific islands as a whole is in excess of 50 per cent, with a range estimated to be between 50 and 90 per cent which significantly reduces the beneficial impact of tourism to the region. This fact was noted back in the early 1970s by the World Bank which estimated that the import content of the Pacific region was 50–60 per cent because of (1) the high propensity to import, (2) the level of expatriate labour and (3) the nature of capital investment (World Bank, 1972).

Short-term crises can severely disrupt the development of tourism, particularly during the early stages of development. So events such as the assassina-

Figure 7.1 *The South Pacific islands*

tion of the Republic of Palau's first president, the destruction caused by hurricane Namu on the Solomon Islands in 1986 and the recent coup in Fiji can set back the development of their tourist industries by years, if not decades.

The plight of the South Pacific islands can be demonstrated by examining, in greater detail, the impact of tourism on three groups of islands—one from Micronesia, one from Melanesia and lastly, one from Polynesia.

The Republic of Palau (Micronesia)

Micronesia is one of the three principal divisions of Oceania, whose main groups are the Caroline, Marshall and Marianas islands. The republic of Palau forms the most western group of islands that make up the Caroline islands. It lies 7°30′ north of the equator, 600 miles east of the Philippines, 722 miles south of Guam, 1,739 miles from Hong Kong and 3,319 miles from Sydney, Australia. There are some 200 islands in the Palauan group, stretching north to south over 400 miles; 197 of the islands are located within a single barrier reef (making local sea transport relatively easy) and the largest island, Babeldaob, is just 27 miles long and 15 miles wide at its widest point.

Palau has been subject to four different colonial administrations since Captain Henry Wilson's ship ran aground there in 1783. The Spanish took control of the islands in 1885 (from the British), but sold them to the Germans in 1899 along with the rest of the Caroline islands and the northern Marianas. The Germans introduced a programme of agricultural development (mainly coconut plantations) and began mining phosphate. The Japanse forces took the Caroline islands in 1914 and by 1920 Koror, the capital of Palau, became the administrative centre for all of the Japanese-controlled islands in the South Pacific.

Colonialization devastated the local population which fell from its 1783 level of over 40,000 to less than 4,000 by 1900 as a result of the introduction of influenza and dysentery. This rapid depopulation resulted in many of Palau's villages being abandoned and the Japanese importing much of their own labour (by 1935, 25,768 Japanese were living in Palau).

In September 1944, the United States invaded Palau and were in control of the Caroline, Marshal and Marianas islands by 1946. Palau, along with the other island groups of Micronesia, achieved significant levels of autonomy in 1956 and 1975 and finally became self-governing in 1980 with the ratification of the 1979 Constitutional Convention.

Tourism in the Republic of Palau

The number of tourist arrivals between 1979 and 1983 was fairly static, fluctuating around 5,000 pleasure and business arrivals per annum. From 1983 onwards the tourism statistics show a rapid increase, 27 per cent increase in 1984 and an impressive 64.3 per cent increase in 1985, but care must be taken when interpreting these increases because of the number of imported workers that were brought in to build the two new international standard hotels. Nevertheless, there has been a significant boost to tourism in Palau and much of the credit for this must go to the private sector which launched major promotional activities in Japan.

Japanese tourists account for just over 50 per cent of all visitors to Palau and 95 per cent of them arrive for pleasure purposes; the United States account for a further 25 per cent of visitor arrivals but 20 per cent of these are business arrivals. Another interesting distinction between the Japanese and the American visitors is that whereas the majority of the Japanese vacationers are general holiday-makers who come to relax in Palau's natural scenic beauty, the majority of the American vacationers are 'special interest' visitors who are attracted to Palau's almost unparalleled marine environment—mainly scuba diving and snorkelling. The remaining 25 per cent of arrivals are distributed amongst the other countries.

Palau has four hotels of international standard but, as recently as 1986, one of the newest hotels was still not operational and the three remaining establishments were only operating with 30–40 per cent occupancy levels. Therefore, the availability of accommodation facilities is not an immediate constraint on future tourism development. On the other hand, the availability of international air transport facilities presents a severe constraint on tourism development. The airport on Babeldaob is not suitable for wide-bodied jets; most visitors must transit through Guam which often necessitates an overnight stay and the flights are far too infrequent.

In 1985 total visitor expenditure was estimated to be US$6 million. Using input–output analysis, the following multiplier values were calculated (Fletcher, 1986a):

Direct plus indirect multiplier effects.[2]
 Income multiplier   = 0.360–0.418
 Government revenue
 multiplier   = 0.234–0.282
 Import multiplier   = 0.499–0.582

In terms of the ability of tourism to create local job opportunities in Palau, for every US$1 million of expenditure, 58.46 full-time equivalent job opportunities are supported. Finally, in terms of imports, more than 53 cents of every tourist dollar leaks out of the economy during the first round of expenditure and this figure increases to more than 82 cents by the time that the tourist dollar has finished circulating in the economy.

The Solomon Islands (Melanesia)

The Solomon Islands form part of Melanesia and the hundreds of islands which make up the Solomons stretch over a distance of almost 1,000 miles. The islands are located between 5° and 12° south of the equator, lying to the east of Papua New Guinea, to the north-east of Australia and to the north-west of Vanuatu. The land area covers 11,500 square miles with a population of 215,000. The economy is largely dependent upon agriculture, forestry and fishing but, whereas the net foreign exchange receipts from these exports have been static or even declining over recent years (despite increases in output in some cases), the net foreign exchange receipts from international tourism have been consistently increasing.

The Solomons were discovered by the Spanish explorer Alvara de Mendana in 1568. By 1899 they were under British administration and remained that way until 1978 when, as part of the British Commonwealth, they achieved political independence.

Tourism in the Solomon Islands

Although tourism in the Solomon Islands is in its infancy, with the exception of a few years the number of visitor arrivals has grown steadily throughout the 1970s and 1980s. In 1985, there were 11,974 visitors plus some 2,294 excursionists who arrived on five cruise ships. The majority of visitors originate from Australia, Papua New Guinea, New Zealand and other South Pacific countries, with the remainder coming from Japan, the United States, the United Kingdom and other European countries. A further point worthy of mention is the lack of any significant seasonal fluctuation in the number of arrivals. The busiest month in terms of tourist arrivals is December (1,179 visitors in 1985) and the quietest month is June (which recorded 828 visitors in 1985).

Pleasure tourists accounted for 58 per cent of all visitor arrivals and 29 per cent were visiting the Solomon Islands for business purposes, while the remaining 13 per cent of visitors were there for other purposes (religion, sport, official government business, etc.).

On the supply side there are 244 rooms available for tourism in the Solomons and almost 80 per cent of these are to be found in hotels. Some 95 per cent of the available rooms are located in the capital, Honiara: there are three hotels which provide 181 rooms plus a small hotel with just 10 rooms. The remaining 53 rooms are to be found in six resorts scattered throughout the area.

Unlike the Republic of Palau, the limited availability of hotel rooms is a severe constraint on the development of tourism in the Solomon Islands. It is not possible to make any future significant advancement in the level of tourism activity without constructing additional hotel bedrooms.

The other major supply-side constraint concerns the transport sector. First,

Table 7.1 *Visitors to the Solomon Islands*

1980	1981	1982	1983	1984	1985[1]
10,517	11,171	11,179	11,113	11,177	11,974

[1] Australia 35.8%, Papua New Guinea 20.4%, New Zealand 10.3%, other Pacific countries 10.9%, USA 7.0%, rest of the world 15.6%.

there is the international air transport constraint, with limited and infrequent flights to the Solomons from tourist-generating countries. This is a problem which is beyond the direct control of the Solomon Islands' government but has a significant influence on the ability of the public and private sectors to expand the number of tourist arrivals. Second, there is a lack of inter-island transport facilities (planes and boats) to transport visitors between Guadalcanal province and the other islands. This seriously hampers the development of the specialist tourist sector (divers, Second World War specialists, etc.) since these visitors must be able to travel between the islands. Finally, there is a shortage of buses and taxis etc. to transport the tourists within and around Honiara.

Tourism expenditure increased by 37 per cent between 1981 and 1985 and the Central Bank of the Solomon Islands estimated total tourist expenditure for the year ending March 1986 to be SI$3.950 million which, although representing only 3.5 per cent of total exports of the Solomons, makes tourism the fastest growing export industry in the economy. For the year 1986/7 it was estimated that tourism expenditure amounted to SI$5.392 million, an increase of more than 36 per cent, but care must be taken when drawing such conclusions because the 1986/7 figure was derived from a business expenditure survey (Fletcher, 1987) as opposed to the Central Bank's estimate, which was derived from foreign exchange transactions. In addition to the SI$5.392 million estimated from the business expenditure survey there was a further SI$2.616 spent on tourist-related services—the breakdown of tourist expenditure during 1986 is shown in Table 7.2. The direct plus indirect tourism multiplier affects are as follows:

Income multiplier   = 0.523
Government revenue
multiplier   = 0.137
Import multiplier   = 0.477

In so far as employment is concerned, tourism activity creates some 435 full-time equivalent job opportunities directly and this number increases to 769 if all of the secondary effects are taken into account.

Table 7.2 *Tourist expenditure in the Solomon Islands, 1986*

	SI$	%
Hotels and resorts	4,201,493	52.47
Restaurants and bars	201,543	2.52
Diving shops	231,347	2.89
Handicrafts	267,504	3.34
Local shops/transport etc.	3,105,854	38.78
Total	8,007,741	100.00

Western Samoa (Polynesia)

Samoa is located 14° south of the equator in the central area of the South Pacific and is often publicized as being the 'gateway to Polynesia' lying to the west of French Polynesia, 1,800 miles north-north east of New Zealand and 2,700 miles to the north-east of Sydney, Australia. The Europeans discovered Samoa in 1722 when the Dutch landed there, but the islands were divided in 1899 when the United States held what is now known as American Samoa and the Germans held Western Samoa. New Zealand took Western Samoa from the Germans during the First World War and it was held by them as UN trust territory until independence in 1962.

Western Samoa consists of two major islands, Upolu (45 by 15 miles) and Savaii (45 by 25 miles), plus a few smaller islands. It has a land area of 1,100 square miles and a population of just over 150,000. The economy is largely dependent upon agriculture, but the range of produce is limited with 65 per cent of their export receipts coming from the sale of copra and copra products. Between 1982 and 1985 the receipts from agricultural exports increased 2.08 times compared with receipts from tourism, which increased 4.4 times.

Tourism in Western Samoa

The tourism statistics relating to Western Samoa were subject to significant distortions prior to the early 1980s; therefore it is not possible to be precise about the trend of tourist arrivals. However in 1984 Western Samoa received some 24,000 tourist arrivals plus visitors from American Samoa and cruise ship passengers. The growth of tourist arrivals throughout the 1970s and 1980s seems to average approximately 500 to 600 additional visitors per annum. Almost half of the tourist arrivals are intra-regional tourists, largely from New Zealand and Australia with a further 25 per cent arriving from North America. It is assumed that a large proportion of these tourists are Samoans now resident in the above countries. European countries seem to provide a further 10–14 per cent of visitor arrivals and the remainder originate from the rest of the world.

There are more than 400 rooms available in the tourist sector but, in 1986, some of these rooms were not on the market because some establishments had ceased operation. More than 75 per cent of the available rooms are located in the capital, Apia, and there is only one beach resort hotel (30 rooms) on the island of Upolu. The other hotels are located on the neighbouring island of Savaii.

In the absence of a visitor expenditure survey, a business expenditure survey undertaken in 1985 estimated that tourist expenditure in the previous 12 months had been $10 million (Fletcher, 1986b). It was estimated that for every $1 million of tourist expenditure $177,675 went directly to local incomes in the form of wages, salaries and locally distributed profits and $27,656 was directly collected as government revenue.

The direct plus tourism multiplier effects are as follows:

Income multiplier $= 0.388$
Government revenue
multiplier $= 0.198$
Import multiplier $= 0.547$

Western Samoa differs from Palau and the Solomons in the sense that it sufers from excess supply in the tourism sector. An example of this is to be found in the restaurant and bar sector: a number of restaurants in Apia were experiencing severe financial difficulties because of a lack of tourists, resulting in a cut-back in the level and quality of service ultimately leading to a fall in visitor satisfaction thus compounding the problem. It also suffers from poor international air contacts which limits the growth in tourist arrivals: additionally there are inadequate promotion and marketing strategies from both the public and private sectors.

Conclusions

The three groups of islands demonstrate the problems facing the South Pacific islands in developing their tourist industries. All three countries have only achieved political independence during the past 26 years. Economic reliance upon agricultural exports such as copra presents extreme difficulties because even though there have been significant advances in output by volume, the world market price has fluctuated reducing the foreign exchange receipts from these exports.

Subsistence farming is evident to a very large degree in all three economies with a consequent lack of organized markets for agricultural products adding to the already high propensities to import associated with tourism activity (ranging from 48 to 58 per cent). High imports by the hotels, restaurants, etc., are exacerbated by the relatively high importing activities of the moneyed household sector. Together, these factors result in low income multipliers, ranging from 0.36 to 0.52. While this situation continues, the economic benefits of tourism will not materialize; whereas the economic, social and cultural costs are only too evident. It is worth mentioning that the level of imports associated with domestic consumption will result in low multiplier values regardless of the vehicle used for economic expansion.

The economic problems facing Australia and New Zealand have most certainly had their repercussions on the development of tourism in the Solomons and Western Samoa and these are factors which, like the world prices for copra, are outside the control of the domestic economies. Equally, many of the factors which have hindered the development of tourism in the South Pacific islands are outside the control of the national governments, for example air traffic constraints, lack of funds for investment in the necessary infrastructure, recently acquired political autonomy, hurricanes. However, the governments themselves have, in some cases, been more than a little ambivalent over the strategies (or even desirability) for developing tourism. Fox (1977) noted that the political leaders of some of the South Pacific islands (including Tonga, the Cook Islands, Samoa and Fiji) had claimed that 'tourism will improve our country's economy and will benefit our islands' people' at the same time complaining, as did the Fijian Minister for Communication, Works and Tourism, that tourism expansion would result in the destruction of their social fabric and that this was unacceptable.

The development of tourism can enhance the economic development of the South Pacific islands, but only if there is an active policy decision to develop tourism in a coordinated fashion. The first issue to be faced is whether or not the countries concerned are prepared to meet the social and cultural costs that are inevitable if they are to enjoy the economic benefits associated with tourism. Although it is possible to minimize the social and cultural costs of tourism development through sound planning and legislative regulation, some costs are unavoidable. Irrespective of the economic and social costs of tourism, the need for careful regulation of tourism development was pointed out by Beed (1961) and Clement (1961), who were both concerned that rapid development of tourism in Tahiti would lead to ecological imbalance on the island. The major problem on this issue is that, although any form of economic development will bring with it social and cultural change, tourism has a much more obvious impact with its *demonstration effect*.

Tourism can provide increased flows of foreign exchange and thereby improve the balance-of-payments' position of an economy. It can create job opportunities and increase income levels, provide social overhead capital which can be enjoyed by the host population and it can increase government revenue. Thus, if the decision to develop tourism is taken, a sound development plan is essential in order to maximize these benefits while keeping the costs to a minimum.

Notes

1. Around 95% of China's arrivals are excursionists.
2. The multiplier values for Palau are given as a range because of the lack of accurate data concerning the precise expenditure pattern of tourists. The range was calculated by using two separate tourist consumption functions covering the feasible range of tourist expenditure.

References

Beed, T. W., 1981, 'Tahiti's recent tourist development', *Geography*, 46: 368.
Clement, H. G., 1961, *The Future of Tourism in the Pacific and the Far East*, US Dept. of Commerce, Washington D.C.

Diamond, J. 1977, 'Tourism's role in economic development: a case reexamined', *Economic and Cultural Change*, 25: 539–53.

Erbes, N., 1973, *International Tourism and the Economy of Developing Countries*, OECD, Paris.

Farrell, B. H. (ed.), 1977, *The Social and Economic Impact of Tourism on Pacific Communities*, Center for South Pacific Studies, University of California, Santa Cruz.

Finney, B. R., Watson, A. (eds), 1977, *A New Kind of Sugar: Tourism in the Pacific*, East–West Technology and Development Institute, East–West Center, Honolulu.

Fletcher, J. E., 1986a, *The Economic Impact of International Tourism on the National Economy of the Republic of Palau*, a report to the government of Palau for the UNDP/WTO (RAS/83/002).

Fletcher, J. E., 1986b, *The Economic Impact of International Tourism on the National Economy of Western Samoa*, a report to the government of Western Samoa for the UNDP/WTO (RAS/83/002).

Fletcher, J. E., 1987, *The Economic Impact of International Tourism on the National Economy of The Solomon Islands*, a report to the government of the Solomon Islands for the UNDP/WTO (RAS/83/002).

Fox, M., 1977, 'The social impact of tourism: a challenge to researchers and planners', in Finney, B. R., Watson, A. (eds), *A New Kind of Sugar: Tourism in the Pacific*, Center for South Pacific Studies, University of California, Santa Cruz, pp. 27–48.

Gray, H. P., 1974, 'Towards an economic analysis of tourism policy', *Social and Economic Studies*, 23: 386–97.

Jonish, J. E., Peterson, R. E., 1973, 'Impact of tourism: Hawaii', *Cornell Hotel and Restaurant Administration Quarterly*, 14: 5–12.

Koea, A., 1977, 'Polynesian migration to New Zealand', in Finney, B. R., Watson, A. (eds), *A New Kind of Sugar: Tourism in the Pacific*, Center for South Pacific Studies, University of California, Santa Cruz.

Knox, J., 1978, *Classification of Hawaii Residents' Attitudes Towards Tourists and Tourism*, Tourism Research Project Occasional Paper No. 1, University of Hawaii at Manoa, Honolulu.

Lundberg, D. E., 1972, *The Tourist Business*, Cahners, Boston. MacKenzie, M., 1977, 'The deviant art of tourism: airport art', in Farrell, B. H. (ed.), *The Social and Economic Impact of Tourism on Pacific Communities*, Center for South Pacific Studies, University of California, Santa Cruz.

Marsh, J. S., 1975, 'Hawaiian tourism: costs, benefits, alternatives', *Alternatives*, 4: 34–9.

Mathieson, A., Wall, G., 1982, *Tourism: Economic, Physical and Social Impacts*, Longman, London.

May, R. J., 1977, 'Tourism and the artefact in Papua New Guinea', in Finney, B. R., and Watson, A. (eds), *A New Kind of Sugar: Tourism in the Pacific*, Center for South Pacific Studies, University of California, Santa Cruz.

Turner, L., 1976, 'The international division of leisure: tourism and the third world', *World Development*, 4: 253–60.

Urbanowicz, C. F., 1977, 'Tourism in Tonga: troubled times', in Smith, V. (ed.), *Hosts and Guests: the Anthropology of Tourism*, University of Pennsylvania Press, Philadelphia, pp. 83–9.

Urbanowicz, C. F., 'Integrating tourism with other industries in Tonga', in Smith, V. (ed.), *Hosts and Guests: the Anthropology of Tourism*, University of Pennsylvania Press, Philadelphia, pp. 89–93.

World Bank, 1972, *Tourism—Sector Working Paper*, Washington D.C.

8 Tourism and island economies: impact analyses

B. H. Archer

The purpose of this chapter is to discuss the contribution which impact analysis can make to understanding the economic effects of tourism in island economies. Discussion is limited to the small- and medium-sized countries and examples are drawn primarily from islands where rigorous analyses have been undertaken. The attention of readers is drawn also to chapter 7, 'Tourism in the South Pacific islands' by J. E. Fletcher in this volume.

The magnitude of the economic impact made by tourism on an island depends upon (1) the volume of tourist expenditure and (2) the direct and secondary effects which this expenditure has on the economy.

The volume of tourism

Tourist expenditure is an invisible export in that it forms an injection of foreign currency into the economy of the destination island. The principal tourist-island destinations outside Europe are shown in Table 8.1.

In terms of tourist and cruise passenger arrivals and also receipts from tourism, the Caribbean and Atlantic area is dominated by the Bahamas and Puerto Rico, with four countries (Jamaica, United States Virgin Islands, Bermuda and Saint Maarten) forming a second significant group. The Pacific area is dominated by Hong Kong and Singapore, with both Indonesia and the Philippines generating significant numbers. The Indian Ocean islands, more distant from their markets, receive relatively smaller numbers. Arrivals and receipts, however, provide only a partial picture of the impact made by tourism on these island economies. Information about the direct and secondary effects can be obtained from impact analysis.

Impact analysis

Impact analysis is an economic approach used to measure *inter alia* the amount of income, government revenue, employment and imports generated in an economy by the direct and secondary effects of tourist expenditure. The direct effects are those created in the establishments which trade directly with tourists; the secondary effects are those created by the further rounds of

Table 8.1 *Major tourist-island-destination countries, 1986*

Country	International tourist arrivals ('000s)	Cruise passenger arrivals ('000s)	International tourist receipts (US$ million)
Caribbean and Atlantic area			
Puerto Rico	1,573	449	720
Bahamas	1,375	1,496	1,114
Jamaica	663	279	516
US Virgin Islands	470	827	509
Bermuda	460	132	407
Saint Maarten	439	314	160
Barbados	370	145	327
Trinidad and Tobago	191	19	190
Martinique	183	217	92
Aruba	181	73	111
Cayman Islands	166	271	94
British Virgin Islands	164	22	122
Antigua	149	123	114
Guadaloupe	148	64	98
Curaçao	128	126	89
Saint Lucia	112	59	68
Haiti	112	na	58
Indian Ocean			
Sri Lanka	230	na	75
Mauritius	165	8	89
Maldives	114	2	42
Seychelles	67	3	56
Pacific area			
Singapore	2,902	9	1,842
Hong Kong	2,589	11	2,211
Indonesia	825	117	591
Philippines	764	17	647
Guam	262	9	308
Fiji	258	49	182
French Polynesia	161	4	146

Note: Care should be taken in the interpretation of these data, not all of which were compiled on the same basis (for details see WTO, op. cit.).

Source: Adapted from World Tourism Organization, 1987, *Compendium of Tourism Statistics*, Madrid. 1987.

economic activity as the money spent by tourists works through the economic system. Thus the hotels, shops, restaurants, transport companies and other businesses re-spend the money which they receive from tourists. This forms business revenue to other establishments, revenue to the government and income to the work-force. In turn, these secondary recipients re-spend some or all of the money and this forms further flows of money through the system. At each stage some money 'leaks' out of the economy to purchase imports and into bank deposits as savings. Thus the amount of money re-circulating in each round diminishes until the volume becomes insignificant. For a more detailed description of impact analysis and of the techniques available to measure the flows, together with their strengths, weaknesses and limitations, see Archer (1977a) and Wanhill (1983).

The most rigorous techniques used for impact analysis are input–output (I–O), Keynesian multiplier models and *ad-hoc* models. I–O analysis involves compiling a table of all transactions which have taken place in an economy for a given period, normally a year. Sales made by each sector of the economy to each of the other sectors and to exports, including tourism, are recorded as rows in the table; purchases made by the same sectors from other sectors and from imports are shown as columns. The economic impact made by tourism can be measured by simple matrix algebra. I–O analysis can be used also to measure the economic effects of changes in the volume and pattern of tourist expenditure.

Such changes can also be measured by Keynesian multiplier analysis. Macroeconomic models developed from the early Keynesian approach are used to measure the effects of changes at the margin, for example the amount of income generated in a country by an additional unit of tourist expenditure. In most cases, however, data limitations have prevented accurate measurements at the margin and such multipliers, like I–O models, normally use average values, that is, it is assumed that small changes will have similar effects to identical expenditures of the same magnitude which have already occurred. Research is attempting to remove these restrictions on I–O and multiplier models (see, for example, Sadler *et al.*, 1973).

Ad-hoc models have been developed in an attempt to overcome some of the inherent problems of I–O analysis and Keynesian multipliers. The first such models, constructed in the early 1970s by Archer and Owen (1971) and Archer (1973), have been extended and improved by later researchers, notably Brownrigg (1971), Brownrigg and Greig (1974 and 1975), Henderson and Cousins (1975), Sinclair and Sutcliffe (1982), Wanhill (1983) and Milne (1987). In essence, *ad-hoc* models are a hybrid form of I–O and Keynesian multipliers. They are constructed to measure the flow of tourist expenditure in a disaggregated form into and through the economy of the destination area. The data requirements are similar to but less demanding than I–O analysis. The approach follows the same conceptual framework as Keynesian multipliers, but with a considerable disaggregation of the model to allow separate flows of expenditure to be traced through the economic system. In their most advanced forms, *ad-hoc* models resemble I–O models and are computed by the same method, although fewer sectors are normally required.

The magnitude of this impact

Economic theory suggests that the principal factors governing the magnitude of the impact made by tourism on an economy are as follows:

— the initial volume of tourist expenditure;
— the size of the economy;
— the value added in the first round;
— the linkages between the tourism establishments and other sectors of the economy;
— the leakages which occur into imports and saving; and
— supply constraints.

Unfortunately the evidence provided by existing impact studies is insufficient to assess the relative influence of some of these factors and to prove or disprove their degree of importance.

The initial volume of tourist expenditure

The initial volume of tourist expenditure is the most important single factor in determining the overall magnitude of the economic impact. The other factors listed above govern the proportion of this expenditure which remains within the economic system at each round of transactions.

Size of the economy

Theory suggests that other things being equal, the larger the economy the larger will be the multiplier effect and the smaller the economy the smaller will be the multiplier. The reasoning is that larger economies normally possess a wider range of economic activities and hence can supply a greater proportion of the goods and services required to provide for a tourist industry; small economies, on the other hand, are unable to supply as large a proportion of the needed goods and services and hence more imports are required. Unfortunately, the available evidence is insufficient to prove or disprove this assertion.

One measure of size is the Gross National Product (GNP). Table 8.2 shows *inter alia* the tourist income multipliers for fourteen island economies in comparison with their GNPs. No statistical analysis is required to demonstrate the lack of correlation (nor is any improvement achieved by comparing the value of the income multipliers with GNP per capita). Indeed the tourist income multipliers do not correlate with any of the other measures shown in Table 8.2. Countries with high tourist densities (international tourist arrivals/ resident population) and high tourist reliance (receipts from international

Table 8.2 *Tourist multiplier, tourist density, tourist receipts and GNP[1]*

Country	Tourist[2] income multiplier[3]	Tourist receipts (US$ million)	GNP (US$ million)	Tourist density[4] (tourists ÷ population)	Tourism reliance[5] (receipts ÷ GNP)%
Sri Lanka	1.59	75	6,448	0.01	1.2
Jamaica	1.27	407*	2,090*	0.29	19.5
Dominica	1.20	8.7*	90*	0.30	9.7
Cyprus	1.14	497	2,821	1.34	17.6
Bermuda	1.09	357*	1,030*	5.75	34.7
Seychelles	1.03	40**	146	0.96	27.4
Malta	1.00	149*	1,190*	1.51	12.5
Mauritius	0.96	89	1,188	0.17	7.5
Antigua	0.88	114	195	1.86	58.5
Hong Kong	0.87	2,211	36,664	0.47	6.0
Philippines	0.82	647	30,800	0.01	2.1
Bahamas	0.78	870*	1,670*	5.73	52.1
Fiji	0.72	169	1,190	0.37	14.2
West Samoa	0.66	7*	110*	0.29	6.4

Notes: 1. The data other than the multipliers relate to the year 1986, except where marked * for 1985 or ** for 1984.
2. In this table 'tourist' means 'international tourist'.
3. The tourist income multipliers were not calculated by the same techniques nor do they all relate to the same year.
4. Tourist density would be better measured in terms of tourist-nights divided by resident population. Unfortunately the source data were insufficient to use this method.
5. Tourist reliance is measured here as tourist receipts divided by GNP (and is expressed as a percentage). It should be remembered, however, that GNP includes net tourist receipts, that is, receipts minus expenditure, and the values in the final column of this table should be used only as a measure of dependence upon tourism. They do not indicate tourism's contribution to GNP.

Source: 1. For tourist income multipliers see list of references.
2. Other data calculated from World Tourism Organization, *Compendium of Tourist Statistics*, WTO, Madrid, 1987.

tourists/GNP) are no more likely to have high income multipliers than those with low densities and reliance.

In essence, insufficient data exists to assess the part played by the size of an economy in influencing the magnitude of the impact in small economies.

The value added in the first round

The early Keynesian models assumed that the entire receipts from international tourism formed income to the destination area. The inappropriateness of this approach has been analysed by several writers, notably Archer and Owen (1971), Archer (1977b), and Sinclair and Sutcliffe (1978 and 1981). In reality some of the revenue leaks immediately out of the system—indeed some may not even pass through the economic system at all. The money which is actually received in the island forms revenue for business establishments. A portion of this revenue becomes first-round value added, that is, it is spent on wages and salaries, rent and interest and some becomes profit. The first-round value added, therefore, might appear to be a significant factor in determining the magnitude of the impact. Unfortunately the available evidence does not support this claim.

From the first two columns of Table 8.3 it can be seen that there is no clear correlation between the tourist income multipliers and the values of the first-round value added. Indeed, Mauritius with a multiplier of almost unity has a first-round value added of only 0.25, whereas Barbados with a multiplier of only 0.6 has a first-round value added of 0.4. It appears that the influence of this factor is not sufficient to offset other influences.

Linkages within the economy

Economic theory postulates that the greater the proportion of goods and services that can be supplied within the economy, the higher will be the value of the multiplier and the greater the impact per unit of receipts from tourism.

In this case the available evidence supports the theory. Indeed Table 8.3 shows that the secondary value added is a more important factor than first-round value added in determining the size of the multiplier. The final column of the same table shows the ratio multiplier values for each island. Whereas

Table 8.3 *Tourist multiplier and value added*

Country	Tourist income multiplier	Value added		Ratio multiplier
		Direct	Secondary	
Sri Lanka	1.59	0.48	1.11	3.31
Bermuda	1.09	0.38	0.71	2.87
Seychelles	1.03	0.41	0.62	2.51
Mauritius	0.96	0.25	0.71	3.84
Antigua	0.88	0.39	0.49	2.26
Hong Kong	0.87	0.47	0.40	1.85
Philippines	0.82	0.37	0.45	2.22
Bahamas	0.78	0.32	0.46	2.44
West Samoa	0.66	0.18	0.48	1.38
Barbados	0.60	0.40	0.20	1.50

Note: The multipliers and value-added figures in this table were calculated from data in the original sources, see references.

ratio multipliers have little practical usefulness (and indeed can be misleading for policy purposes), they are a measure of the extent of the internal linkages within an economy. In general, the greater the linkages within an economy, the higher is the ratio multiplier and the greater are the secondary impacts of tourist receipts.

Leakages

At each round of transactions some money leaks abroad to purchase imports or into bank deposits as savings. Insufficient evidence is available about most island economies to assess the influence of leakages into bank deposits, but import leakages have been measured in many studies.

Economic theory postulates that the lower the proportion of goods and services that can be supplied from within the destination economy, the greater will be the import bill and the lower the magnitude of the impact made by tourist receipts. To some extent this is complementary to the linkages proposition.

Unfortunately, the available evidence on import leakages is not conclusive. Table 8.4 shows the value of the tourist income multipliers for eight islands in relation to the direct and indirect imports needed to provide for the tourist industry. It should be remembered, however, that in each case further imports are needed also to provide for the increased domestic consumption among the resident population occasioned by the tourist receipts—these induced imports are not included in Table 8.4. With these induced imports included in the analysis the leakage element increases substantially (see Chapter 7 by J. E. Fletcher in this volume).

The values of the direct and import leakages do not correlate with the values of the multiplier for these eight countries. It appears that in some cases the high linkages between sectors within the domestic economy are not necessarily

Table 8.4 *Tourist multiplier and import leakages*

Country	Tourist income multiplier	Import coefficients (direct and indirect)
Sri Lanka	1.59	0.27
Bermuda	1.09	0.44
Seychelles	1.03	0.30
Mauritius	0.96	0.43
Hong Kong	0.87	0.41
Philippines	0.82	0.11
Bahamas	0.78	0.45
West Samoa	0.66	0.55

Note: The multipliers and import coefficients in this table were calculated from data in the original sources, see references.

generating correspondingly high value-added coefficients. That is value-added margins are relatively low for some rounds of transactions. Bermuda, for example, with a high import content has a high income multiplier (total value added), whereas the Bahamas with almost the same import coefficient has a much lower income multiplier. The two 'larger' economies, Sri Lanka and the Philippines, both have small import coefficients. Sri Lanka, however, has a much higher multiplier than the Philippines which indicates that the value-added margins are higher as the money works through the economic system. Recent work (Milne, 1987) has shown that leakages vary substantially by size of firm and that analyses at the micro level can reveal useful information about the part played by leakages in determining the magnitude of the impact.

Supply constraints

The magnitude of the impact and consequently the value of the income multiplier is reduced if domestic supply constraints inhibit the ability of an island to provide sufficient goods and services to meet the needs of an increase in tourism. This problem was first addressed by Bryden (1973), who showed in the case of Antigua that if domestic agriculture was unable to supply the increased demand from hotels as tourism expanded, the value of the income multiplier would fall from 0.88 to 0.81 and that the value of the multiplier was sensitive to levels of occupancy and utilization of capacity in hotels. Indeed this argument applies to all sectors of the economy. If capacity is already fully utilized and insufficient labour exists to support an increase in tourism activity, further expenditure creates inflation and additional goods and services may have to be imported.

Recent research (Wanhill, 1988) has involved constructing a matrix of supply constraints for each sector to channel the effects of additional demand into import sectors once full capacity is reached.

Conclusions

Impact models have revealed a great deal about the amount of income, employment, government revenue and net foreign exchange created by tourism in island economies. Most studies have been concerned with assessing the existing situation in terms of the total impact made by tourism over a given period. The technique, however, is capable of generating data about possible changes in the volume and value of tourism and of the effect of new developments on the economy. Recent modelling improvements, particularly those relating to problems of supply constraints (Wanhill, 1988), have made input–output analysis a more powerful tool for examining in advance the effects of policy changes.

It is hoped that future studies may also reveal more clearly the relative influences of the major factors thought to influence the magnitude of the impact made by tourism.

References

Abhaya Attanayake, Samaranayake, H. M. S., and Nandasena Ratnapala, 'Sri Lanka', in Pye, E. A., Tzong-Biau, Lin (eds), 1983, *Tourism in Asia: The Economic Impact*, Singapore University Press, Singapore, pp. 241–35.

Archer, B. H., 1973, *The Impact of Domestic Tourism*, University of Wales Press, Cardiff.

Archer, B. H., 1977a, *Tourism Multipliers: The State of the Art*, University of Wales Press, Cardiff.

Archer, B. H., 1977b, *Tourism in the Bahamas and Bermuda*, University of Wales Press, Cardiff.

Archer, B. H., 1982, *The Economic Impact of Tourism in Seychelles*, Commonwealth Secretariat, CFTC/SEY/51.

Archer, B. H., Owen, C., 1971, 'Towards a tourist regional multiplier', *Regional Studies*, 5(4): 289–94.

Archer, B. H., and Wanhill, S. R. C., 1981, *The Economic Impact of Tourism in Mauritius*, World Bank, MAR/80/004/A/01/42.

Archer, B. H., and Wanhill, S. R. C., 1985, *Tourism in Bermuda: An Economic Impact Study*, Government of Bermuda.

Armstrong, W. E., David, S., and Francis, A. A., 1974, 'A structural analysis of the Barbados economy, 1968, with an application to the tourist industry', *Social and Economic Studies*, 23(4): 493–520.

Brownrigg, M., 1971, 'The regional income multiplier: an attempt to complete the model', *Scottish Journal of Political Economy*, 18(3): 281–97.

Brownrigg, M., Greig, M. A., 1974, *The Economic Impact of Tourist Spending in Skye*, Special Report No. 13, Highlands and Islands Development Board, Inverness.

Brownrigg, M., Greig, M. A., 1975, 'Differential multipliers for tourism', *Scottish Journal of Political Economy*, 22(3): 261–75.

Bryden, J. M., 1973, *Tourism and Development*, Cambridge University Press, Cambridge.

Bryden, J. M., Faber, M., 1971, 'Multiplying the tourist multiplier', *Social and Economic Studies*, 20(1): 61–82.

Delia, E. P., 'The multiplier for tourism and export of goods in the Maltese economy: a comment', discussion paper, Department of Economics, University of Malta.

Fletcher, J. E., 1985, *The Economic Impact of Tourism on Jamaica*, WTO/UNDP.

Fletcher, J. E., 1986, *The Economic Impact of Tourism on Western Samoa*, WTO/UNDP.

Fletcher, J. E., 1986b, *The Economic Impact of International Tourism on the National Economy of the Republic of Palau*, WTO/UNDP.

Fletcher, J. E., 1987, *The Economic Impact of International Tourism on the National Economy of the Solomon Islands*, WTO/UNDP.

Henderson, D. M., Cousins, R. L., 1975, *The Economic Impact of Tourism in Greater Tayside*, Tourism and Recreation Research Unit, University of Edinburgh.

Levitt, K., Gulati, I., 1970, 'Income effect of tourist spending: mystification multiplied', *Social and Economic Studies*, 19(3): 326–43.

Lin, Tzong-Biau, Yun-Wing, Sung, 1983, 'Hong Kong' in Pye E. A. and Tzang-Biau, Lin (eds), *Tourism in Asia: The Economic Impact*, Singapore University Press, Singapore, pp. 1–99.

Milne, S. S., 1987, 'Differential multipliers', *Annals of Tourism Research*, 14(4): 499–515.

Sadler, P., Archer, B. H., and Owens, C., 1973, *Regional Income Multipliers*, University of Wales Press, Cardiff.

Santos, J. S. D., Ortiz, E. M., Huang, E., and Secretario, F., 1983, 'Philippines' in Pye,

E. A. and Tzang-Biau, Lin (eds), *Tourism in Asia: The Economic Impact*, Singapore University Press, Singapore, pp. 173–240.

Sinclair, M. T., Sutcliffe, C. M. S., 1978, 'The first round of the Keynesian income multiplier', *Scottish Journal of Political Economy*, 25(2): 177–86.

Sinclair, M. T., Sutcliffe, C. M. S., 1982, 'Keynesian income multipliers with first and second round effects: an application to tourist expenditure', *Oxford Bulletin of Economics and Statistics*, 44(4): 321–38.

Varley, R. C. G., 1976, *Tourism in Fiji: Some Economic and Social Problems*, University of Wales Press, Cardiff.

Wanhill, S. R. C., 1983, 'Measuring the economic impact of tourism', *Service Industries Journal*, 3(1): 9–20.

Wanhill, S. R. C., 1988, 'Tourism multipliers under capacity constraints', *Service Industries Journal*, 8(2): 136–42.

World Tourism Organization, 1987, *Compendium of Tourism Statistics*, WTO, Madrid.

9 Recreational resource management

S. Glyptis

Introduction

Defining the bounds of a subject is an obvious prerequisite for reviewing its progress. In the case of recreational resource management their choice is usually hazardous, inviting legitimate attack for sins of omission and inclusion. The difficulties begin with recreation. A simple listing of recreational activities is not appropriate, for recreation essentially is a matter of personal perception. The activity which is recreational to one person may be a chore and a drudge to another. Gardening and do-it-yourself activities are oft-quoted examples, but the point applies much more widely: recreation encompasses almost every conceivable activity. This review will concentrate on those which make particular demands upon natural and man-made resources.

To couple 'recreational' with 'resources' complicates definitions still further. In a recreational context the obvious resources are the 'natural resources' of land, water and landscape, together with man-made resources including sports centres, swimming pools, parks and playing fields. These are the prime focus of this review. However, two further factors must be noted, the first for clarity, the second for completeness. First, relatively few recreational activities make use of resources which are solely recreational. Much recreation takes place alongside other uses such as farming, forestry, water supply and wildlife conservation. Many recreation management issues are therefore concerned with the management of multiple use, and the promotion, provision and containment of recreation alongside the claims of other, prime, uses. Second, many forms of recreation require little by way of land or facilities, but need resources of organization, leadership and coordination. Brief mention is therefore made in this review of the role of human resources in providing for recreation.

The diffuseness and multi-disciplinary nature of the subject are paralleled by a fragmented pattern of research activity and sponsorship. As other reviewers have noted (Collins and Patmore, 1982; Goodale and Witt, 1985; Owens, 1984; Patmore and Collins, 1980), much of the research is funded by providing agencies, each forming part of a complex mosaic of public, private and voluntary sector bodies whose interests in recreation variously coincide, overlap and even conflict (Travis, 1979). This has a threefold ramification for research. First, the field is dominated by applied, descriptive research concerned with informing, evaluating and reviewing existing policies and management approaches. Critical appraisals of strategic uses, and the development of concepts and theories aimed at a fundamental understanding of recreational behaviour, motivations and rewards have received much less attention. Second, research focuses repeatedly on a few well-worn themes (such as site catchment areas), while others are neglected. Third, the research output is fragmented: much is found in reports published by the commissioning agencies, the remainder dispersed throughout the geography, planning, environmental studies, biology, sociology, psychology, economics and marketing literature.

Recreational resource management: the contemporary context

Research priorities reflect the economic, political and social climate of the time. In the 1980s, four broad influences have been evident. First, belief in the view that recreation is a right of every citizen has become enshrined in the policies of government and statutory agencies. Issues of equity and social welfare therefore underpin much research on the management of recreational resources. Issues of social control, too, have lent added impetus from time to time, for example in the additional government funding earmarked for inner city recreation following the urban riots of 1981. The intriguing and uneasy alliance of social welfare and social control objectives in recreation policy has been skilfully charted by Coalter *et al*. (1986). Second, priorities reflect social change. These include, in the United Kingdom, dramatic changes in the age structure of the population; an increasingly diverse recreation market due to a decrease in household size and more varied household structures; and the migration of people away from metropolitan centres to areas of high-technology industry, and rural and retirement areas. These changes pose a host of research questions concerning effective service delivery for the recreational needs of specific sectors of the community, and about the mismatch of supply and demand in areas of rapidly expanding or contracting population. Third, the 1980s bear marked contrast to previous decades in economic terms. With low growth, structural unemployment, the demise of traditional manufacturing industries and inner city decay, the age of leisure, so eagerly anticipated in the earlier expansionist era, has been reinterpreted as the collapse of work (Jenkins and Sherman, 1979). For the recreation manager, the challenges are greater and financial resources fewer.

The fourth contextual theme, the emergence of strategic planning in public sector recreation agencies, stems from the first three. In the United Kingdom, collective recognition of the challenges ahead came with the publication of *Leisure Policy for the Future* (1983) by the Chairmen's Policy Group, the umbrella body for statutory agencies involved in leisure provision. The translation of vision into reality, however, rests with individual agencies. In this respect the

Sports Council has shown an impressive lead in strategy formulation and review, based on painstaking analysis of social and economic trends and the evaluation of past policy measures (Sports Council, 1982, 1988). Others have followed suit (Countryside Commission, 1983, 1987; English Tourist Board, 1987), with rather less presentation of research evidence but with equally fluent statements of intent.

In addition to these established trends, mention must be made of two further changes in prospect which will affect the management of particular types of recreational resources. The first is agricultural change, resulting from the concern in EEC countries to reduce beef and cereal surpluses. The main solutions advocated are extensified farming, and land set aside to develop new crops or other sources of income such as forestry, craft industries, tourism and recreation (Bell, 1986; Ministry of Agriculture, Fisheries and Food, 1987). The other change is the British government's concern to privatize, or open up to competitive tendering, the provision of certain public services. Most of these have repercussions for recreation opportunities, and two have direct effects—the water industry, and sport and recreation facilities (Department of the Environment/Ministry of Agriculture, Fisheries and Food/Welsh Office, 1987; Department of the Environment/Scottish Education Department/Welsh Office, 1987). The effects are as yet difficult to anticipate: the benefits should be greater efficiency and effectiveness in management; the costs might be an overall reduction of recreational opportunities, particularly for low-income groups.

Recreational resource management: general appraisals

The diversity of recreation, and its interdependence with resource management for other purposes, means that periodic appraisals of the field as a whole are particularly welcome. Few have attempted as broad a view as the Americans, Chubb and Chubb (1981) who cover both recreational behaviour and its resource requirements, providing an excellent discussion of the nature and resources, and their planning and management in the commercial, voluntary and public sectors. On resource issues, the British counterpart is Patmore (1983). Here the perspective is specifically geographical, but with full recognition of the interplay of social, economic and political factors, and with a wealth of data, often retrieved and reworked from little known sources. The bulk of the text concerns contemporary patterns of recreational activity and the demands they place on land and water resources, with myriad references to management issues and solutions.

Less questioning in approach, but valuable for its breadth, is Torkildsen's *Leisure and Recreation Management* (1986), which focuses on resources which are managed specifically for recreation. The many lists of 'does and don'ts for managers' are apt to hide the complexities on occasions, but they serve as effective abstractions for textbook purposes. Others, less managerialist in stance, can pose the fundamental questions, Goodale and Witt (1985) being a worthy case in point. Contending that research to date has concentrated 'on how more than what, and what more than why' (p. xi), they debate where leisure and recreation services fit into the overall scheme of human welfare and service provision; who is to be enabled, and to do what; whether providers manipulate needs; and what should be the basis of recreational resource management in an era of financial and energy limits. Some of these issues are also addressed by Lieber and Fesenmaier (1983).

The era of limits brings greater recognition of the value of sound business principles. Setting and achieving targets, and monitoring effectiveness are essential to good management, whether returns are sought in the form of financial profits or social or environmental benefits. A welcome spate of texts and articles has applied traditional economic and marketing principles to the management of recreational resources, most notably Cowell (1984), Curry (1987), Department of the Environment Audit Inspectorate (1983), and Gratton and Taylor (1985). Increasingly, too, public-sector providers are arguing their own case for resources in terms of economic benefits (for example, Ellis, 1985; Henley Centre for Forecasting, 1986).

An understanding of relevant aspects of the law is an important tool of management. These have for long been inaccessible, but in a British context, three valuable recent publications have begun to fill the void (Collins, 1984; Grayson, 1988; Scott, 1985). Collins explains in lay terms the many areas of the law which are relevant to recreational activities, including that governing the use of premises, fund raising, risk to others, protection of belongings, the sale of food and alcohol, health and safety, public liability and nuisance. Scott provides a detailed compilation of those points of law which form the framework in which public leisure services are operated.

Demand appraisals

The starting-point for many resource management discussions is present and likely future demand. Even this apparently simple information is hard to obtain. There are two main methods of doing so: household surveys and site surveys. Site surveys will be considered in more detail under 'countryside recreation' below, but their inherent limitations must be sketched at the outset. By their very nature, site surveys deal only with participants (not non-participants), and they are preoccupied with the use of the particular site under study, rather than with the broader leisure lifestyles of visitors. If information is required on overall levels of participation, or on the characteristics and aspirations of non-participants, then a population sample, rather than a user sample, is required. Recreation surveys are notoriously difficult to design and expensive to conduct: the diversity of recreation, and the fact that, individually, most recreational activities attract only a minority of the population, mean that survey pro formas must be long and samples large. Not surprisingly, the specialist surveys of the 1960s (British Travel Association/University of Keele, 1967; Sillitoe, 1969) were the first and, to date, last at national scale, and there have been none at regional scale since 1973. From that date, however, questions on leisure have been included from time to time in the government's annual *General Household Survey*, and the evolving series begins to afford insights into trends over time. The most recently published statistics, for 1983 (Office of Population Censuses and Surveys, 1985), reaffirm the importance of home-based, passive and social pursuits, but also demonstrate a steady increase in involvement in many sports and countryside activities. Disaggregation of the data by demographic and social characteristics shows the continuing dominance of men, young people, car owners and the professional and managerial classes in most forms of outdoor recreation.

Since 1977 the Countryside Commission has carried out its own periodic national surveys of countryside recreation (for example, Countryside Commission, 1985a), which afford fuller insight into destinations visited. Participation again is socially selective. Seventeen per cent of the population make 68 per cent of all countryside trips, although, interestingly, among participants there are few contrasts between the social classes in the frequency of trip making.

These data provide essential planning information but reveal little of latent demand, constraints or motivations. Even the analysis of expressed demand is in some ways more rudimentary than that of the earlier surveys; none since, for example, has matched the methodological sophistication of *Leisure in the North West* (Rodgers and Patmore, 1973) in using multiple regression to identify the relative effects of different social indicators as predictors of participation.

Participation is not a static pattern but a dynamic process. Activities are taken up, pursued for a while and then abandoned, perhaps with others taking their place. Few researchers, however, have addressed these processes of recruitment, turnover and wastage, and the factors which trigger them. Rodgers' (1977) ingenious manipulation of participation data from several European countries remains unsurpassed as a means of inferring process from cross-sectional data, though many of his ideas were applied effectively in a local study of sports participation over the life-span among two communities in Teesside (Boothby *et al.*, 1981). Hedges (1986) discusses the methodo-logical prospects and limitations of adopting this life-history approach more generally, and Jackson and Dunn (1988) relate dropping out of particular activities to other aspects of leisure behaviour, classifying people into continuers, adders, replacers and quitters. Such applications go beyond mere academic amusement. An understanding of the circumstances in which people are likely to adopt or abandon an activity, and the duration for which they might pursue it, are fundamentally important to agencies concerned with promoting participation and with allocating grant-aid to support activities which will be more than mere passing interests.

Countryside recreation

The recreation research literature has long been dominated by investigations of the scale, character, problems and impact of countryside recreation. In the more general appraisals recreation is rarely the main interest (Patmore, 1983 and Wall and Marsh, 1982 are exceptions to this), but is discussed alongside the requirements of agriculture, forestry, water supply and conservation (Blacksell and Gilg, 1981; Blunden and Curry, 1985; Cloke, 1987; Cloke and Park, 1986; Green, 1981; Lowe *et al.*, 1986; Parker and Penning-Rowsell, 1980). From all of these sources the impossibility of divorcing recreation from wider issues of land management and of landscape and wildlife conservation is made plain. Inevitably, management and research tend to concentrate on the use of existing resources and on the problems, rather than the opportunities, of recreational use. The near ubiquitous site study remains the mainstay of management information. Little different from the pioneer studies of the 1960s and early 1970s, site surveys concentrate mainly on visitor characteristics, catchment areas, methods of travel and frequency of visiting. This basic, site-specific information is vital for the management of particular sites. Nonetheless, site studies remain oddly isolated and incomplete. Most are designed as one-off enquiries with no thought of comparison with other sites or other times; furthermore, such comparisons are thwarted by a lack of standardization in the questions asked, the definitions used and the samples selected (Elson, 1977; Tourism and Recreation Research Unit, 1983a). Despite their undoubted value in a parochial sense, in terms of cumulative understanding the assemblage of site surveys amounts to little more than the sum of the parts.

The preoccupation of site surveys with visitor characteristics calls into question their completeness even for site management purposes. Only a few (Burton, 1974; Glyptis, 1981a, 1981b) have examined visitor behaviour on site and how this relates to the configuration of landscape features, the siting of facilities and the presence of other users. Recent surveys of the use of country parks (Locke, 1985) have gone some way towards this in asking people about their use of visitor centres, their spending on site and their likes and dislikes. Another modest but important innovation of Locke's study is its ready identification of marketing and management practices arising from the results. An example is the discovery that as many as one in five visitors had not decided where to go on setting out from home, but decided to visit the country parks upon seeing signposts as they drove along. As a result, greater attention is now paid to the importance of local roadside information in influencing visitors' decisions.

Ownership, management and access

Research and policy attention tend to focus on managed sites. Paradoxically, in the United Kingdom, the bulk of countryside recreation takes place elsewhere, on land in private ownership. The 1984 *National Countryside Recreation Survey* found that 44 per cent of all recreation trips had as their destinations farmland, woodland and other inland coastal areas not managed primarily for recreation. A further 11 per cent involved stopping in villages, at country pubs and cafés and at roadside viewpoints.

Public rights of access to private land for recreation have been the cause of feverish campaign, and remain a matter of consternation and confusion. The dedication and the deeds of the early campaigners are recalled by the Council for National Parks (1986a, 1986b), and the continuing significance of pressure groups in access and amenity debates is well recognized (Cherry, 1985; Lowe and Goyder, 1983). Marion Shoard (1987), in a powerful polemic, employs forceful and skilful advocacy, and no little supporting evidence, for the public 'right to roam'. She proposes a twofold 'social contract for the countryside', recommending a rural land tax, whereby owners managing their land in the public interest (for example, adopting sound habitat management) would be subsidized by a tax on those who fail to act in the public good. This would be coupled with an access charter akin to the Swedish *Allemanstatten*, allowing unrestricted access on foot to the countryside. Such a claim is more easily asked for than achieved, though tentative beginnings are under way in relation to public access to 'common' land (Countryside Commission, 1986; Land Use Consultants, 1985).

A recent empirical study of the attitudes of individuals and organizations affected by access underpins the gist of Shoard's analysis (Centre for Leisure Research, 1986; Sidaway *et al.*, 1986). The emphasis is on the political science, rather than the laws, of access, examining the ways in which access is negotiated between competing interest groups. The evidence dispels some well-worn myths about unruly urban hordes wreaking havoc on private land. While 36 per cent of farmers reported severe problems, these were caused mostly by local users regularly walking, rambling, scrambling and poaching. Even with the offer of financial incentives, virtually all farmers were opposed to any increase in public access to farmed land. The study concluded that farmers and landowners have such strong feelings about private property, privacy and control that if they could communicate more easily with recreationists there would be more conflict, not less!

Legal rights of way are in many cases poorly maintained. Evidence collated by the Countryside Commission (1988) showed that in 1986–7 over half of the local authorities in England and Wales spent less than 15 pence per capita maintaining rights of way, an average of 3 pence per walk made. Some, though, have taken positive measures to promote rights of way and to create public confidence in using the countryside by designing attractive walks suited to a variety of needs and limitations (Wilkinson *et al.*, 1985).

As on the land, so too on the water the legal rights of recreationists are complex and keenly contested, involving both the rights of passage along the water, and of access to the banks. On the basis of a painstaking analysis of 21 rivers, Telling and Smith (1985) recommended a registration system for navigation rights, backed up by management to ensure the use of registered waterways with due regard to the interests of anglers, navigation and riparian owners.

Impact, conflict and capacity

The manager's concern for recreation is not merely with its presence but with its impact. Sidaway and O'Connor's (1978) review remains a valuable reminder of its diversity, including direct impacts on natural resources and the disturbance of wildlife habitats, and social and psychological impacts arising from traffic congestion, overcrowding, nuisance, noise, aesthetic intrusions and conflict between different forms of recreation. The direct, physical impact, although restricted to a few heavily used areas, can be severe in both visual and ecological terms. Patmore (1987) cites the example of the Lyke Wake Walk, where in parts of its route through the North York Moors National Park the path is over 300 feet wide. Evidence generally shows that visitors themselves care about the visual quality of the environment and its conservation (Jackson, 1986; McAvory *et al.*, 1986). Several studies have sought to relate levels of erosion or habitat disturbance to the nature and types of recreation taking place (Cole, 1986; Kuss, 1986). The concern is not just with diagnosing damage, but with recovery rates (Harrison, 1980–1).

The impact of recreation on wildlife tends to be judged more on allegation than on evidence, as interest groups defend their causes, and claims become polarized. Two recent studies on the impact of recreation on waterfowl are therefore especially welcome. Tuite (1982) clearly had more sympathy with the birds than with the people, but from a review based largely on desk research he concluded that, while recreation may influence the distribution of birds locally, there is no evidence of population declines nationally being attributable to recreation. More detailed in its management prescriptions and more innovative in its approach was Watmough's (1983) research on reservoirs in the Trent Valley. Accepting as a truism that birds will fly away when disturbed, the study sought to establish the response of birds to different types and amounts of recreational activity, and the time taken to recover. Observations were made, with controlled amounts of sailing on the reservoirs, of the distance at which birds took flight, their behaviour when displaced, and the time taken to resume normal behaviour. Watmough concluded that if a large enough refuge area can be designated far enough from sources of disturbance, recreation and conservation interests can coexist as long as there is effective site management to ensure that restrictions are respected.

Compatibility and capacity are largely matters of personal perception and priority. Interest in visitors' tolerance of crowding continues (for example, Glyptis, 1981a, 1981b; West, 1981), but Burton's (1974) study of the carrying capacity of Cannock Chase remains unchallenged both for its conceptual and methodological sophistication and its management insights. Together with related studies it provided the foundation for the Cannock Chase Management Plan (Countryside Commission, 1985b).

Tolerance, of course, relates not just to the numbers present, but to what they are doing, and the extent to which they impinge on other people. In a British context O'Riordan and Paget's (1978) study of the views of anglers and boaters is the most thorough and perceptive. Elsewhere, other activities have been addressed, including water-skiing and angling (Gramann and Burdge, 1981), and cross-country skiing and snowmobiling (Jackson and Wong, 1982).

The activities which evoke the greatest controversy tend to be the noisiest, fastest and most mechanized. They also evoke sweeping generalization. Motor sports are associated with conflict and improper use of the countryside, and their adherents are often branded as unruly and deviant. The reality behind the stereotype is uncovered in a recent appraisal by Elson *et al*. (1986a). The study outlines the scale and diversity of motor sports activity; reviews associated legal, financial and managerial problems; evaluates examples of good practice in provision; and makes recommendations for the more effective planning and management of land for motor sports. Detailed site requirements and management considerations for 19 different motor sports' disciplines are set out in an accompanying handbook for providers (Elson *et al*., 1986b).

Management approaches

Increasing concern to make countryside recreation resources accessible to town dwellers without cars, and to encourage car owners to leave their cars at home, have spawned a number of transport experiments such as the Wayfarer project in Greater Manchester and West Yorkshire. These provide useful guidance on the organization, running and usage of such schemes (Countryside Commission, 1985c). As Duffield (1982) reminds us, household car ownership is a poor indicator of individual mobility; rather than seeking the solution in public transport schemes for recreation, he advocates enhancing public transport for journeys to work, so that the household car can be left at home for others to use during the day.

Particularly in the more sensitive environments, management objectives may be geared less towards attracting visitors than to educating them. Countryside interpretation seeks not merely to inform but to educate, and to awaken the visitor's desire to contribute to environmental conservation. The bulk of research in this field has evaluated the effectiveness of the communications media, but Uzzell (1985) takes a refreshingly critical look at management issues. Based on evidence from several visitor centres, he concludes that interpretive objectives are ill-formulated, and the composition of actual and intended audiences often ignored. Greater user-orientation is called for, including the involvement of the public as providers, as well as passive absorbers, of interpretive skills.

Reference has already been made to the increased recognition of business methods in providing recreational services, but attitudes to pricing remain ambivalent. Countryside recreation in Britain is generally available at no direct charge to the user, and indeed in the open countryside and on open access sites, charging is impracticable. There is evidence, however, that demand is price-inelastic, and several authors in the United Kingdom and elsewhere argue in favour of the more widespread adoption of pricing (Bovaird *et al.*, 1984; Leuschner *et al.*, 1987; Stoakes, 1982). However, as Patmore (1987) demonstrates, tactic must be tailored to circumstance. In a year when admission charges were levied at an interpretive centre in the North York Moors, the facility cost approximately £1.27 per visitor to run and, arguably, the charge excluded those whom the National Park Authority would particularly want its interpretive messages to reach. In 1984, with free admission, visitor numbers increased by 25 per cent, there was greater expenditure on guide books and other items at the centre and the subsidy decreased to 14 pence per visit.

Special resources

Whether special by designation, by use, or by location, certain categories of resources generate specific management problems. National Parks have perhaps the most delicate balance to strike between conserving the environment and coping with public access. In England and Wales the balancing act is compounded by the fact that the designated areas are neither national nor parks: most national park land is privately owned, or publicly owned for non-recreational purposes such as military training; most is in productive agricultural use; and all ten national parks have local economies and populations to sustain. Recent years have seen a spate of scholarly and lively appraisals, both of the parks system generally (MacEwen and MacEwen, 1982, 1987) and of its workings at local level (Patmore, 1987). The MacEwens' earlier book is provocative and pessimistic, citing many instances in which the national park purpose has been overridden, and concluding that government policies actually work against the interests of conservation management. The national park system is described as essentially cosmetic. The later book turns pessimism into positive prescription, urging the need to strengthen and extend the national park system, and to make the conservation of landscape and resources an integral part of social and economic development policy.

In the urban fringe, the pressures are different in scale and in kind. The green belt, in particular, is a fast-changing scene and a fascinating arena of competing claims and conflicting interests. Its recreational importance has long been stressed, both in statements of support for green belt creation and expansion, and in the policies of government agencies. A decade ago the Countryside Commission launched a series of countryside management experiments in the urban fringes of London and Manchester, introducing project officers to work with local landowners, farmers, recreation and conservation interests and residents to reach practical compromises between private interests and public pressures (Countryside Commission, 1981). More recently, in an attempt to attract financial and other support from the major interests spending money in such areas, the mechanism of environmental trusts has been developed, the first as Operation Groundwork in Merseyside.

In addition to studies for purely pragmatic purpose, two major academic appraisals of the green belt have recently been published, both including, but not restricted to, recreational considerations. Munton (1983) quantifies the recreational use of London's green belt and argues that the capacity of existing sites to absorb greater use could be extended through improved management. Demonstrating the inaccessibility of the green belt to inner city residents, he questions the conventional wisdom that it provides a countryside recreation experience for deprived town dwellers. Elson's (1986c) scholarly appraisal of conflict mediation in the urban fringe takes a broader and more dynamic view. He concludes that the recreation interest appears weak, and provision is largely opportunistic, based more on the seizing of available sites than on technical assessments of demand and a strategic view of need.

The recreational resources closest to home tend to be the least researched. Urban parks are a good example, commanding well over a third of local authority recreation expenditure, but their form little changed and their function little questioned. An excellent review by the Tourism and Recreation Research Unit (1983b) discusses the provenance and provision of parks to date, and stresses the need to study their use and people's attitudes towards them and to evaluate the effectiveness of management approaches. Gold (1985) also outlines the need for broader thinking on the future role of urban parks.

Mention must also be made of the home itself, the best used and most neglected recreational resource of all. The indoor and outdoor space of the home, the social context of the household and the increasing range and sophistication of leisure equipment and labour-saving devices make the home the most versatile and accessible of leisure centres, and the recreational resource where there is greatest freedom to exercise personal preference. Given the proportion of free time spent at home, and the amount of money invested in equipping and maintaining it, there is a need for a much fuller understanding of its recreational role. Cherry (1982) provides a fascinating historical account of the changing nature of the home and household, highlighting the revolutionary impact on leisure of new inventions such as electric lighting and central heating. An exploratory study of contemporary usage (Glyptis *et al.*, 1987) examines the impact of house type and household type on the recreational opportunities, activities and constraints of household members. Through the use of time–space activity diagrams insight is gained into the activity patterns of individuals, and the convergence or divergence of activities between different members of the same household.

Built facilities

Many of the research themes relating to the use of built facilities echo those of the countryside. In Britain, participation data for facility-based activities are gleaned mainly from the *General Household Survey* and from user surveys equivalent to the countryside recreation site survey. Their proliferation paralleled the massive growth of facility provision in the 1970s, and focused on indoor sports centres, swimming pools and leisure pools (for example, Built Environment Research Group, 1977; Public Attitude Surveys, 1979). Several aimed to establish the catchment areas of facilities (Cowling *et al.*, 1982), and the mutual impact of neighbouring centres (Atkinson and Collins, 1980). Another major theme has been the use of community recreation facilities on school sites (Built Environment Research Group, 1978; Murphy and Veal, 1977).

The harsher economic climate of the 1980s underscores the need for efficiency in resource use. The promotion of facility provision jointly by education and recreation authorities and the opening up of underused school sports facilities, remain major policy thrusts of the Sports Council. The economic and social costs and benefits of shared use were analysed by Coopers and Lybrand Associates (1981). The local need for low-cost, small-scale facility provision has prompted the development by the Sports Council in the 1980s of standardized sports hall designs in the form of SASH (Standardised Approach to Sports Halls) and SCRC (Small Community Recreation Centres) facilities. These are currently being monitored in terms of both usage and building design and performance.

The evidence of the 1970s that, virtually regardless of location, the use of sports facilities was dominated by young middle-class male car owners prompted a new policy orientation in the 1980s. Less emphasis was to be placed on facilities, and more on community needs. In contrast to countryside recreation, where the interest of most public-sector providers is to contain rather than positively encourage public use, the Sports Council has a more vigorous development role, enshrined in its slogan 'Sport for All'. The extent of non-participation, and the concentration of non-participants among particular sectors of society showed that, even with substantial facility provision, certain barriers to participation existed which the public sector should identify and take steps to remove. Needs and barriers are reviewed in general terms by Boothby *et al.* (1981) and Dower *et al.* (1981). Several studies have focused on particular social groups, notably women (Bialeschki and Henderson, 1986; Green *et al.*, 1987; Shaw, 1985; Talbot, 1979), school leavers (Hendry, 1981; Roberts, 1983), ethnic minorities (Carrington *et al.*, 1987; Kew, 1979), and the elderly (Long and Wimbush, 1985). Some have addressed the needs and problems of provision in inner city (Roberts, 1978) and rural (Glyptis, 1987; Ventris, 1979) areas.

In many cases it was clear that the removal of tangible barriers to participation—such as lack of transport, lack of facilities, lack of awareness, inability to pay—was not sufficient to motivate non-participants to take part. Throughout the 1980s, therefore, much greater emphasis has been placed on investment in leadership and outreach workers to forge effective links between community needs and the provision of services. This approach was first piloted on a large scale in three national experimental schemes of sports provision for the unemployed, launched by the Sports Council in 1981. Teams of sports leaders were appointed to provide activity sessions in a wide range of sports, and to work at neighbourhood level to get to know local unemployed people, discuss their interests and encourage them to come along to the activities provided. A similar approach directed at inner city communities more generally was launched in 1982 as Action Sport. Further developments of the same approach have been tested in smaller towns and rural locations, using existing facilities and networks such as Working Men's Clubs, Women's Institutes and pubs as the initial base for the leaders. All of these initiatives have been monitored and evaluated (Glyptis *et al.*, 1986a, 1986b; Rigg, 1986; Sports Council, 1984–6). Given the upsurge in unemployment in the 1980s, and its likely future persistence, many local authorities have also devised specific recreation policies and provisions for the unemployed; these are reviewed by Glyptis and Riddington (1983) and Glyptis and Pack (1988).

Conclusions

Drawing the salient threads from a wide-ranging review might present problems of over-generalization, but with recreational resource management the risks are relatively few. In all aspects of the subject, research is dominated by applied, descriptive studies, most of which are site or facility based, geared to the short-term needs of managers, and concerned with the working of present policies. Usefulness has been the guiding hand behind the greater part of recreation research. The dominance of policy makers as research sponsors ensures that research remains firmly focused on tactics rather than strategy, on pattern rather than process and on activities rather than aspirations, meanings and motivations. Earlier reviewers have drawn similar conclusions, and lamented the lack of fundamental progress and theoretical insight (Owens, 1984). However, relevance is a strength to be cherished, not a weakness to be chided. The need is not to replace existing approaches with new orientation to theory and sophisticated methodology for its own sake, but rather to strike a balance in the research questions asked between the evaluation of policies and provisions already made, and the assessment of fundamental needs, approaches and service delivery systems.

One eminent policy maker in countryside recreation in Britain espoused the view in the early 1980s that 'the practitioners in the field are not receiving from the academics enough criticism or ideas' (Hookway, 1984: 10). The academics in turn are too few in number, too dispersed in location and too dependent on agency funding to be tackling many of the broader questions with the intellectual vigour they deserve. The academic research funding councils have their own financial limits and priorities, but have generally failed to respond to the future social and economic importance of recreation. The academic institutions must take recreation research as seriously as the practitioners do, and stimulate the underpinning of concept, theory and understanding that three decades of research have so far failed to yield.

References

Atkinson, J., Collins, M. F., 1980, *The Impact of Neighbouring Sports and Leisure Centres*, Research Working Paper 18, Sports Council, London.

Bell, M., 1986, 'Changing contexts in agriculture and rural life', in Countryside Recreation Research Advisory Group, *New Approaches to Access in the Countryside*, Proceedings of CRRAG Conference, CRRAG, Bristol.

Bialeschki, M. D., Henderson, K., 1986, 'Leisure in the common world of women', *Leisure Studies*, 5(3): 299–308.

Blacksell, M., Gilg, A., 1981, *The Countryside: Planning and Change*, George Allen and Unwin, London.

Blunden, J., Curry, N. (eds), 1985, *The Changing Countryside*, Croom Helm, London.

Boothby, J., Tungatt, M. F., Townsend, A. R., and Collins, M. F., 1981, *A Sporting Chance?* Study 21, Sports Council, London.

Bovaird, A. G., Tricker, M. J., and Stoakes, R., 1984, *Recreational Management and Pricing*, Gower, Aldershot.

British Travel Association/University of Keele, 1967, *Pilot National Recreation Survey*, Report no. 1, British Travel Association, London.

Built Environment Research Group, 1977, *The Changing Indoor Sports Centre*, Study 13, Sports Council, London.

Built Environment Research Group, 1978, *Sport for All in the Inner City*, Study 15, Sports Council, London.

Burton, R. C. J., 1974, *The Recreational Carrying Capacity of the Countryside*, Keele University Library Occasional Publications No. 11, Keele.

Carrington, B., Chivers, T., and Williams, T., 1987, 'Gender, leisure and sport: a case study of young people of South Asian descent', *Leisure Studies*, 6(3): 265–79.

Centre for Leisure Research, 1986, *Access to the Countryside for Recreation and Sport*, CCP 217, Countryside Commission and Sports Council.

Chairmen's Policy Group, 1983, *Leisure Policy for the Future*, Sports Council, London.

Cherry, G. E., 1982, *Leisure in the Home*, Sports Council/Social Science Research Council Joint Panel on Leisure and Recreation Research, London.

Cherry, G. E., 1985, 'Scenic heritage and national parks lobbies and legislation in England and Wales', *Leisure Studies*, 4(2): 127–39.

Chubb, M., Chubb, H. R., 1981, *One Third of Our Time? An Introduction to Recreation Behavior and Resources*, Wiley, New York.

Cloke, P. (ed.), 1987, *Rural Planning: Policy into Action*, Harper and Row, London.

Cloke, P., Park, C. C., 1986, *Rural Resource Management*, Croom Helm, London.

Coalter, F., Long, J., and Duffield, B. S., 1986, *Rationale for Public Sector Investment in Leisure*, Sports Council/Economic and Social Research Council Joint Panel on Leisure and Recreation Research, London.

Cole, D. N., 1986, 'Recreational impacts on backcountry campsites in Grand Canyon National Park, Arizona, USA', *Environmental Management*, 10(5): 651–9.

Collins, M. F., Patmore, J. A., 1982, 'Recreation and leisure', *Progress in Human Geography*, 6(2): 254–9.

Collins, V., 1984, *Recreation and the Law*, E. & F. N. Spon, London.

Coopers and Lybrand Associates, 1981, *Sharing Does Work*, Study 21, Sports Council, London.

Council for National Parks, 1986a, *50 Years for National parks*, CNP, London.

Council for National Parks, 1986b, *National Parks: The Celebration and the Challenge*, Proceedings of the 50th anniversary conference, CNP, London.

Countryside Commission, 1981, *Countryside Management in the Urban Fringe*, CCP 136, Countryside Commission, Cheltenham.

Countryside Commission, 1983, *Our Programme for the Countryside 1983–88*, Countryside Commission, Cheltenham.

Countryside Commission, 1985a, *National Countryside Recreation Survey: 1984*, CCP 201, Countryside Commission, Cheltenham.

Countryside Commission, 1985b, *Cannock Chase 1979–84: A Country Park Plan on Trial*, CCP 181, Countryside Commission, Cheltenham.

Countryside Commission, 1985c, *The Wayfarer Project*, CCP 193, Countryside Commission, Cheltenham.

Countryside Commission, 1986, *Common Land: The Report of the Common Land Forum*, CCP 215, Countryside Commission, Cheltenham.

Countryside Commission, 1987, *Policies for Enjoying the Countryside*, CCP 234, Countryside Commission, Cheltenham.

Countryside Commission, 1988, 'Rights of Way', *Countryside Commission News*, 32 (Summer): 6.

Cowell, D. W., 1984, *The Marketing of Services*, Heinemann, London.

Cowling, D., Fitzjohn, M., and Tungatt, M., 1982, *Identifying the Market: Catchment Areas of Sports Centres and Swimming Pools*, Study 24, Sports Council, London.

Curry, N., 1987, 'Recreation cost–benefit analysis and the equity effect', *Journal of Environmental Management*, 25(4): 363–75.

Department of the Environment, Ministry of Agriculture, Fisheries and Food, Welsh Office, 1987, *The National Rivers Authority: The Government's Policies for a Public Regulatory Body in a Privatised Water Industry*, DOE, London.

Department of the Environment, Scottish Education Department, Welsh Office, 1987, *Competition in the Management of Local Authority Sport and Leisure Facilities*, Consultation Paper, DOE, London.

Department of the Environment, Audit Inspectorate, 1983, *Development and Operation of Leisure Centres: Selected Case Studies*, HMSO, London.

Dower, M., Rapoport, R., Strelitz, Z., and Kew, S., 1981, *Leisure Provision and People's Needs*, HMSO, London.

Duffield, B. S., 1982, 'A review of mobility and countryside recreation', in Countryside Recreation Research Advisory Group, *Countryside Recreation in the 1980s: Current Research and Future Challenges*, Proceedings of CRRAG Conference, CRRAG, Cheltenham.

Ellis, J. B., 1985, 'The leisure economy of Ontario—some dimensions and measures', *Society and Leisure*, 8(2): 493–512.

Elson, M. J., 1977, *A Review and Evaluation of Countryside Recreation Site Surveys*, Countryside Commission, Cheltenham.

Elson, M. J., Buller, H., and Stanley, P., 1986a, *Providing for Motorsports: From Image to Reality*, Study 28, Sports Council, London.

Elson, M. J., Buller, H., and Stanley P., 1986b, *Motorsports and Motor Recreation: A Handbook for Providers*, Study 29, Sports Council, London.

Elson, M. J., 1986c, *Green Belts: Conflict Mediation in the Urban Fringe*, Heinemann, London.

English Tourist Board, 1987, *A Vision for England*, English Tourist Board, London.

Glyptis, S. A., 1981a, 'Room to relax in the countryside', *The Planner*, 67(5): 120–2.

Glyptis, S. A., 1981b, 'People at play in the countryside', *Geography*, 66(4): 277–85.

Glyptis, S. A., 1987, *Sport and Recreation in Rural Areas: A Sample Study of Ryedale and Swaledale*, Yorkshire and Humberside Council for Sport and Recreation, Leeds.

Glyptis, S. A., Kay, T. A., and Donkin, D., 1986a, *Sport for the Unemployed: The Monitoring of Schemes in Leicester, Derwentside and Hockley Port*, Sports Council, London.

Glyptis, S. A., Kay, T. A., and Donkin, D., 1986b, *Sport for the Unemployed: Lessons from Schemes in Leicester, Derwentside and Hockley Port*, Sports Council, London.

Glyptis, S. A., McInnes, H. A., and Patmore, J. A., 1987, *Leisure and the Home*, Sports Council/Economic and Social Reseach Council Joint Panel on Leisure and Recreation Research, London.

Glyptis, S. A., Pack, C. M., 1988, *Local Authority Sports Provision for the Unemployed*, Study 31, Sports Council, London.

Glyptis, S. A., Riddington, A. C., 1983, *Sport for the Unemployed: A Review of Local Authority Projects*, Research Working Paper 21, Sports Council, London.

Gold, S. M., 1985, 'Future leisure environments in cities', in Goodale, T. L., and Witt, P. A. (eds), *Recreation and Leisure: Issues in an Era of Change*, Venture Publishing, State College, Pennsylvania, pp. 135–51.

Goodale, T. L., Witt, P. A. (eds), 1985, *Recreation and Leisure: Issues in an Era of Change*, Venture Publishing, State College, Pennsylvania.

Gramann, J. H., Burdge, R. J., 1981, 'The effect of recreation goals on conflict perception: the case of water skiers and fishermen', *Journal of Leisure Research*, 13(1): 115–27.

Gratton, C., Taylor, P. (1985), *Sport and Recreation: An Economic Analysis*, E. & F. N. Spon, London.

Grayson, E., 1988, *Sport and the Law*, Butterworths, London.

Green, B., 1981, *Countryside Conservation*, George Allen & Unwin, London.

Green, E., Hebron, S., and Woodward, D., 1987, *Leisure and Gender: A Study of Sheffield Women's Leisure Experiences*, Sports Council/Economic and Social Research Council Joint Panel on Leisure and Recreation Research, London.

Harrison, C. M., 1980–1, 'Recovery of lowland grassland and heathland in Southern England from disturbance by seasonal trampling', *Biological Conservation*, 19: 119–30.

Hedges, B., 1986, *Personal Leisure Histories*, Sports Council/Economic and Social Research Council Joint Panel on Leisure and Recreation Research, London.

Hendry, L. B., 1981, *Adolescents and Leisure*, Sports Council/Social Science Research Council Joint Panel on Leisure and Recreation Research, London.

Henley Centre for Forecasting, 1986, *The Economic Impact and Importance of Sport in the UK*, Study 30, Sports Council, London.

Hookway, R., 1984, 'A challenging horizon', in *Planning for Leisure in the Countryside*, Journal of Planning and Environmental Law Occasional Paper, pp. 1–19.

Jackson, E. L., 1986, 'Outdoor recreation participation and attitudes to the environment', *Leisure Studies*, 5(1): 1–23.

Jackson, E. L., Dunn, E., 1988, 'Integrating ceasing participation with other aspects of leisure behaviour', *Journal of Leisure Research*, 20(1): 31–45.

Jackson, E. L., Wong, R. A. G., 1982, 'Perceived conflict between urban cross-country skiers and snowmobilers in Alberta', *Journal of Leisure Research*, 14(1): 47–62.

Jenkins, C., Sherman, B., 1979, *The Collapse of Work*, Eyre Methuen, London.

Kew, S., 1979, *Ethnic Groups and Leisure*, Sports Council/Social Science Research Council Joint Panel on Leisure and Recreation Research, London.

Kuss, F. R., 1986, 'A review of major factors influencing plant responses to recreation impacts', *Environmental Management*, 10(5): 637–50.

Land Use Consultants Ltd, 1985, *Management Schemes for Commons*, CCP 197, Countryside Commission, Cheltenham.

Leuschner, W. A., Cook, P. S., Roggenbuck, J. W., and Oderwald, R. G., 1987, 'A comparative analysis for wilderness user fee policy', *Journal of Leisure Research*, 19(2): 101–14.

Lieber, S. R., Fesenmaier, D. R. (eds), 1983, *Recreation Planning and Management*, E. & F. N. Spon, London.

Locke, S., 1985, *Country Park Visitor Surveys: Lessons from a Study at Sherwood Forest and Rufford Country Parks, Nottinghamshire*, CCP 180, Countryside Commission, Cheltenham.

Long, J. A., Wimbush, E., 1985, *Continuity and Change: Leisure Around Retirement*, Sports Council/Economic and Social Research Council Joint Panel on Leisure and Recreation Research, London.

Lowe, P., Cox, G., MacEwen, M., O'Riordan, T., and Winter, M., 1986, *Countryside Conflicts: The Politics of Farming, Forestry and Conservation*, Gower/Maurice Temple Smith, Aldershot.

Lowe, P., Goyder, J., 1983, *Environmental Groups in Politics*, George Allen and Unwin, London.

McAvory, L. H., Burdge, R. J., Absher, J., and Gramann, J., 1986, 'The importance of visual environmental quality in site selection for water-based and water-enhanced recreation activities', *Recreation Research Review*, 12(3): 41–8.

MacEwen, A., MacEwen, M., 1982, *National Parks: Conservation or Cosmetics?* George Allen and Unwin, London.

MacEwen, A., MacEwen, M., 1987, *Greenprints for the Countryside? The Story of Britain's National Parks*, George Allen and Unwin, London.

Ministry of Agriculture, Fisheries and Food, 1987, *An Extensification Scheme: A Consultation Document by the Agriculture Departments*, MAFF, London.

Munton, R. J., 1983, *London's Green Belt: Containment in Practice*, George Allen and Unwin, London.

Murphy, B. J., Veal, A. J., 1977, *Community Use of Community Schools at the Primary Level: Two Case Studies in Walsall*, Research Working Paper 5, Sports Council, London.

Office of Population Censuses and Surveys, 1985, *General Household Survey 1983*, HMSO, London.

O'Riordan, T., Paget, G., 1978, *Sharing Rivers and Canals*, Study 16, Sports Council, London.

Owens, P. L., 1984, 'Rural leisure and recreation', *Progress in Human Geography*, 8(2): 157–88.

Parker, D. J., Penning-Rowsell, E. C., 1980, *Water Planning in Britain*, George Allen and Unwin, London.

Patmore, J. A., 1983, *Recreation and Resources*, Basil Blackwell, Oxford.

Patmore, J. A., 1987, 'A case study in national park planning', in Cloke, P. (ed.), *Rural Planning: Policy into Action*, Harper and Row, London, pp. 88–101.

Patmore, J. A., Collins, M. F., 1980, 'Recreation and leisure', *Progress in Human Geography*, 4(1): 91–7.

Public Attitude Surveys, 1979, *Leisure Pools*, Study 19, Sports Council, London.

Rigg, M., 1986, *Action Sport: An Evaluation*, Sports Council, London.

Roberts, J., 1978, *A Review of Studies of Sport and Recreation in the Inner City*, Study 17, Sports Council, London.

Roberts, K., 1983, *Youth and Leisure*, George Allen and Unwin, London.

Rodgers, H. B., 1977, *Rationalising Sports Policies: Sport in its Social Context*, Council of Europe, Strasbourg.

Rodgers, H. B., Patmore, J. A., 1972, *Leisure in the North West*, Manchester, North West Sports Council.

Scott, M., 1985, *The Law of Public Leisure Services*, Sweet and Maxwell, London.

Shaw, S. M., 1985, 'Gender and leisure: inequality in the distribution of leisure time', *Journal of Leisure Research*, 17(4): 266–82.

Shoard, M., 1987, *This Land is Our Land: The Struggle for Britain's Countryside*, Paladin, London.

Sidaway, R. M., Coalter, J. A., Rennick, I. M., and Scott, P. G., 1986, *Access Study: Summary Report*, CCP 216, Countryside Commission and Sports Council, Cheltenham.

Sidaway, R. M., O'Connor, F. B., 1978, 'Recreation pressures in the countryside', in Countryside Recreation Research Advisory Group, *Countryside for All?* Proceedings of CRRAG Conference, CRRAG, Cheltenham.

Sillitoe, K. K., 1969, *Planning for Leisure*, HMSO, London.

Sports Council, 1982, *Sport in the Community: The Next Ten Years*, Sports Council, London.

Sports Council, 1984–6, *Participation Demonstration Projects: Phase 1 Reports*, Sports Council, Manchester.

Sports Council, 1988, *Sport in the Community: Into the 90s: A Strategy for Sport 1988–1993*, Sports Council, London.

Stoakes, R., 1982, 'Charging and pricing for countryside recreation', in Countryside Recreation Research Advisory Group, *Countryside Recreation in the 1980s: Current Research and Future Challenges*, Proceedings of CRRAG Conference, CRRAG, Cheltenham.

Talbot, M., 1979, *Women and Leisure*, Sports Council/Social Science Research Council Joint Panel on Leisure and Recreation Research, London.

Telling, A., Smith, R., 1985, *The Public Right of Navigation*, Study 27, Sports Council, London.

Torkildsen, G., 1986, *Leisure and Recreation Management*, E. & F. N. Spon, London.

Tourism and Recreation Research Unit, 1983a, *Recreation Site Survey Manual: Methods and Techniques for Conducting Visitor Surveys*, Countryside Commission for Scotland, Perth.

Tourism and Recreation Research Unit, 1983b, *Urban Parks and Open Spaces—a Review*, Sports Council/Economic and Social Research Council Joint Panel on Leisure and Recreation Research, London.

Travis, A. S., 1979, *The State and Leisure Provision*, Sports Council/Social Science Research Council Joint Panel on Leisure and Recreation Research, London.

Tuite, C. H., 1982, *The Impact of Water-Based Recreation on the Waterfowl of Enclosed Inland*

Waters in Britain, Report to The Sports Council and Nature Conservancy Council, Wildfowl Trust, Slimbridge.

Uzzell, D. L., 1985, 'Management issues in the provision of countryside interpretation', *Leisure Studies*, 4(2): 159–74.

Ventris, N. (ed.), 1979, *Leisure and Rural Society*, Conference papers no. 10, Leisure Studies Association, London.

Wall, G., Marsh, J. S. (eds), 1982, *Recreational Land Use: Perspectives on its Evolution*, Carleton University Press, Ottawa.

Watmough, B., 1983, *The Effects on Wildfowl of Recreation at Reservoirs in the Mid Trent Valley*, Severn–Trent Water Authority, Birmingham.

West, P. C., 1981, 'Perceived crowding and attitudes toward limiting use in back-country recreation areas', *Leisure Sciences*, 4(4): 419–25.

Wilkinson, J., Atkins, B., and Brewer, E., 1985, *A Step in the Right Direction: The Marketing of Circular Walks*, Countryside Commission and Sports Council, Cheltenham.

10 Perspectives on temporal change and the history of recreation

G. Wall

Investigations of the history of recreation, be they studies of activities, events, places or participants, may be undertaken for many reasons. Curiosity and the intrinsic interest of the subject combine to encourage some to study the history of recreation for its own sake, and such researchers may require no further justification for their activities. However, if such studies are not placed within a broader context, there is a danger that they will be merely antiquarian and that they will fail to make the full contribution to the understanding of society which they have the potential to make. Activities undertaken in leisure, while not free of constraints, by definition, involve a large element of choice. In consequence, their investigation may reveal different and complementary insights into the workings of a society when compared with other areas of life where choices may be more constrained.

For too long it has been common, almost fashionable, to begin academic papers on outdoor recreation with references to growing population, expanded leisure, rising incomes, improved transportation and greater urbanization, and to attribute rapid rates of growth in participation in outdoor recreation to expansion of these causal factors. Attention is drawn to growth, to the relative neglect of activities or areas which are stagnant or in decline. Such perspectives ignore many recent trends in Western societies which have implications for both supply and demand such as declining birth rates and greater longevity, increased unemployment, economic vagaries, traffic congestion and changes in the structure of metropolitan areas, making such assertions both simplistic and dated. There is also every reason to believe that even the recent past was much more complex than these generalizations imply. Such statements gloss over the real importance of fluctuations in such variables and imply that the nature of their influence upon leisure and recreation are well understood when, in fact, such relationships continue to be fruitful areas of research. Furthermore, the emphasis on the rapidity of change, which often accompanies such assertions, suggests a break with the past rather than the considerable continuities which more careful analyses reveal. Thus, it is argued that recreation researchers should be much more cognisant than they frequently have been of the temporal contexts of their studies.

There are also sound practical reasons why recreation researchers should understand the temporal dimensions of their topics. Processes of change may be best understood through studies which are more than cross-sections in time, and policy recommendations must acknowledge the existence of preceding situations which place limitations on options. The world is not a *tabula rasa* and possible futures are very much constrained by decisions which have been made in the past. An understanding of past patterns of recreation and the evolution of recreational activities and areas can also lead to the development of interpretive materials to cater to the considerable interest in heritage. Thus, the history of recreation need not be a purely academic enterprise for it also has its applied aspects.

While more recreation and leisure studies should be more firmly placed in their temporal contexts, there is also a need for researchers with a predominantly historical focus to look beyond the narrow bounds of their subject matter. If the antiquarian trap is to be avoided then researchers must strive to move beyond the case study. This is not to suggest that good case studies are not needed, for accurate factual information must be acquired, and examples must be developed to test hypotheses and to illuminate and illustrate generalizations. The point is that case studies will be most useful if they are linked to broader themes and serve a higher purpose rather than being ends in themselves.

If progress is to be made and studies are to be cumulative in their contribution to knowledge then it is necessary to impose a structure upon information. Of course, many such structures are possible, no one structure will suit all needs and the utility of different structures will vary with the objectives for the study. One relatively straightforward means of categorizing information is by topic (Marsh and Wall, 1982; Butler and Wall, 1985). Thus, one might be interested in spas or seaside resorts, in urban or rural recreation, in public or private provision, in recreations of the élite or the experiences of the proletariat, in the evolution of particular activities or in a multitude of other topics. Perhaps not surprisingly, topical coverage is very uneven. For example, there is excellent documentation on seaside resorts (Walvin, 1978; Walton, 1983) but the definitive work on spas has yet to be written. Similarly, there is a vast academic and popular literature on national parks in many parts of the world (Bella, 1987; MacEwen and MacEwen, 1982; Runte, 1979; Foresta, 1984; Wirth, 1980), but much less extensive documentation of parks at regional, provincial and state levels, or of the evolution of urban park systems, although documentation of the latter is beginning to emerge (Cranz, 1982; Schuyler, 1986). The histories of sports and recreation usually concentrate upon the élite performers, winners and professional athletes to the relative neglect of the recreational participant but, again, this is beginning to change (Bailey, 1980; Lowerson and Myerscough, 1977; Malcolmson, 1973).

If the history of recreation is to be more than a collection of disparate topics then a means of integrating the topics must be found. One such means is the application of themes which cut across the various topics. Examples of such themes include the roles of health, religion, technological change, socio-economic influences, landscape evaluation and cultural transfer. Regardless of the topics, it is likely that one or more of these themes will be relevant to most historical studies of outdoor recreation.

History is the study of change through time. A considerable and growing body of literature is concerned with understanding such changes, although only a limited proportion of this work has been contributed by professional historians. The time-scales of such investigations vary greatly and the nature and availability of data also vary with time (Towner, 1984 and 1988). Considerable attention has been given to seasonality and the various problems associated with it, and weekly and diurnal patterns of recreation have also received consideration (Murphy, 1982). The Rapoports (1975) have found the family life cycle to be a useful concept for understanding changes in individual recreational behaviour and associated changes in society and demands upon facilities and resources. Other authors have considered the possibility of displacement and succession as initial users of a site elect to go elsewhere and are replaced by newcomers with different expectations as the experiences available at that site are modified (Schreyer, 1979; Roggenbuch et al., 1980). Similarly, authors interested in the ecological impacts of recreation have been concerned with changes in the numbers of users, the extent to which they modify the resources and the potential for its recovery. They conclude that most impact takes place at relatively low levels of use, successive increments of use generally being associated with diminishing marginal rates of change, but that periods required for recovery are much longer than those for impact, and may number in hundreds of years in some fragile environments (Hammitt and Cole, 1987). Thus, temporal frames of reference employed by researchers vary widely.

While the studies which have been mentioned in the preceding paragraph are all concerned with change through time, because of the short periods investigated and the recency of the times under consideration, some, with justification, may not consider them to be historical. This doubt should not exist in the case of resort cycles which are concerned with changes over decades and even centuries. Butler (1980) has suggested that the history of resorts exhibits considerable similarities to the S-shaped product life cycle. Numbers of visitors change over time as resorts go through successive stages which Butler has called exploration, involvement, development, consolidation, stagnation and decline or rejuvenation, the latter depending upon the availability of previously untapped resources. One great value of the resort cycle is that it succeeds in incorporating a number of other concepts and ideas. Thus, it encompasses changes in the numbers and types of visitors (Plog, 1974), modifications in sources of investment and control over development (Brown, 1985), alterations in resident attitudes (Doxey, 1976) and it could, potentially, include notions of landscape change.

Although instant resorts, such as Cancun, and some resorts in developing countries which were pioneered by colonial élites, do not fit the model, the resort cycle has great intuitive appeal and, as a descriptive model, it appears to fit a large number of cases more than superficially. It would be unwise to employ the model for predictive purposes but it does have some applied utility in that it encourages one to question the inevitability of the cycle and to search for strategies which might arrest the cycle at a desirable stage.

The resort cycle has spawned a rapidly growing body of literature. Some researchers have questioned the validity and utility of the model, are concerned about the data with which it might be tested and question if it can be proved or disproved (Haywood, 1986). Others have found it to provide a useful organizing framework for their studies and have attempted to test it in particular situations (Stansfield, 1978; Hovinen, 1981). There is potential to incorporate additional concepts into the model. For example, Meyer-Arendt (1985), using a series of studies in the Gulf of Mexico, associated changes in resort morphology and environmental modification with different stages of the model. The reconciliation and linking of seemingly disparate concepts may be a fruitful path to follow in the search for more broadly based understanding.

While Butler's cycle has received most attention in the literature there are others whch are less widely known. Krakover (1985), drawing upon the experiences of arid areas in Israel, has suggested a different series of situations which may be common to evolving resorts in remote areas. In contrast to Butler, he stresses the importance of government investment in the early stages of development when infrastructure must be constructed. Government involvement changes to a regulatory role in later stages when business opportunities may be more attractive to private investors.

There may also be other cycles which operate at different time-scales and have yet to be documented. Investment in many forms of recreation is lumpy. For example, the size of hotels is now such that the construction of a large new hotel may change the accommodation situation of under-supply to over-supply with resulting implications for occupancy rates, pricing and visitor behaviour. Demand may have to rise considerably to increase occupancy rates to a level at which there is excess demand and sufficiently high prices to merit the installation of new supply when the cycle may start again. Such speculation awaits empirical verification.

Investigations of changes through time in recreation have been both cause and effect of increased interest in the history of recreation and have been associated with the integration of concepts and the development of generalizations. However, if historians of recreation are to make a major contribution to knowledge it is necessary that they not only strive to link concepts and generalize, they must also address issues which are of interest to other disciplines. Examples of such issues abound. They include evolving class structures, economic cycles, technological change, quality of life, people–environment interaction, gender roles and national identity. The evolution of leisure and recreation is itself a phenomenon with implications for many other areas. The growing literature on recreation as a means of social control, though controversial, is a good example of the kind of approach that is needed (Cunningham, 1980; Clarke and Crichter, 1985; Golby and Purdue, 1984). Although the concept has received only limited attention in North America, it has generated considerable debate in Britain and encouraged re-assessment of the significance of leisure with implications for a number of the issues mentioned above. If historians of recreation are to do justice to their subject matter they must set themselves lofty goals, reach out beyond the narrow confines of their sub-discipline and relate their findings to major themes which challenge intellects across disciplines. Wadsworth (1975) suggested that: 'As the prevailing culture and attitudes of a society change, so also do its leisure pursuits; by studying the pursuits it is possible to increase our understanding of the progress and development of that society.' His ideas are not new for Josiah Strutt, writing in 1801, indicated that:

In order to form a just estimation of the character of any particular people, it is absolutely necessary to investigate the sports and pastimes most generally prevalent among them ... When we follow them to their retirements, where no disguise is necessary, we are most likely to see them in their true state, and may best judge of their natural dispositions.

There are signs that the challenges of such demanding, but far-reaching, questions are being taken up. However, should recreational historians shy away from using their expertise to illuminate the broader questions of society, there is a danger that they will fail to make the contributions to knowledge of which they are capable, and that they will end up merely talking to themselves.

References

Bailey, P., 1978, *Leisure and Class in Victorian England: Rational Recreation and the Contest for Control, 1830–1885*, Routledge & Kegan Paul, London.

Bella, L., 1987, *Parks for Profit*, Harvest House, Montreal.

Brown, B. J. H., 1985, 'Personal perception and community speculation: a British resort in the 19th century', *Annals of Tourism Research*, 12(3): 355–69.

Butler, R., 1980, 'The concept of a tourist area cycle of evolution: implications for the management of resources', *Canadian Geographer*, 24(1): 5–12.

Butler, R., Wall, G., 1985, 'Introduction: themes in research on the evolution of tourism', *Annals of Tourism Research*, 12(3): 287–96.

Clarke, J., Chrichter, C., 1985, *The Devil Makes Work: Leisure in Capitalist Britain*, Macmillan, London.

Cohen, E., 1985, 'Towards a sociology of tourism', *Annals of Tourism Research*, 39(1): 104–22.

Cranz, G., 1982, *The Politics of Park Design: A History of Urban Parks in America*, The MIT Press, Cambridge, Mass.

Cunningham, H., 1980, *Leisure in the Industrial Revolution*, Croom Helm, London.

Doxey, G., 1976, 'When enough's enough: the natives are restless in old Niagara', *Heritage Canada*, 2(2): 26–7.

Foresta, R. A., 1984, *America's National Parks and Their Keepers*, Resources for the Future, Washington DC.

Golby, J. M., Purdue, A. W., 1984, *The Civilisation of the Crowd: Popular Culture in England 1750–1900*, Batsford, London.

Hammitt, W. E., Cole, D. N., 1987, *Wildland Recreation: Ecology and Management*, Wiley, New York.

Haywood, K. M., 1986, 'Can the tourist-area life cycle be made operational?' *Tourism Management*, 7(3): 154–67.

Hovinen, G., 1981, 'A tourist cycle in Lancaster County, Pennsylvania', *Canadian Geographer*, 25(3): 283–5.

Krakover, S., 1985, 'Development of tourism resort areas in arid regions', in Gradus, Y., *Desert Development: Man and Technology in Sparse-lands*, D. Reidel, Dordrecht, pp. 271–84.

Lowerson, J., Myerscough, J., 1977, *Time to Spare in Victorian England*, Harvester, Hassocks, Sussex.

MacEwen, A., MacEwen, M., 1982, *National Parks: Conservation or Cosmetics?* George Allen and Unwin, Hemel Hempstead.

Malcolmson, R. W., 1973, *Popular Recreations in English Society 1700–1850*, Cambridge University Press, Cambridge.

Marsh, J., Wall, G., 1982, 'Themes in the investigation of the evolution of outdoor recreation', in Wall, G., Marsh, J. (eds), *Recreational Land Use: Perspectives on its Evolution in Canada*, Carleton Library Series 126, Carleton University, Ottawa, pp. 1–12.

Meyer-Arendt, K. J., 1985, 'The Grand Isle, Louisiana resort cycle', *Annals of Tourism Research*, 12(3): 449–65.

Murphy, P., 1982, 'Tourism planning in London: an exercise in spatial and seasonal management', *Tourist Review*, 1: 19–23.

Plog, S. C., 1974, 'Why destination areas rise and fall in popularity', *The Cornell Hotel and Restaurant Association Quarterly*, 14(4): 55–8.

Rapoport, R., Rapoport, R. N., 1975, *Leisure and the Family Life Cycle*, Routledge & Kegan Paul, London.

Roggenbuck, J. W., Smith, A. C., and Wellman, A. D., 1980, *Specialization, Displacement and Definition of Depreciative Behaviour among Virginia Canoeists*, North Central Forest Experiment Station, U.S. Department of Agriculture, St. Paul, Minn.

Runte, A., 1979, *National Parks: The American Experience*, University of Nebraska Press, Lincoln.

Schreyer, R., 1979, *Succession and Displacement in River Recreation: Problem Definition and Analysis*, North Central Forest Experiment Station, US Department of Agriculture, St. Paul, Minn.

Schuyler, D., 1986, *New Urban Landscape: The Redefinition of City Form in Nineteenth-Century America*, Johns Hopkins University Press, Baltimore.

Stansfield, C., 1978, 'Atlantic City and the resort cycle: background to the legalization of gambling', *Annals of Tourism Research*, 5(2): 238–51.

Strutt, J., 1801, *The Sports and Pastimes of the People of England*, William Tegg, London.

Towner, J., 1984, 'The grand tour: sources and a methodology for an historical study of tourism', *Tourism Management*, 5(3): 215–22.

Towner, J., 1988, 'Approaches to tourism history', *Annals of Tourism Research*, 15(1): 47–62.

Wadsworth, P. M., 1975, 'Leisure pursuits in nineteenth-century Bath', unpublished MA thesis, University of Kent.

Walton, J. K., 1983, *The English Seaside Resort: A Social History 1750—1914*, Leicester University Press, Leicester.

Walvin, J., 1978, *Beside the Seaside: A Social History of the Popular Seaside Holiday*, Allen Lane, London.

Wirth, C. L., 1980, *Parks, Politics and the People*, University of Oklahoma Press, Oklahoma.

11 The practice of human resource management within the hospitality industry

R. C. Mill

Introduction

Human resource management is concerned with obtaining, organizing, training and motivating the people needed by an organization.

The changing role of human resource management

Title change

The human resource function has, of late, gone through a name change and is in the process of going through a role change (Umbreit, 1987: 343–4). As little as five years ago the term universally used to describe the **people function** was 'personnel management'. In the field of tourism and hospitality, personnel management at the unit level consisted of little more than recruitment advertising, selection screening, fringe benefit administration and orientation. Personnel managers themselves received little training and most were not responsible for conducting training sessions (apart from orientation). The term now used is **human resource management**. Human resource management suggests a greater concern for recognizing the importance of the human resources of a company. The name change is important for it sets an image of what the function is all about. Yet the roles associated with human resource managers are changing more slowly (Pickworth, 1981: 44).

It is a transition similar to the one experienced two decades ago as 'sales' evolved into 'marketing'. In the beginning sales managers were called marketing managers yet they still performed the role of the traditional sales manager—they sold the product. Slowly the role has evolved into a true marketing manager concerned with determining the needs of the market, developing products and services to meet those needs, presenting those services to the market and ensuring the satisfaction of the customers afterwards. A similar evolution is occurring in human resource management.

Role change

A change in the role of human resource manager is under way, albeit rather slowly. The factors that precipitated this change were external to the company. The major factors were an increase in government regulations and the changing structure of the labor force (Umbreit, 1986: 344–6).

There has been a movement to protect the rights and safety of employees in the workplace. Regulations exist to protect workers from discrimination in hiring, promotion, daily treatment and in firing. Similarly, employers must provide a safe environment for their employees to work in. Keeping up with new government regulations requires an expertise that line managers do not have the time to cultivate. They have turned to the staff specialist to assist them (and keep them out of trouble). In so doing the human resource function begins to get more respect from line managers.

The other major factor influencing the changing role of human resources is the structure of the labor force (Leposky, 1987). The hospitality industry has traditionally relied upon teenagers as a prime employee group. Yet, due to changing demographic trends there are fewer teenagers in the work-force. Additionally, the employee of today is better educated and more demanding. More employees want more out of the job than a pay check. The 'quality of life' concerns of the 1970s and 1980s will enhance the move towards more employee participation in the affairs and decisions of the workplace.

To find and motivate the 'new' employee of the 1980s, line management is beginning to turn to the human resource specialist. As a result human resource management is beginning to take on greater importance to companies. Long-range plans and strategic analyses are beginning to include the human resource element. The new approach is to see employees as assets, and money spent on hiring and training as capital investments (Ferguson and Berger, 1985). The role change is most evident in the fast food (or fast service) companies in the United States. Perhaps this is because the fast food industry is into the maturity stage of its life cycle and is experiencing problems now that will be faced by the rest of the industry later.

The personnel function in the smaller property and in the independent property is still given too little attention. Personnel activities are too often performed by someone who has 'personnel' added to their main responsibilities. Little or no formal training is provided. As a result personnel in the smaller property concentrates on recruitment of employees (Pickworth, 1981).

It appears that personnel or human resource managers differ in the United States and Great Britain in a major respect. In Britain personnel managers are much more involved in the training function than are their counterparts in the United States. This is true even in smaller hotels. Largely because of the involvement of the Hotel and Catering Industry Training Board many department heads have trainer-skills qualifications. This has allowed the personnel department to concentrate on the design and evaluation of training (Boella, 1986).

The changing hospitality employee

The hospitality industry is seeing a movement away from an adequate supply of low-skilled entry level employees to a shortage of such workers. There are four reasons for this (Leposky, 1987; Elder, 1987). First, as mentioned above, there is the importance of demographic trends. The hospitality industry, especially the restaurant industry, has relied heavily on the 16–24-year-old age group. As the baby boomers—those born in the 15 years following the Second World War—grow up this source of employees is diminishing. Automation will make up for only some of this loss.

Second, there is evidence that the image of the hospitality industry is not a positive one for many potential employees. Employees are increasingly concerned with getting personal fulfillment from their job and are looking for more benefits from the organization. Many feel they cannot get this from the hospitality industry. Third, economic expansion in many countries has reduced the unemployment rate, making it even more difficult to recruit for low-paying entry level positions.

Last, evidence indicates that turnover is still a major problem for hospitality companies—a problem that many companies seem unable to do anything about. As the labor market shifts from a demand to a supply orientation employees will find it easier to get better jobs in other areas. As a result, by the mid-1990s, there will be a shortage of hourly employees in the hospitality industry. Employers will have to become more aggressive and innovative in their recruiting practices.

Employers will have to turn to four groups for their future workers: women, seniors, minorities and the handicapped (Mill, 1988).

Women

Several factors combine to indicate the growing importance of women to the hospitality industry (Jafari, 1986–7). More women are marrying at a later age, postponing or eliminating entirely the idea of having children. Those women with children face increased economic pressure to work outside the home. In fact, one of the fastest growing labor groups is mothers with young children. For this group part-time work is preferable. Major problems are the low pay and the odd hours. By the time day care is paid for there may be little money left from the pay check. The needs of the children often clash with the busiest hours of operation.

At the managerial level women are slowly beginning to make their presence felt. The proportion of females in degree courses in hotel and restaurant management has increased significantly over the past decade.

The growing importance of women to the industry has resulted in more attention being paid to several matters (Mill, 1988). Guidelines have been issued on the subject of sexual harassment. Management is responsible for protecting its employees from unwelcome sexual conduct on the part of supervisors, fellow employees, suppliers or customers. Regulations require that pregnancy be treated as a temporary condition. Employees are protected from losing their jobs because they become pregnant. Currently attempts are being made in the United States to follow Europe's lead in providing parental leave to both spouses on an unpaid leave basis.

Others feel that the benefit of the immediate future will be for employers to provide child-care centers (Boyle, 1987). Some proponents point out that such centers would allow employees to be available for longer hours while also being an attractive feature for guests with small children. The United States' government, in fact, offers tax incentives for corporate child-care programs.

Seniors

There will be more older people in the next ten years. The fast food companies seem to be better at utilizing this group of potential employees (Elder, 1987). Several companies have realized that seniors show better judgment, are more accurate, make better decisions and are more committed to quality than are younger workers. Legislation is making it easier for seniors to earn more money without pensions being adversely affected.

Companies like McDonalds have successfully attracted seniors by developing special programs just for them. Older workers are kept together, thereby making the group a cohesive unit; one-to-one on-the-job-training is provided and employees are made to feel a purpose or responsibility in their work. Discounted meals, the provision of transportation to and from work and the availability of medical benefits are other factors of importance to this group (Dee, 1987).

Handicapped

As society encourages the integration of the handicapped into mainstream society many companies are turning to this group to help solve the labor problem (Elder, 1987). Various tax and monetary incentives are available to encourage businesses to spend the time and effort in assisting the handicapped into the workforce. Companies must overcome the prejudice of existing employees together with the biggest fear—will this person be able to perform the job? Initial training must be personalized and tight supervision is necessary at first. Thereafter, the employee is generally loyal and dependable. Turnover tends to be low, safety records are good and the employee may perform tedious work that no one else is willing to do. If the employee is made to feel needed he/she is thankful for the opportunity to contribute to society.

Minorities

The hospitality industry has traditionally relied upon minority employees to perform its most tedious low-level jobs. The hospitality employer will find more restrictions in such areas as allowing minority employees to speak their own language on the job. From a management perspective it may make sense to hire supervisors who can speak the language of the minority or to train them in such skills.

In the United States it is expected that blacks will play a bigger role in the workplace (Peters, 1987). The 1986 Immigration Bill makes it illegal to hire aliens who do not have the right to work in the United States. This will impact a large number of Hispanics in the workforce and may open up additional opportunities for black employees.

Unions

Union density in the hospitality industry is low. Many explanations have been offered for this fact—the fragmented structure of the industry, high turnover, foreign labor and the practice of tipping (Riley, 1985). Historically, hotel workers have been outside of the main labor movement. It is argued that the idea of 'service' is inconsistent with the ideals of trade unionism. Whatever the reasons, the fact is that only approximately 10 per cent of the more than four million hotel and restaurant employees in the United States are represented by the Hotels and Restaurant Employees International Union (Kohl and Stephens, 1985). Unions are concentrated in large cities in California, Florida, the northeast and the upper midwest.

The hiring process

Discrimination

Hospitality companies have been fortunate to escape problems in the areas of discrimination. Discrimination in hiring undoubtedly goes on. Generally, people who feel that they have been unfairly treated simply apply at another property. The law quite clearly states, however, that employees should be hired on the basis of job-related criteria only and without regard to age, sex, race, religion, handicap or national origin. National origin has recently been broadened to include citizenship.

At the corporate level the major companies are taking the law to heart by setting policies which they hope will result in fewer complaints of discrimination. For the independent operator, however, hiring remains a subjective and often discriminatory process (Adu-Kwansa *et al*., 1986). It should be pointed out that the employee is protected against discrimination not only in the hiring process but also in the areas of pay, job assignment, promotion, use of facilities, training, retirement plans, disability leaves and firing.

Sexual harassment

Early court decisions on discrimination on the basis of sex limited liability to cases where an employee was denied a position, promotion or some other economic benefit on the basis of sex. That idea was broadened in the United States in 1981 to include an atmosphere of sexual harassment. Sexual harassment consists of unwelcome sexual advances of a verbal or physical nature.

To provide a working environment free of sexual harassment the following steps are suggested:

1. Evaluate the existing atmosphere in all work locations to determine whether any element of a sexually offensive environment is present.
2. Institute a forceful and precise policy statement forbidding all types of sexual harassment.
3. Educate all managers about the policy and the type of conduct considered to be sexual harassment.
4. Communicate the policy forcefully to all employees through meetings, bulletins and newsletters.
5. Act firmly and promptly when faced with any violations, no matter by whom or how slight (Johnson, 1985).

Testing

One way to make the hiring process more objective is through the use of tests. In order to be above challenge tests should be valid and reliable. A valid test is one which is a solid predictor of a person's likely performance on the job. If a potential employee fails the test it is likely that he/she will not perform well on the job. A test is reliable if it yields approximately the same results over time if taken by the same individual. If a test meets both criteria then it can safely be used in the hiring process.

Three types of test are of particular concern to the hospitality industry— honesty tests, drug and alcohol tests and tests for AIDS (Chon and Jacob, 1987).

Honesty tests are important because hospitality employees come into contact with money and/or guest belongings. Innkeepers have had a historically strong obligation to ensure the safety of their guests. Increasingly polygraphs are being outlawed. Many employers are reverting to pencil and paper questionnaires designed to inventory a person's attitude about honesty and their previous behavior.

Drug and alcohol tests are important for two reasons. First, various studies have demonstrated that the employee under the influence or control of alcohol and/or other drugs costs the business money through a lack of productivity and an increase in absenteeism, accidents and lateness. Second, the availability of alcohol in the hospitality industry means that the temptation to abuse it is strong.

Before administering such tests it is vital to ensure their reliability. The reliability of urinalysis, for example, runs from 80 to 95 per cent. Some laboratories are more effective than others in reading the results. The major concern about drug and alcohol tests concerns possible discrimination suits. If an employee is refused employment because of the test results the property must prove that the employee was not qualified to perform the job even if 'reasonable accommodations' were made by the employer to compensate for the employee's habit. Increasingly an addict is being classified as a handicapped individual and is protected by the law. The safest course is to provide an opportunity for rehabilitation of the employee's addiction before refusing that employee for employment.

Given the increase in numbers of people with AIDS, employers have had to formulate policies concerning AIDS victims and virus-infected individuals. Recent court decisions suggest that AIDS victims are protected as handicapped employees. The burden is on the employer to prove that the employee cannot physically perform the job because of the virus. There have been no documented cases of AIDS being transmitted through casual contact or food preparation. Since there are no foolproof methods of testing for the virus, pre-employment testing for AIDS is strongly discouraged.

Interviewing

The interview remains the most widely used method of selecting employees. At the same time it is time consuming, costly and subjective. The interview can be more objective if it is structured. A structured interview is one which focuses strongly on job-related questions. The process begins with an analysis of a specific job. The knowledge, skills and competencies needed for successful job performances are identified. For each essential competency key behavioral questions are determined that will elicit examples of past accomplishments, activities and performances.

Questions may be oral, in writing or the interviewee may be asked to perform part of the job. The same questions should be asked of all potential employees. Sample answers will have been developed beforehand so that the interviewer knows what he/she is looking for. To improve reliability some companies are using more than one interviewer. The entire process is documented in writing and kept as reference in case of future complaints of discrimination. The interview is, after all, a test and is subject to the strictures of validity and reliability mentioned above.

Because of the changing demographics outlined above the interviewer often has to 'sell' the job to the employee as well as vice versa. In some situations company representatives have oversold the company, the position and the opportunities. Being realistic about the job will result in fewer acceptances. Those who do accept, however, are likely to remain longer and be happier in their positions.

Reference checks

It is generally agreed that managers should check employee references before making the decision to hire (Marshall and Bellucci, 1985). The rationale is that past peformance is an effective predictor of future performance. However, it is becoming more and more difficult to get useful information from a reference check. The reason is that employees are beginning to sue employers for giving poor references that (they feel) prevented them from getting a job. As such, most companies instruct management to do no more than confirm the dates the individual was employed and the job the person did. It is possible by talking to the direct supervisor of the employee rather than the personnel office to obtain more pertinent information.

Assessment centers

Assessment centers are not places but a selection and development program composed of a series of exercises and tests followed by evaluations (Berger, 1985). The tests usually last from one and a half to two days with groups of participants of up to 12 in number. The participants are usually nominated for this program by their supervisor and are evaluated by a panel of trained evaluators who are usually two to three levels of management above the participants. The most common use of the assessment center is the identification of potential for first-level management.

The first center was begun by A. T. T. in the 1950s. Becuse of the costs involved—from $600 to $6,000 per participant—most companies who use this technique are large. Hospitality companies such as the Holiday Corporation have begun developing assessment centers to identify potential general managers. The technique will likely become more popular among hospitality companies in the future.

Orientation and training

If employers did a perfect job of hiring employees there would be no need for any other human resource functions. The fact that companies do not recruit perfectly gives rise to two types of problems—either employees are hired who do not have the skills to perform or do not have the motivation to perform. In the former case the answer is training. Training actually begins in the orientation process.

Orientation

Many companies still do not take advantage of one of the most effective means for holding on to employees—a well-planned orientation program. The orientation process historically practiced in most companies has proven ineffective (Reid, 1985). Because the first days on the job are critical to the holding process between company and employee an orientation program is critical to cutting down on employee turnover.

The scope of the orientation program should focus on the following:

1. Knowledge and understanding of company history, values, functions, type of customers served, services provided and the kind of contribution the company seeks to provide to society.
2. Compensation package and benefits.
3. Specifics of job duties and the relevant relationships to others in the department and the company.
4. Performance standards and expectations.
5. Salary increases and advancement opportunities based on job performance.

For best results orientation sessions should be short and spread over a few days. This structuring of the sessions will not overload the employee with too much information at one time. Certain criteria are common to the development of any worthwhile program. First, all elements of the orientation should convey an accurate impression of the company's character. Second, the written and visual information should be well organized, clearly articulated and presented in a way that is easy to understand. Third, the information should be structured in a way that is interesting and will keep the attention of the employee. Fourth, a program should be flexible, incorporating the internal and external changes affecting the company. Last, the program's content should convey the message that the company's employees are the most important asset to the firm's success.

Training

More and more companies are recognizing the importance of training. In the 1970s in Great Britain the Hotel and Catering Industry Training Board introduced a levy exemption scheme whereby companies could avoid paying the statutory training levy of 1 per cent of payroll by showing that they were meeting their own needs. The result was that, in many cases, professionals were hired from outside the hospitality industry and charged with upgrading the quality of the training function (Kelliher and Johnson, 1987). Because of the interrelationship between training and other personnel functions the entire human resource activity was improved.

In the United States over 70 per cent of the membership of the National Restaurant Association have formal training programs for hourly employees. The average length of the program is eight days although almost 60 per cent of the training programs last from one to five days. The most popular training methods used are:

1. Training conducted by a manager or specific supervisor;
2. Training conducted by a peer employee;
3. Training which makes use of a training manual which the trainee studies (Reid, 1986).

A variety of management training programs exist. Management training programs of food service organizations in the United States exhibit the following characteristics:

1. The average length of the program is 13 weeks with a range from two weeks to 65 weeks.
2. Two-thirds of the programs are held at company-owned properties while one-third involve training at corporate headquarters or regional training sites.
3. On-the-job training is the favored technique used while over a third involve some type of rotation through all the positions in the operation. Formal classroom work is a common method for 20 per cent of the organizations while less than 10 per cent use video as a training device (Reid, 1985).

It is generally agreed that, while training is important, not enough is done. That which is done is often poorly done and ineffective. In fact there is no consistent pattern for training costs in the United States by type of establishment, sales size or years in operation. Nor is there a consistent relationship with turnover or the ratio of full- to part-time employees (*Restaurants USA*, 1986).

More role playing needs to be done to improve the realism of the training. The methods used must be tailored to the needs of the individual employee, and the employee given more control over the pace at which training is conducted. The latter two points have both been linked to turnover (Foucar-Szocki, 1987). Management still too often see training as an expense rather than as an investment. When business is good there is no need for training. When business is bad the training that occurs is conducted in a rushed, crisis atmosphere. The result is poorly trained employees. Management will often use this as a rationale that training does not work. The seasonality of many hospitality business certainly makes training much more difficult. Employees have to be recruited and trained each season. The cost is often difficult to rationalize.

Good training can occur when managers establish an overall climate within which trainees want to learn and are reinforced for learning. It must be on-going, goal oriented and supported by top management (Knight and Salter, 1985). Training in the hospitality industry is essentially on-the-job training. The only exception is training for the front office which, because of the emphasis on computers, occurs in the classroom.

Two recent concerns that involve training are developing a quality assurance program and improving the service skills of employees. For a quality assurance program to work certain progressive steps are in order. Management sets goals and policies for guest service. From these, quantitative and qualitative standards are written and reviewed with employees. Training for new employees in the skills of the job is instituted and the standards constantly monitored and evaluated. Based on these same standards productivity and performance can be measured and reported to department heads and quality assurance committees made up of representatives of the various departments in the property. The impetus for a program of quality assurance came in the United States from a 1982 survey of the characteristics of lodging properties known for the high quality of their operation. Based on the findings, the American Hotel and Motel Association developed a quality assurance program suitable for implementation in lodging properties.

An increasing consideration of the social and service skills of hospitality has recently complemented the past and total emphasis on job skills. The steps to improving customer service are: define standards of quality service with measurable indicators; assess the current situation; develop effective service-improvement strategies; initiate the solutions carefully; provide feedback, recognition and rewards (Martin, 1986). The key is to define service in terms that employees can relate to and to institute procedures to train employees in the skills they lack. Service in the dining-room, for example, consists of procedural and convivial dimensions (Martin, 1986). Procedural skills include such things as ensuring that service is timely, customers' needs are anticipated and customer feedback is sought; the convivial dimension of service involves the servers making helpful suggestions to customers, communicating in a friendly, personal tone of voice and calling customers by name (Martin, 1986). Once standards are defined, often with the help of employees, training can take place to develop these skills within employees.

Much work needs to be done in persuading businesses, particularly small businesses, of the need to train and on improving the quality of the training itself.

Employee motivation

When employees have the skills to perform but are not producing what management expects, the problem has to do with the motivation of the employee. Surveys of hospitality executives have consistently indicated that they feel the success of their properties is directly related to their ability to motivate employees. Yet, despite claims that employee motivation is a major concern, in practice it is given little weight (Mill, 1985).

The key to producing motivated employees is for the manager to set a climate within which employees motivate themselves to produce. Such a climate is produced when employees feel that the company sets high goals; they know what is expected of them; they are committed to the goals of the company; they have some input in to the parts of the job that affect them; they receive recognition for their efforts; and they operate within an atmosphere of trust (Mill, 1988).

For managers this means involving employees in the setting of objectives for the property. Contrary to popular belief, involving employees in the setting of objectives results in objectives being set that are higher than if set by management alone. Employee involvement can be increased by emphasizing non-financial objectives such as quality, service and hospitality. Employees can better relate to such goals and, thus, will be more committed to achieving them. Employees become part of the team when they are encouraged to show initiative and are recognized for their efforts.

A related problem that management will face in the near future is the problem of motivating middle managers who cannot be promoted because of a lack of upper-level positions. This situation is beginning to manifest itself as the baby boomers crowd the ranks of management. Companies are faced with a large number of qualified, ambitious prospects aiming for a relatively small number of upper management slots. Some companies are experimenting with lateral transfers, supporting employee educational efforts, direct counseling and job rotation (Foucar-Szocki, 1987).

Pay and benefits

The hospitality industry has historically been a poor compensator of its employees. Pressure to increase wages will come from the projected labor shortage of the 1990s.

While employee benefits have increased, hospitality companies are still far behind other industries. While benefits can cost a corporation up to an additional one-third of its wage bill, American restaurants spend a median of 5 per cent of payroll on non-wage benefits. Paid meals and uniforms are provided immediately while, for benefits like life insurance and paid vacations, employees have had to meet restrictions based on such things as longevity, position and performance (National Restaurant Association, 1982).

A major development has been the adoption of *cafeteria benefit plans* whereby the company sets aside a certain amount for benefits for each employee. Within that sum of money employees are free to choose which benefits they want based on their particular needs.

Restaurants that are part of a chain provide better benefits than do independents. A survey of American chain operations indicated that 95 per cent of the respondents provided meals, uniforms and paid vacations for their employees; almost 95 per cent provided a medical plan. By contrast, less than 80 per cent of independent restaurants offered paid vacations or meals and less than two-thirds provided uniforms or a health plan.

While only four out of ten of the chains provided a dental plan only one in five of the independents did so. This benefit was rarely seen several years ago. Eighty per cent of the chains provided group life insurance coverage while slightly less than half offered a profit-sharing or thrift-sharing savings plan to hourly employees. The figures for independents were 40 per cent and 16 per cent respectively (Jackson, 1986).

Three out of ten chains offered assistance to employees with related educational expenses while one quarter provided a pension plan. The benefit least likely to be offered hourly employees was a stock purchase plan. Education expense was provided by about one out of six independents while less than 10 per cent offered a pension plan.

Non-traditional rewards

In an effort to produce motivated employees businesses are turning to non-traditional reward systems. Among these are:

1. Information sharing—most commonly through a newsletter or bulletin board.
2. Participative work practices—employee involvement programs such as small problem-solving groups and suggestion systems.
3. Employment security—including a written commitment to no layoffs and a guaranteed minimum number of work days or hours.
4. Pay for performance—such as lump sum bonuses, individual incentives and profit sharing (National Restaurant Association, 1986).

Summary

Changes in the way human resources are managed in the hospitality industry have occurred because of pressures external to the industry. This trend continues. Despite protestations by management that human resource management is important to the financial success of their properties, the practice of enlightened human resource management is lacking.

The situation is changing, albeit slowly. As management faces the crisis of an imminent staff shortage, external pressures will again force hospitality managers to change not only the titles of the people responsible for human resources but also their functions and responsibilities.

References

Adelman, S., 1986, 'The need for employees remains strong', *N.R.A. News*, 6(6): 42–3.

Adu-Kwansa *et al.*, 1986, *An Analysis of Major Trends and their Impact Potential Affecting the Hospitality Industry as Identified by the Method of Content Analysis*, Proceedings of the 1986 Annual CHRIE Conference.

Albrecht, K., Zemke, R., 1985, *Service America: Doing Business in the New Economy*, Dow Jones-Irwin, Homewood, Illinois.

Bamford, R. D., 1981, 'The impact of recent employment legislation on the United Kingdom's Hotel and Catering Industry', *Hospitality Education and Research Journal*, 5(2): 81–94.

Berger, E., 1985, 'Assessing assessment centers for hospitality organizations', *The Cornell Hotel and Restaurant Quarterly*, 26(2): 56–61.

Berger, F., Evans, M. E. and Farber, B., 1986, 'Human resources management: applying managerial-profile databases', *The Cornell Hotel and Restaurant Administration Quarterly*, 27(3): 44–50.

Boella, M. J., 1986, 'A review of personnel management in the private sector of the British hospitality industry', *International Journal of Hospitality Management*, 5(1): 29–36.

Boyle, K., 1987, 'Child care: the fringe benefit of the 1990s', *Restaurants U.S.A.*, 7(5): 20–2.

Chon, Kye-Sung, Jacob, L. F., 1987, 'Implementing employee drug and alcohol testing: implications for hotel managers', *Florida University Hospitality Review*, 5(2): 79–86.

Czepiel, J. A., Solomon, M. R. and Superenant, C. F., 1986, *The Service Encounter: Managing Employee/Customer Interaction in Service Businesses*, D. C. Heath and Company, Lexington, Maine.

Dee, D., 1986, 'Older workers: the industry work force of the future?' *Restaurants U.S.A.*, 7(10): 10–13.

Elder, M. 1987, 'The image issue', *Restaurant Business*, 86(13): 180–5.

Fanning, J. J., 1981, 'Training and employment of the handicapped foodservice employee', *Hospitality Education and Research Journal*, 6(1): 79–81.

Foucar-Szocki, R., 1987, 'Management training in the food service industry: a state of the art', *Hospitality Education and Research Journal*, 11(2): 217–22.

Ferguson, D. H., Berger, F., 1985, 'Employees as assets: a fresh approach to human-resources accounting', *The Cornell Hotel and Restaurant Administration Quarterly*, 25(4): 24–9.

Jackson, D., 1986, 'Benefits and eligibility requirements', *Independent Restaurants*, 48(10): 29–31.

Jafari, J., 1986/7, 'Women in hospitality and tourism', *Hospitality Education and Research Journal*, 10(2) and 11(11): 139–42.

Johnson, D. C., 1985, 'Legal time bomb of the 1980s: sexual harassment in the workplace', *Independent Restaurants*, 47(4): 98–100.

Kelliher, C., Johnson, K., 1987, 'Personnel management in hotels—some empirical observations', *International Journal of Hospitality Management*, 6(2): 103–8.

Knight, J. B., Salter, C. A., 1985, 'Some considerations for hospitality training programs', *The Cornell Hotel and Restaurant Administration Quarterly*, 25(4): 38–43.

Kohl, J. P., Stephens, D. B., 1985, 'On strike: legal developments in labor-management relations', *The Cornell Hotel and Restaurant Administration Quarterly*, 25(4): 71–5.

Kreck, L. A., 1985, 'Evaluating training through work performance standards', *International Journal of Hospitality Management*, 4(1): 27–37.

Leposky, G., 1987, 'Tapping new labour sources', *Lodging*, 12(7): 23–9.

Liberson, M. J., 1987, 'AIDS: a managerial perspective', *The Cornell Hotel and Restaurant Administration Quarterly*, 28(3): 57–61.

Marshall, A. G., Bellucci, E. C., 1985, 'The high cost of hasty firing', *Florida International University Hospitality Review*, 3(1): 5–14.

Martin, W. B., 1986, *Quality Service: The Restaurant Manager's Bible*, Cornell School of Hotel and Restaurant Administration, Ithaca, New York.

Mill, R. C., 1985, 'Upping the organization: enhancing employee performance through an improved work climate', *The Cornell Hotel and Restaurant Administration Quarterly*, 25(4): 30–7.

Mill, R. C., 1988, *Managing for Productivity in the Hospitality Industry*, Van Nostrand Reinhold, New York.

National Restaurant Association, 1982, *A Foodservice Operator's Guide to Benefit Plans for Hourly Wage Employees*.

National Restaurant Association, 1986, Current Issues Report, *Foodservice and the Labour Shortage*.

National Restaurant Association, 1987, Current Issues Report, *Non-traditional Reward System for Foodservice Employees*.

Normann, R., 1984, *Service Management: Strategy and Leadership in Service Businesses*, John Wiley & Sons, New York.

Papa, A., 1985, 'Protecting your staff from sexual harassment', *N.R.A. News*, 5(1): 18–19.

Peters, J., 1987, 'Alternative labor pool', *Restaurant Business*, 86(13): 183–7.

Pickworth, J. R., 1981, 'A profile of the hotel personnel manager', *The Cornell Hotel and Restaurant Administration Quarterly*, 22(1): 42–6.

Reid, R. D., Pond, S. L., 1986, *Human Resource Management: Training Issues Confronting Hospitality Industry Managers and Educators*, Proceedings of the 1986 CHRIE Conference.

Reid, R. D., 1985, 'Older workers: are they a viable labor force in the foodservice industry?' *Hospitality Education and Research Journal*, 10(1): 1–11.

Restaurants U.S.A., 1986, 'No pattern for employee training costs', 6(11): 44.

Riley, M., 1985, 'Some social and historical perspectives on unionization in the U.K. hotel industry', *International Journal of Hospitality Management*, 4(3): 99–104.

Robinson, W., 1984, 'Earnings in the hotel and catering industry in Great Britain', *Service Industry Journal*, 4(2): 143–60.

Stutts, A. T., 1986, 'Productivity: a review for the hospitality manager', *Florida International University Hospital Review*, 4(1): 38–47.

Susser, P. A., 1987, 'AIDS: legal considerations', *The Cornell Hotel and Restaurant Administration Quarterly*, 28(2): 81–5.

Umbreit, W. T., Eder, R. W. and McConnell, J. P., 1986, 'Performance appraisals; making them fair and making them work', *The Cornell Hotel and Restaurant Administration Quarterly*, 26(4): 58–69.

Umbreit, W. T., 1987, 'When will the hospitality industry pay attention to effective personnel practices?', *Hospitality Education and Research Journal*, 11(2): 343–50.

12 Developments in food technology

G. Glew

Introduction

Food technology is a subject that has developed rapidly in the past 50 years. This development has been demand-led in the sense that urbanization of populations world-wide and the advance of industrialization, particularly in third world countries, has created a demand for processed food. In agricultural communities the problem of keeping food from season to season, from times of plenty to times of scarcity, has always existed. That problem remains with us today in addition to a demand for food in a more convenient-to-use form than the raw agricultural product. Food manufacturing therefore involves a transformation from agricultural products to edible products and is a process of adding value. Food manufacturing, together with the drink industry, produces 18.4 per cent (1984) of total United Kingdom manufacturing gross output, and 13.2 per cent of gross value added. In gross output terms it is a larger industry than mechanical engineering, the chemical industry or electrical and electronic engineering. It is almost three times as large as the motor vehicle industry (Stocker, 1987). Within the European Economic Community food and drink processing is by far the largest industry in gross output terms.

The growth in eating outside the home in the past 30 years has been due partly to an increase in disposable incomes but also to urbanization and advances in technology in other fields. Economies of scale have led to the development of larger manufacturing complexes, larger educational complexes, and larger tourism and leisure complexes. Business activity related to these manufacturing and service industries has expanded as travel has become more necessary and easier. Furthermore, international trade has exploded with the development of containerization of shipping cargoes which, in turn, generates more business activity. These developments have created demand for food to be available outside the home in factories, schools and colleges, hotels and restaurants, hospitals and tourist resorts and leisure complexes.

In this chapter an attempt will be made to summarize the developments in food technology which increasingly allow the catering industry to provide a food service for consumers in a variety of work and leisure situations. The last 20 years has also seen an increasing public concern for both the safety of food and its nutritional quality. The part that caterers play in this situation will be discussed first.

The growth in the use of processed foods

Agricultural surpluses are a feature of the economies of most developed nations. Research expenditure on agriculture is high in such countries and new and more efficient methods of animal husbandry and crop production are in constant development. The proportion of annual research budgets spent on food research as opposed to agricultural research is small. In 1986 in the United Kingdom 14 per cent of the Ministry of Agriculture, Fisheries and Food research budget was spent on food research, the rest on agricultural or fisheries research. Hence, money spent on research on agricultural products as food is very small compared with expenditure on agricultural production. In the United States the Land Grant Colleges were established nearly 100 years ago to teach and study better agricultural practices. The emphasis was on crop production and animal husbandry. Agricultural research in all developed countries has been very successful. It is common for less than 10 per cent of the working population in developed countries to be engaged in agriculture; in the United Kingdom and the United States it is less than 3 per cent. In the United Kingdom only 2.7 per cent of the workforce is engaged in agriculture with a further 2.7 per cent in food, drink and tobacco processing, whereas in the Economic Community (1983, 10 member states) 7.6 per cent were in agriculture and 2.9 per cent in food, drink and tobacco processing (Stocker, 1987). Hence, the quantitative imbalance between food production and need has historical roots, is difficult to change and political will is required to tackle the overall problem.

Furthermore, the emphasis in the agriculture industry is on improving yield. Farmers are usually paid on the basis of the quantity of food they produce and quality, other than visual quality, is often forgotten. Agricultural research on new varieties of plants or new husbandry regimes for animals is aimed at improving yield. Research on the flavour of food derived from these new products rarely takes place. In the catering industry the sensory properties of food are of much greater importance than the yield, particularly if the price is also higher than is needed because of political as opposed to economic reasons.

Meanwhile, due to industrialization and urbanization, the proportion of food consumed in developed countries which is processed as opposed to being a raw agricultural product is now very large. It has been estimated that 85 per cent of food consumed in the United Kingdom is processed in some way. In 1986 caterers spent £4,160 million on all food and beverage items of which expenditure 50 per cent was on chilled and frozen items. In addition, canned and dehydrated foods were used and it is difficult to identify products, apart from so-called 'fresh' vegetables, that are not now processed. The term 'fresh' is now misused and the use of this term in relation to food is changing. In the past the term meant 'gathered, picked or killed and used within a few hours'. Time was an important factor with shortness of time between cropping and consumption being crucial in relation to the perceived freshness of a foodstuff. Now the use of the term 'fresh' is more related to concepts of wholesomeness. Foods may have been processed and preserved and remain wholesome for many months whereas foods described as fresh in the true sense of the word may now be unwholesome and unacceptable. Vegetables and fruit gathered in France or Spain and transported by road to wholesale markets in Britain, then to retailers and eventually to the home, cannot be described as 'fresh' and are sometimes coming to the end of their useful life as a wholesome product. Fish if improperly stored during transport and distribution, particularly in summer, can be unwholesome by the time it is consumed, but it is still described as 'fresh'. In all these cases—fruit, vegetables and fish—a product which is processed is likely to be more wholesome, and in that sense 'fresher' than traditionally fresh products.

Consumer concerns about processed foods

Sociological and psychological factors make the consumer feel that unprocessed foods must be better in every way than processed foods. This is partly a question of whether a product is new in the experience of that consumer. The most basic ingredient, flour, is a processed product and has been for millenia. Margarine and pasteurized milk are examples of processed products more recently available but accepted readily by the majority of the population. However, the insidious growth of new products made from basic ingredients, the growth of the retailing industry based on the supermarket concept which relies on processing and preservation techniques for its existence and the growth of interest of the media in matters related to food, have raised awareness, particularly among educated sectors of the population, of food processing as a feature of present-day life.

Concerns about food safety

Concerns with the safety of food, its nutritional content and increased expectations of its sensory properties have focused attention on the technological changes in food processing techniques which have occurred in the last 50 years. Food processing has come to be regarded as interference with something which should be 'natural' and a sector of the population, who can afford to do so, have espoused this cause with vigour, and an anti-additive, anti-processing lobby associated with the growth of the health food industry has developed. Our increasing knowledge of the physiological effects of food on man, for example knowledge of the effects of certain foodstuffs on allergic reactions, has increased awareness that food does not only satisfy hunger.

Improved scientific techniques for alerting us to possible future food-related health risks are now available. This material is interpreted, often by journalists with no specialized knowledge, in a way which causes alarm. The simplification of these scientific messages often distorts what, at that moment, the scientist believes to be the truth of the matter. In addition, there are a few scientists who may believe that their career prospects may be enhanced by interpreting data in ways which cause alarm. Scientific truths develop from painstaking repetitive work, often in many countries, open to peer criticism and open to different interpretations. Food is a complex material chemically, physically and biologically (nutritionally) which has been the subject of close study for less than half a century and hence it is not surprising that our knowledge about its physiological effects is imperfect.

This stage in the development of the subject leaves us in the position where there is an improving understanding of what we do not know about food. Scientific knowledge and its application to food will not stop. The demands for new and different culinary experiences will increase. We can only try to ensure that food is safe and nutritious based on what we know is an imperfect understanding of the processes we use. A discovery is made and we use the process: for example, insecticide and herbicide sprays will be used by farmers to improve yield in various ways until such time as doubt is cast on their safety. Similarly with food additives; food processors use additives which are believed to be safe to perform some function in the processing, preserving or marketing of a food until such time as doubt is thrown on the safety of that additive. There is no other way of proceeding.

Those who fear the effects of the iterative nature of technological development are thrown into the 'natural' food lobby which has its own dangers. The use of the word 'natural' is coming under scrutiny as it is very difficult to define precisely. It is not always certain that all members of the health food industry have the knowledge and technical expertise to ensure the absence of naturally occurring aflatoxins from their products. It is known that aflatoxin contamination can occur in untreated legumes and nuts imported from tropical areas. Aflatoxins are formed by moulds and are highly carcinogenic. Considerable care has to be taken to ensure they are absent. Furthermore, some additives are used to ensure the microbiological safety of many traditional products such as cured meats. High salt concentrations create an inhospitable environment for microorganisms and the use of mixtures of salts ultimately gives these products their attractive and familiar pinkish colour. However, other compounds are formed during the curing process including nitrosamines which are known carcinogens. However, there is no direct evidence of consumers contracting cancer as a result of eating cured products. Another example of a potentially dangerous traditional process is the smoking of food. Smoking food using oak chips leads to the deposition in the food of benzpyrene from the wood smoke. This compound is a known carcinogen which also occurs in tobacco smoke. Liquid smokes can now be used which do not contain this compound but do impart a smoky flavour; hence modern technology has replaced a potentially dangerous traditional practice. It is therefore unwise to assume that traditional processes and foods labelled 'natural' are safe and that modern processes are less safe.

Concerns about nutrition

Epidemiological observations have shown an uneven distribution of some diseases in different parts of the world which is difficult to explain. Some nutritionists have suggested that atherosclerosis and coronary heart disease, which is common in Europe and North America, is in some way related to dietary habits. It has been suggested that in those countries where the disease is common, consumption of fat, particularly saturated fats of animal origin, is the culprit. The incidence of these arterial diseases is much lower in Africa and Asia where the diet has a much lower animal fat content. In addition, fat consumption has risen and fibre consumption has fallen as the incidence of arterial and lower bowel disease has risen respectively. High blood pressure is associated with stroke and high salt intake has been related to raised blood pressure in some patients; disease of the lower bowel has been associated with a diet low in dietary fibre.

In many countries, these observations have led to the establishment of committees to make recommendations on modifications to the diet of the population with the aim of reducing the incidence of these diseases. In the United Kingdom the Committee on Medical Aspects of Food Policy (DHSS, 1984) recommended in its report on *Diet and Cardiovascular Disease* that:

— the consumption of fat, particularly saturated, should be decreased;
— intake of common salt should not be increased further and consideration should be given to ways of decreasing it;
— reduced fat intake should be compensated for by increasing the intake of complex carbohydrates;
— obesity should be avoided and exercise undertaken;
— cigarettes should be avoided; and
— excessive alcohol intake should be avoided.

However, establishing a direct causal relationship between disease and diet is not easy (Cottrell and Sommerville, 1987). The causes of these diseases are likely to be multifactorial and aspects of lifestyle other than diet could have a major influence. The study of nutrition is not an exact science and it is unfortunate that the general public have accepted some messages about diet without fully understanding the opposing ideas. Nevertheless, interest in the nutritional factors associated with food has grown substantially during recent years and this is very desirable. The effect of this interest on the catering industry is clear as menus have appeared with 'healthy alternatives'.

Community Health Councils have developed nutrition policies to encourage consumption of 'healthy' food and the popular press, especially the women's press, has espoused the cause of 'healthy food'. It is unfortunate that these campaigns give the impression that, by inference, if certain foods are healthy then other foods must be unhealthy. This is not necessarily the case. All foods make a contribution in some way to the diet and it is the balance of foods consumed that is important.

There is a popular misconception that the fast food industry are purveyors of 'junk' and the term 'junk foods' has become synonymous with fast food. In most cases, fast foods are not junk. Analysis of fast foods has shown that they are generally well balanced with the exception that the fried foods tend to be higher in fat than some nutritionists would recommend and Chinese food tends to have a high salt content. Pizza was shown to be well balanced with percentage of total energy from fat tending to be in the recommended range. The effects of catering techniques on the nutritional quality of food have been reviewed by Glew *et al.* (1987).

Concerns about sensory quality

The sensory quality of food includes those properties of food which affect our senses and embrace its appearance, odour, texture and flavour. There is concern that food processing destroys those natural properties of food which make it pleasurable to eat. This is a difficult argument to sustain when considering the main process used which is heat treatment in the form of cooking. Many uncooked foods are inedible in the raw state. Heat treatment changes the texture and appearance and often enhances the odour and flavour characteristics as well as improving digestibility. The baking of flour-based products and roasting of meat are examples of improvement of the sensory properties of food due to cooking. Concern is often expressed that processed food is of inferior quality to home-cooked food, that is the sensory properties are of a lower order. It is difficult to support this view when consideration is given to the many hundreds of products which appear annually on the market, each one offering a slightly different range of sensations. It is often older people who make this type of remark and they forget that the sensory faculties dull with age, as do all our senses.

The sensory properties of food are of primary importance to the caterer as these properties determine whether a customer will buy and consume the product. Customers assume that the product is safe to eat and nutritious as they are usually unable to judge from the sensory properties that these criteria are fulfilled. However, there are sometimes areas of conflict between what nutritionists believe is good for us and what people find attractive to eat. The main area is in relation to fat consumption. Fat in food usually adds to the pleasure of eating a foodstuff. It improves the mouthfeel of many dishes and aids swallowing. In addition, many fats have an attractive flavour. Fried foods are very popular because of the crisp texture resulting from the frying process. Crispness is a modern attribute of high-fat foods, such as many snack products, which consumers find desirable. However, with regard to microbiological safety, no compromise is possible and it is incumbent on all caterers to ensure that their products are microbiologically safe.

A further factor in relation to eating out which is of considerable importance is the ambience within which the food is consumed. At the upper end of the market the ambience has always been important. The decor, the table setting and the quality of the service are as important as the quality of the food. Close attention to these environmental factors is now a feature at all levels of catering. Factory canteens, hospital dining-rooms and other workers' eating places are no longer dreary, dull and noisy places. They are bright and cheerful if also bustling. Fast food chains adopt a design posture which enables the customer immediately to recognize the outlet anywhere in the world and, furthermore, to know the type, quality and price range of the product being served. This projection of a brand image for a restaurant is likely to expand as new concepts in popular catering are evolved. It is also necessary, in relation to ambience, to recognize the importance of the company with whom one is eating. The relationship one has with such eating companions, whether it is business, friends or family, influences the quality and impact of the whole meal experience. Hence, any consideration of food processing must not neglect factors other than the sensory quality of the food served.

Processes used by food manufacturers

Most of the basic processes used to process and preserve food have been known for centuries. Drying food, including using smoke as a preservative, is a very old process. For many centuries it has been known that lowering the temperature of food by freezing or chilling reduces the rate of deterioration. Heating food in a closed container was shown by Nicholas Appert to prevent deterioration. All these processes were discovered before the scientific knowledge was developed to explain why these processes were successful: for example, the invention of canning by Appert in the late eighteenth century preceded by nearly 100 years the discovery by Pasteur of micro-organisms. Milling and baking are transformation processes not preservation processes, but make grains into an edible form and their origins as processes are ancient. Fermentation processes are still widely used as preservation processes for food in addition to the very old process of yeast fermentation to produce alcoholic drinks. Again, it is only recently that the scientific basis for successful fermentation was discovered.

The only forms of preservation to be developed from fundamental knowledge, that is the science coming before the technology, are those involving the use of certain radiations such as microwave radiations and ionizing radiations.

The fundamental basis of the industry

Food spoilage

The term 'food spoilage' is used to describe the processes of deterioration which takes place in food after harvesting. Such processes usually make the food unacceptable but rarely cause the food to become toxic, that is, cause food poisoning. Food can become spoiled in a number of ways:

(i) *Microbiological spoilage*   Bacteria, yeasts and moulds use food as a growth medium. Some bacteria, when they grow, produce gas or acid which sours the food. Moulds form a characteristic filamentous, often greenish growth on the surface of foods and yeast causes undesirable fermentations to take place in food. Foods in which microbes have grown and multiplied usually become unfit to eat though rarely poisonous if they are eaten. In order to multiply rapidly micro-organisms require moisture, a food source and warmth; they often grow best between 10°C and 60°C although some types of organism will grow at −1°C and some will grow above 60°C. Given the optimum conditions for growth, some bacteria can divide every 20 minutes, hence, within a few hours, a single organism can produce many millions of cells.

(ii) *Enzymic spoilage*   Enzymes are not living entities but form an essential part of the chemically organized system which forms the phenomenon of life. Enzymes catalyse the chemical reactions which take place in living cells. Living cells are highly organized but when the membrane, which forms the barrier between one cell and another, is broken the cell contents become disorganized and the enzymes start to catalyse chemical reactions resulting in the development of off-odours and off-flavours, hence altering the sensory properties of food. All enzymes are proteins and can be destroyed by heat, that is the structure of the enzyme is disrupted so destroying its catalytic activity.

(iii) *Oxidative spoilage*   Oxygen, which forms 21 per cent of the atmosphere, can chemically react with various food components to cause spoilage. Oxygen can react with naturally occurring colours in foods thereby altering their appearance. Oxygen can also react with flavour and odour compounds in food and hence affect the sensory properties. A common problem is rancidity of fatty foods which is caused by oxygen combining with certain fats to form chemical compounds which result in foods with rancid off-odours and off-flavours. In some cases, the effect of oxygen is enhanced by certain enzymes which therefore speed up the development of rancidity in food.

Microbiological, enzymic and oxidative spoilage are the main causes of deterioration of food and a major element of the food manufacturer's job is to produce conditions in which deterioration will not occur. This is done in three main processes by heating, drying or cooling food. Other processes such as fermentation, salting and curing also assist in food preservation. Newer techniques including the irradiation of food and packing food in an inert gas atmosphere can also be effective. In addition to preventing deterioration, food manufacturers convert raw agricultural products, such as all forms of cereal grains, to an edible form by milling, then further processing these milled products into baked and extruded products. These processes will be considered in detail in a later section.

Food poisoning

Most micro-organisms are completely harmless to man but there are a few types of organisms that grow in food and cause poisoning after the food is eaten. One of the main tasks of the food processor is to ensure that precautions are taken to prevent these food poisoning organisims growing in food. Very few outbreaks of food poisoning are associated with food processed by food manufacturers: many outbreaks are associated with food produced by caterers because the latter do not understand the conditions under which micro-organisms grow best and do not always exercise the necessary control procedures to ensure that growth does not occur. A wide range of foods are produced by caterers, often by unskilled and poorly trained staff. The diversity of foodstuffs, the low level of hygiene education in some establishments, the rush to prepare food for consumer deadlines which sometimes means that foods are prepared too far in advance, all contribute to food poisoning outbreaks. Food processes ensure that their products are microbiologically safe by processing the food in such a way that food poisoning organisms are killed or by ensuring that the storage conditions are such that the organisms, if present, cannot grow.

Two main types of food poisoning organism occur. First, organisms may grow in food and produce a toxin and the toxin when consumed then causes the illness; the micro-organism may be dead but the toxin persists. Such poisoning is called intoxication. In the second type of food poisoning, the living cells must be consumed in the food to cause illness, and such poisoning is called an infection.

(i) *Intoxications.*   *Staphylococcus aureus* is widely present in the nose and on the skin of most people and will grow in cuts and abrasions, hence the need to cover such wounds in food handling situations. The organism gets into the food and multiplies and produces a toxin which if consumed causes the rapid onset of diarrhoea and vomiting. Some of the toxins produced are not destroyed rapidly by boiling. Food processors try to ensure that this organism does not get into the food.

   The most dangerous organism is *Clostridium botulinum*. Fortunately, poisoning due to this organism is rare because it grows best in the absence of oxygen, but a tin can or other hermetically sealed container can form an ideal place in which to grow. Much of the effort of canners of meat, vegetable and dairy products goes into ensuring that the heat process is such as to ensure that the chance of one cell surviving in such a canned product is less than one in 10^{12}. This organism cannot grow in acid products such as canned fruit. If the organism does grow in food it produces a toxin which, if consumed, can be fatal. However, the toxin is readily destroyed by heat, and boiling food before consumption is sufficient to get rid of it. A relative of this organism, *Clostridium perfringens*, also produces a toxin. It is released in the human gut when live cells are consumed, which is rarely fatal, but illness caused by it is more common. Again the organism does not grow well in the presence of oxygen so will grow, for example, during the night in a warm stock pot at the bottom of which oxygen cannot penetrate.

(ii) *Infections*.   The most well-known infection is caused by a large variety of different types of *Salmonellae*. *Salmonellae* can occur in most foods but are practically associated with meat products. The organisms must be consumed in the living state and cause diarrhoea and vomiting. The illness is debilitating and, in the elderly, very young or ill people can cause death. The organism is easily destroyed by heating to 63 °C therefore poisoning occurs when improperly cooked food is consumed, for example, rare meat or cooked meat which has not been cooled rapidly. A further source of poisoning occurs due to cross-contamination, for example when cooked meat is handled after handling raw meat or when poultry is allowed to thaw in the same refrigerator as cream cakes or other cooked food which will not be reheated before consumption; the watery drip from the poultry is the source of contamination. These situations rarely occur in food processing plants but frequently occur in catering establishments.

Other organisms that can cause infections are *Bacillus cereus*, *Campylobacter*, *Lysteria monocytogenes* and *Yersinia enterolytica*. *Lysteria* and *Yersinia* are cold-loving organisms and grow well at below 5 °C, hence will grow in chilled food. The most dangerous is *Listeria* which can cause a form of meningitis. However, both organisms are easily killed by heat and will not survive a few minutes above 70 °C. A number of food poisoning outbreaks have been reported from the United States and the United Kingdom, implicating *Campylobacter* particularly in milk products. *Bacillus cereus* is a commonly occurring organism which is found in cereal products, particularly rice. Its spores can survive the cooking process and they may germinate and grow in the cooked food. Rice dishes left overnight unrefrigerated and consumed the next day are a common source of poisoning from this organism.

There are a number of viruses which appear to cause enteritis and can be found in raw shellfish, but little is known about these organisms as yet. Viruses cannot grow outside the living cell and are destroyed by cooking.

Outbreaks of food poisoning originating from food processed by food manufacturers are rare.

Application of fundamental concepts in food technology

Heating, drying and cooling food are the main processes used by food technologists to preserve food from deterioration. Operations such as salting, curing and packing food in an inert gas may be considered as adjuncts to the main processes. The only new process based on fundamental principles is the using of ionizing radiations.

Heat processing

When foods are heated to a temperature above 70°C most micro-organisms are killed and most enzymes are destroyed. However, the disorganization of the natural structure of a food product which takes place when it is heated or cooked may result in greater susceptibility to oxidative deterioration. In addition, there are a group of oxidative enzymes that are even resistant to boiling.

Because our whole environment is full of micro-organisms, when the organisms in the food have been killed by heating, methods to prevent recontamination must be used. This is achieved in several ways as outlined below.

(i) *Canning*   Nicholas Appert discovered this process in France during the Napoleonic Wars at the beginning of the nineteenth century while trying to find a way to preserve food for use by the army. He found that if food was heated in a hermetically sealed container it did not suffer from the natural deterioration processes thereafter. Although he did not understand the reasons for his success the process he used was killing those micro-organisms which cause food spoilage and preventing recontamination from the environment. At the same time, the raised temperature destroyed enzymes in the food and the closed container prevented oxidation by atmospheric oxygen.

As previously mentioned, *Clostridium botulinum* will grow in non-acid foods such as meat, fish, vegetables and dairy products and may cause a serious form of food poisoning. This organism, as part of its life cycle can surround itself with a horny protective coat which makes it more difficult to kill by heat. This state of life of the organism is called the 'spore' state as opposed to the 'vegetative' state during which the organism can multiply. Such spores are common and it must be assumed that all non-acid foods may potentially contain them. *Clostridium botulinum* will not grow in air, hence the oxygen-free environment of a can forms ideal conditions for the spore to turn back into the vegetative state, multiply and produce toxin. Canners therefore need to heat the sealed tin-plated steel cans to a high enough temperature and for a time long enough to reduce the number of living spores to such a low level that poisoning from this source is extremely unlikely (Hersom and Hulland, 1980). Such a process is known as a 'botulinum cook' and would require about 10 hours in water boiling at 100°C. This would be uneconomic apart from grossly overcooking the food; therefore canners use temperatures higher than 100°C for shorter times. Processing temperatures of 120–130°C are achieved by processing under steam pressure in a large pressure cooker. The principle being used is that the higher the processing temperature then the shorter the time required to achieve a botulinum cook. The limiting factor is the rate at which the heat is transferred through the product. Food is a poor conductor of heat and large cans, such as those used in catering, require many hours of steam pressure cooking to ensure safety.

(ii) *Aseptic canning*   An alternative to heat processing the food after sealing it in a can is to heat process outside the can and fill and seal the cans aseptically. Clearly solid food such as canned salmon cannot be processed in this way. But food slurries containing pieces up to 2.5 cm. across can now be heat treated and pumped into cans aseptically. Most liquid products can be treated by this method. The most commonly seen is the range of milk products aseptically processed into cartons and stable for many months at ambient storage temperatures.

(iii) *Pasteurization*   The heat processes so far discussed achieve a state of 'commercial sterility', that is, under normal room temperature storage conditions they will remain stable for many months or even years because all micro-organisms capable of growth have been destroyed. Many foods do not require to be kept for such long periods but must be safe from food poisoning organisms.

The process of heat pasteurization ensures that food poisoning organisms are destroyed but other food spoilage organisms survive although their numbers are severely reduced. Because the product is not commercially sterile these surviving spoilage organisms will grow and spoil the product within a few days. The shelf-life (the period during which the product will remain safe and wholesome) of such pasteurized products can be extended by refrigeration. Pasteurized milk has been treated at a temperature of 72°C for 15 seconds to ensure its microbiological safety, but even when refrigerated will sour, as a result of the growth of acid-producing bacteria, in a few days. Sour milk is not poisonous and indeed is a product in its own right when prepared specifically by using lactic-acid-producing bacteria.

(iv) *Pouch and tray processing*   The advent of heat resistant plastic materials has allowed the development of pouch sterilized foods. These products are processed to botulinum cook standards and hence are as safe as canned foods. New manufacturing methods for aluminium sheet have allowed the production of shallow containers which can be sealed and also heat processed to botulinum cook standards. The advantage of such containers is that, being thin in one dimension, they require a shorter time for heat processing because the heat has a much thinner layer of food to penetrate than in a cylindrical tin can. However, the disadvantage of such food containers is that they are not as mechanically strong as tin cans, are easily punctured and are therefore usually marketed in a protective card outer pack.

Products processed in pouches or trays should be better in sensory qualities than canned products because they have been subjected to a less severe heat process. However, at present this advantage is more in theory than in fact because during the cooling of these products with cold water an overpressure of air must be used in the pressure vessel to prevent the pouches or trays bursting. The operation of the plant, though automatic, tends to be slow and the products therefore tend to be overcooked. Engineering developments in the processing equipment may overcome these problems.

Drying

Most raw foods have a very high water content: lettuce contains over 90 per cent by weight of water, meat nearly 70 per cent water. If water is removed from a foodstuff then a state can be reached where there is insufficient water left to support the growth of micro-organisms (Ashworth, 1988). Enzymes are not always destroyed by dehydrating a food unless the product is heated during the process to above about 70°C. Oxidative changes are often enhanced by dehydrating a foodstuff because structural changes can occur which increase the surface area exposed to the oxygen in the air. Hence, dehydrated foods are now often packed for storage in an inert gas such as nitrogen. There are a number of ways which can be used either to remove water from food or ensure that it is unavailable for use by micro-organisms.

(i) *Air drying*   This ancient food preservation process is still used in many parts of the world. Food is simply hung out to dry in the sun and can then be stored for many months. Alternatively the water can be driven out by artificially heating the food. However, such methods result in a dried product which is difficult to rehydrate and is usually extremely tough and chewy, for example, the dried reindeer meat of Lapland and dried fish of the Middle East. The basic structure of tissue, whether animal or vegetable, relies on water for its integrity. Heating food to 100°C to drive out the water not only cooks it but causes flavour changes and also results in the collapse and denaturization of the structure. More successful methods of drying rely on heating the food in a vacuum. In such conditions, the water in the food will boil and evaporate at a temperature lower than 100°C and hence do less chemical and physical damage to the foodstuff.

(ii) *Spray and roller drying*   Liquid foods, such as milk, with a low solids content can be formed into a fine spray of droplets. The droplets have a very large surface area and, when mixed with hot air in a large closed chamber, the water evaporates almost instantly and the solid particles fall to the bottom of the chamber. Alternatively, the product can be deposited onto one side of a large heated roller which rotates slowly. The water evaporates and the dried product is scraped off at the other side of the roller. Products of fairly stiff consistency, such as mashed potato, can be applied to a heated roller and dried in this way. Spray dried products are usually of better quality than roller dried because they suffer less heat damage during the process; roller drying is being replaced by other processes.

(iii) *Freeze drying* This is the least damaging dehydration process and results in high-quality preserved products (Loventzen, 1981). The process involves freezing the food then gently heating it in a vacuum at less than 3 mm of mercury atmospheric pressure (as opposed to atmospheric pressure at 760 mm). Under these conditions, the water sublimes from the ice crystals in the food, going from solid to water vapour without melting and going through the liquid water phase. This results in a dried foodstuff which has not lost its structure; for example a 1 cm slice of meat does not shrink and collapse as in air drying. Since it is brittle it is difficult to package and transport, but it is easy to rehydrate and requires cooking as it is still raw. The spaces left in the food after the water has sublimed out result in a product with an enormous surface area which, if exposed to air, will cause oxidative deterioration very rapidly. It is therefore usual to break the vacuum at the end of the process with an inert gas such as nitrogen rather than air so that all the spaces in the food are nitrogen-filled rather than air-filled. The process is expensive to operate, hence only expensive products are treated in this way, for example, shrimps and some liquid products such as coffee. Because the process is gentler than air drying there is less change in flavour. Coffee is a good example; the freeze-dried product, which is packed for storage in an inert gas atmosphere, commands a price premium because it has a better flavour than spray-dried coffee.

Cooling

If the temperature of a foodstuff is reduced to just above its freezing point (about 2 °C) then the rate of multiplication of most micro-organisms is reduced. Hence, chilling food and keeping it refrigerated can increase the time that it remains in edible condition (known as the shelf-life of a food). In many chilled foods, enzymic and oxidative changes will occur and also the slow growth of both spoilage and some food poisoning organisms such that the storage life is limited to a matter of a few days. If the temperature of the food is lowered even further so that the water it contains is frozen out as ice, and it is then stored at −18 °C, no micro-organisms can grow and it will remain microbiologically sound indefinitely. However, enzyme-catalysed and oxidative changes can still take place very slowly even in frozen food in addition to changes due to the migration of water, resulting in slow deterioration and ultimately reducing the sensory quality to the point of inedibility. Chilling and freezing food, as preservation methods, can be applied in catering establishments as opposed to canning and drying. The use of chilling and freezing in the catering industry has been developed into systems for feeding people which have become known as 'cook-chill' and 'cook-freeze' methods (Glew, 1985).

(i) *Chilling*   Chilling as a method of short-term storage has developed very rapidly in the past 10 years. Chilled foods are regarded by consumers as 'fresh' and hence do not carry the stigma of being 'processed'. In addition, there is now a refrigerator in most homes and the development of the supermarket system enables rapid and controlled temperature distribution with rapid turnover of chilled stock in the store. In the catering industry a similar development has taken place for similar reasons. Chilling of raw food has been routinely used for many years but the chilling, distribution and sale of precooked chilled food is a more recent development. Precooked chilled food is an added-value product in the retail market and a method of rationalizing production and containing or reducing costs in the catering market.

When used in catering the food is cooked, portioned and blast chilled. In a blast chiller, air at about $-6\,^{\circ}C$ is circulated over the chilled food in shallow trays. The heat is rapidly removed and the temperature reduced to between $0\,^{\circ}C$ and $3\,^{\circ}C$. Distribution and storage between these two temperatures then takes place followed by reheating immediately prior to consumption. This method allows caterers to centralize food production and distribute to numerous satellite restaurants where reheating takes place. The requirements for skilled cooking staff is reduced because food production is continuous at the central production unit and staff productivity is high. At the satellite unit high food production skills are not required but staff training in the storage, reheating and service of food is essential.

Some chilled food stored in air can develop off-flavours due to oxidation. In addition, micro-organisms can grow at chilled storage temperatures; hence the shelf-life is limited. Most organisms which grow in chilled food cause only spoilage, but there are some which, if present, can cause food poisoning. These organisms are *Listeria monocytogenes* and *Yersinia enterolytica*. Both should be killed in the initial cooking process and, if contamination of the cooked food occurs, both will be killed during the reheating period provided that the temperature in all parts of the reheated food reaches $70\,^{\circ}C$.

The possible dangers of the system in the hands of caterers, who normally are not educated in food technology, were recognized by the British government who issued guidelines in 1980 with a revision in 1983. A complete revision of the guidelines was published in 1989 (DHSS, 1989). The main recommendations were that during cooking the temperature of all parts of the food should reach 70°C; chilling to between 0°C and 3°C should take place within two hours of leaving the cooking process; storage between 0°C and 3°C should not exceed five days including the day of production and the day of consumption; and reheating to 70°C should follow within 30 minutes of leaving chilled storage with service commencing within 15 minutes of removal from the reheating device. No food poisoning outbreaks, as a result of the use of the cook-chill system in catering, have been reported to date and should not occur if the guidelines are strictly observed.

Other systems involving the use of precooked chilled foods have been developed. One system known as *sous vide* was developed in France and involves packaging raw food in a plastic pouch followed by cooking in the pouch. Chilling is then achieved rapidly by immersion of the pouches in iced water. It is claimed that storage for 21 days at 3°C is possible. The use of this system in the United States by caterers in establishments not subject to US Food and Drugs Administration control is prohibited under the FDA Retail Code 1976. However, the method is gaining acceptance in Europe. The main danger occurs from the possible growth of *Clostridium botulinum* in the oxygen-free conditions in the pouch. Another method, developed in the United States, involves pasteurizing food prior to pumping into large plastic cylindrical casings. The casings are then ice-water chilled and storage periods up to 45 days at 3°C are claimed for the method. Similar arguments to those raised against the *sous vide* method could be used against this system. However, one advantage in packaging in oxygen-free conditions is that oxidative deterioration of the food will be minimized.

(ii) *Freezing* The microbiological disadvantages of chilled food are avoided if the cooked food is frozen and stored at −18°C. Furthermore, oxidative deterioration and enzyme activity is reduced compared with chilled foods. However, frozen food does not carry the 'fresh food' image and hence is regarded as less desirable than chilled food. So far as caterers are concerned, the cook-freeze system frees them from the problems of a short storage period as frozen foods can be kept wholesome for months, and distribution and use at the satellite units is not constrained by time. Nevertheless, such precooked frozen food should be used as soon as convenient and it is rarely necessary to store such food for more than eight weeks in catering operations.

Frozen food purchased from food manufacturers should be used within a few months and not stored indefinitely. During storage, water migrates from the food and crystallises as ice in other parts of the packaging giving rise to the phenomenon of 'freezer burn'. The surface of raw food becomes desiccated and its quality is impaired. Fluctuations in storage temperature accelerate this process and frozen food should always be stored in water-vapour-proof packaging (Jul, 1984).

Cooking food prior to freezing, as in the cook-freeze process, destroys enzyme activity, hence deterioration from this source is not a problem.

New processes

(i) *Intermediate moisture foods* Preserves such as jam do not suffer microbiological deterioration other than the occasional growth of mould in improperly processed and stored home produced preserves. Furthermore, such products are stable at room temperature. The reason for this phenomenon is that the water in the product is bound by the high sugar concentration and is not available for use by micro-organisms. In addition, the acid from the fruit in jam has a preservative effect. Compounds other than sugar have also been used to produce such shelf-stable, intermediate-moisture products but, as yet, are not available for human consumption although moist ambient temperature stable pet foods fall into this category (Davies *et al*., 1977).

(ii) *Processes using ionizing radiation* Gamma rays from certain radioactive isotopes and electrons produced by machines can be used to process many foods (Anon, 1985). The energy of the radiation used is not high enough to produce nuclear changes hence there is no danger of the food becoming radioactive. The radiation, however, can kill all types of micro-organisms depending on the dose applied. The Gray (Gy) is the unit of radiation dose; 1 Gy is equivalent to an energy deposition of 1 J/ kg. Low-dose treatments (up to 2.5 KGy) can be used for extending the shelf-life of soft fruit by killing yeasts and moulds. Somewhat higher doses (5–7 KGy) can pasteurize fish and increase its shelf life. *Salmonellae* can be eliminated from poultry by a dose of 5.0 KGy. High-dose treatments (50.0 KGy) result in commercial sterility equivalent to the botulinum cook used by the canning industry. The radiation has its effect by causing molecules to ionize. If this happens within a micro-organism, it is damaged or killed. Unfortunately, the radiation is not selective and food molecules are affected causing the development of off-flavour compounds. In general, the higher the dose the greater the off-flavour development, hence sterilizing treatments are not a practical proposition at present. Enzyme activity is not destroyed by radiation treatment.

Other uses of radiation include the prevention of sprouting in root vegetables such as potatoes and the killing of insects infesting stored grain products. Irradiated food products are now on sale in many countries after 30 years of intensive animal feeding trials. No untoward effects of the consumption of irradiated food have been observed in numerous different animal species fed for many generations on irradiated food. At present no test exists to indicate whether a food has been irradiated or not, hence abuse could occur by unscrupulous traders. For example, badly contaminated food could be irradiated and remain undetected; hence Britain maintains its ban on the sale of such products until a suitable test has been developed.

(iii) *Other forms of radiation*   Non-ionizing radiations such as microwaves and radiofrequency heating can be used for food processing. They are usually used as adjuncts to other processes as opposed to methods in themselves. Rather than heat the foodstuff by conduction from the outside these forms of radiation generate heat within the foodstuff.

(iv) *Extrusion processing*   This is not a preservation process in itself but many new products are appearing resulting from this phenomenon. A very wide range of snack foods are produced by extrusion processes. Mixtures of ingredients are forced at very high pressures through specially designed nozzle heads. In puffed products the almost instantaneous drop in pressure as the mixture is extruded to atmospheric pressure causes minute explosions in the mixture. This type of processing has great potential for the development of new products based on new combinations of ingredients with unusual textural and other sensory properties. Food manufacturers are interested in this form of processing because it cooks, imparts texture and shapes the product in one machine (Baker, 1988).

Combination processes and operations

Combinations of the basic processes can offer advantages. Preserving food with salt is a very old process but such products are normally too salty for the modern palate hence lower salt concentrations are now used combined with refrigeration to enhance shelf-life. Smoking raw food in wood smoke is also an old process with preservative effects partly due to the dehydration which occurs and partly to the effect of the chemicals in the wood smoke. Refrigeration is also used with smoked and salted products. Curing of bacon, ham and other meat products to preserve the product and give the desirable red colour is another very old process which now requires the assistance of refrigeration to enhance shelf-life.

The combination of drying and packaging in an inert gas has been mentioned. Extruded products are also frequently gas-packed and precooked chilled products retain quality better if packed in an inert gas. Gas packing is also used to delay senescence in salad vegetables.

Ionizing radiation combined with a heat treatment designed to inactivate enzymes provides a useful combination. Irradiation in the frozen state is also possible as ionizing radiation does not raise the temperature of the food. Hence, frozen poultry could be irradiated to eliminate *salmonellae* and thereby reduce the incidence of food poisoning from this source.

Fermentation processes are now usually controlled by employing inoculums of known micro-organisms in controlled time and temperature conditions. Lactic acid fermentation results in acid production which has a preservative effect as well as introducing a desirable sensory effect. Similarly cheese production is now highly controlled to ensure that high quality consistent products are available. Acid products with a vinegar base in the form of chutneys and similar products also have a long shelf-life. Although many types of product are shelf stable at ambient temperature, refrigeration can improve their life as a high-quality product.

References

Anon, 1985, *Food Irradiation Processing*, Proceedings of Joint FAO/IAEA Symposium Washington, International Atomic Energy Agency, Vienna.

Ashworth, J. C., 1988, 'Drying for quality and efficiency', in Turner, A. (ed.), *Food Technology International Europe*, Sterling Publications, London, pp. 79–85.

Baker, R. W., 1988, 'Cereal ingredients from extrusion processes', in Turner, A. (ed.), *Food Technology International Europe*, Sterling Publications, London, pp. 203–7.

Cottrell, R. C., Sommerville, M., 1987, 'Styles of life and death', *British Nutrition Foundation Bulletin*, 12(2): 70–86.

Davies, R., Birch, G. G., and Parker, K. J., 1977, *Intermediate Moisture Foods*, Applied Science Publishers, London.

Department of Health and Social Security, 1984, 'Report on Health and Social Subjects 28, Diet and Cardiovascular Disease', Committee on Medical Aspects of Food Policy, HMSO, London.

Department of Health and Social Security, 1989, *Guidelines on Precooked Meals in Catering: Chilled and Frozen*, HMSO, London.

Glew, G., 1985, 'Refrigeration and the catering industry', *Proceedings of the Institute of Refrigeration*, 6(1):

Glew, G., Lawson, J., & Hunt, C., 1987, 'The effect of catering techniques on the nutritional value of food', in Cottrell, R. (ed.), *Nutrition in Catering*, Parthenon Publishing, London, pp. 53–74.

Herson, A. C., Hulland, E. D., 1980, *Canned Foods: Thermal Processing and Microbiology*, 7th ed., Churchill Livingstone, Edinburgh.

Jul, M., 1984, *The Quality of Frozen Foods*, Academic Press, London.

Lorentzen, J., 1981, 'Freeze drying: the process, equipment and products', in Thorne, S. (ed), *Developments in Food Preservation—1*, Applied Science Publishers, London.

Stocker, T., 1987, 'Food manufacture in the UK: current and perceived trends', in Turner, A. (ed.), *Food Technology International Europe*, Sterling Publications, London, pp. 41–17.

13 The hotel feasibility study— principles and practice

T. J. Ward

Introduction

That there is no such thing as a standard feasibility study is a concept well known (and often quoted) by practitioners of the art, but one which tends not to be understood by others. Certainly in some circles, the existence of a feasibility study by a reputable consultancy is regarded as valid proof of viability, almost regardless of content—so long as the projected available cash flow is sufficient to cover debt service for example, the substantiation of that projection is secondary. In those same circles, we as a firm are satisfied with the knowledge that our reputation enables people to rely on our work without cause for examination and we are prepared to accept that to those people, a Horwath and Horwath study may be a standard product. But, as professionals, we can also justifiably claim that no two feasibility studies are (for different projects) the same, and that we do not consciously sell a standard study to our clients.

This chapter seeks to provide an examination of what a hotel feasibility study is, the variables which determine the content of any study and, broadly, a common approach to a study. Readers seeking a more detailed description of how to undertake a study should refer to other, more detailed, texts (Laventhol and Horwath, 1984; Doswell and Gamble, 1979).

What is a feasibility study?

Working from the basis that there is no standard feasibility study, it is difficult to establish a standard definition, particularly given that our perception of each is different, as is that of most of our clients. What a hotel feasibility study should do (provided it is positive) is to give support to a development proposal—that proposal can be vague or specific, as we shall see later. A study can only conclude that a project is feasible if the measurement of feasibility is predetermined and that, as we shall also see later, will vary according to who makes the decision. A definitive conclusion can therefore be reached from one viewpoint (for example, the projected income streams are at an acceptable level according to specific criteria), while the project may not be considered feasible from another viewpoint (for example, because the projected net foreign exchange earnings of the proposed hotel are insufficient to compensate for environmental disbenefits).

It is because of this that feasibility studies seldom reach a definitive conclusion, but this should not be considered as a failure on the part of the consultant, nor as in any way detracting from the content of the study. I maintain that the purpose of a hotel feasibility study is to provide an objective, independent appraisal of a development opportunity, providing sufficient information for the client (or others involved in the project) to make a decision as to whether the project should or should not proceed, and in what form. At the request of the client, and given the unit of measurement, the consultant can reach a conclusion as to the feasibility, and this can, indeed, be included in the report, but this is rare; that conclusion should, in practice, be reached by the client based on the evidence presented. A hotel developer who himself reaches a conclusion of feasibility, and therefore a decision to proceed, will have more credibility, and is more likely to have a successful project, than one who adopts another's conclusion as his own.

If a feasibility study does not conclude whether a project is feasible or not, can it then in truth be called a feasibility study? While a more accurate description may be appraisal, common practice within the consultancy profession, including clients who request such studies, is to use the term 'feasibility study'. Therefore it can be said that precisely because of this lack of definition there is no standard project—the argument has come full circle but will be expanded later. Academic papers such as this one generally demand a definition from the outset and this author may have taken longer than most in reaching this point, but for good reasons previously explained. A feasibility study might be defined as an appraisal (it need not be independent, a point which is examined later) of a development proposal providing a measurement of the return on investment. This is deliberately a loose definition. 'A measurement of the return on investment' can be defined in many ways: it is a measurement which might be precise, and therefore can itself be a measure of feasibility for example, the Internal Rate of Return (IRR—expressed as a percentage) or which might require further analysis (for example, income before fixed charges). In non-monetary terms, the measurement may be the number of jobs created, but it is more often stated as a monetary amount. I am therefore deliberately excluding from the term 'feasibility study' those pieces of work undertaken by consultants which either identify (rather than appraise) a development opportunity, or which appraise an opportunity without reaching a measurement of the return on the investment, for example, those which project occupancy and average room rate (measurements of *performance*) only. Such studies, of which we carry out a large number, are most commonly used by clients in the preparation of their own internal feasibility studies.

I have restricted, at this stage, my definition to include only development proposals, that is new projects, for which the bulk of feasibility studies are commissioned. There is no reason, however, why a hotel feasibility study cannot be carried out to appraise the future of an existing hotel, thus enabling a decision to be taken regarding whether or not it is feasible to continue with that operation. The scope work and methodology for such a study, as described later, is similar in most respects.

Why commission a feasibility study?

In general terms, it is possible to categorize the reasons that feasibility studies are commissioned into five groups. Few hotel feasibility studies fall into one group only, some cover the entire range.

— To support an application for finance;
— To support an application for planning permission;
— To attract potential operators;
— To define optimum land use; and/or
— To define a concept.

These are primary reasons for commissioning and could be the sole purpose of the study. Most studies will also have one or more secondary purposes, which could include, for example:

— To provide marketing information;
— To identify market opportunities;
— To analyse specific operational aspects, for example local labour laws; and/or
— To identify potential sources of development finance.

These secondary reasons are, by and large, by-products of the feasibility study and, while a study should as a matter of course provide information in these areas, this information could also be obtained in other ways.

Reverting back to the primary reason, it is of value to consider the part a feasibility study will play in achieving these objectives.

To support an application for finance

This is the most common reason for commissioning a study, and indeed nearly all studies are used for this purpose to some degree. The source of finance could be a number of different types: a lending institution, equity investors (including hotel operating companies), a public-sector grant-aiding body or even the client himself, who is considering investing his own capital in the hotel project and wishes to obtain an independent third-party assessment of the rate of return and the risk involved. The measure of feasibility used could differ from one source of finance to another, and the same study may well be presented to more than one source; hence the difficulty faced by the consultant in reaching any conclusion. A commercial lending institution's prime interest will be the project's ability to service its (and other) loans throughout the term of those loans. Equity investors will mainly be interested in the level of the return they will receive on their capital, and will probably expect an element of risk return, while the developer investing his own money may be satisfied with only a commercial (or even lower than commercial) return. A public-sector grant-aiding body, on the other hand, may be primarily concerned with certain specific criteria such as the number of jobs created, or the volume of tourist spend attracted to the area; clearly they will also require comfort that the hotel can continue to meet these criteria for a reasonable period. Proof of a specific project's need for grant aiding may also be required.

To support an application for planning permission

Although this is rarely the only primary consideration for commissioning a feasibility study, it can be a major use for a study. Those planning bodies which operate on a higher level than merely ensuring the adherence to regulations will wish to be assured that the built environment they are creating is one of stability and prosperity, and not subject to decline. They may well, therefore, require independent evidence to prove the market need, and to support a developer's claims of guaranteed success.

To attract potential operators

A study used to support an application for finance can be commissioned either by the applicant—most often the developer—or by the source of finance itself. Equally, a study required in order to attract a potential operator can be commissioned by a developer or by the operator itself. While the former approach could be said to be mistimed (and the timing of feasibility studies is discussed below) it is an approach commonly used in the hotel business, particularly when the tourism sector is immature. A feasibility study would provide evidence to a potential operator of the desirability of managing that hotel, but unless the study is written specifically for that operator, it cannot provide all the evidence. Where a study is commissioned by a potential operator (and in our experience, where the number of hotel projects looking for operators generally exceeds those operators' demands, this is becoming less common) or in order to attract a designated operator, then that study can be specific to the operator and can incorporate their requirements (for example, the hotel operator may require an assessment of the impact of their managing this unit on another existing hotel). An operator may also be a potential source of equity or loan finance and therefore that operator will be looking to the report to provide market justification in the long term.

To define optimum land use

This may well be the objective of a pre-feasibility study, which leads onto a subsequent feasibility study, but remains a primary reason for commissioning. By definition, this implies the appraisal of alternatives, whether between different types of hotel, or between the scale and mix of components, of which hotel use is one, or whether a hotel should be developed at all, in the face of other possibilities (office, residential, retail, etc.). In these circumstances, the pre-feasibility study must reach a conclusion—that is, the optimum land use— by applying a measure of feasibility to the alternatives. Although this will most certainly be in terms of the internal rate of return, in many cases another factor to be considered will be the attitude of local and/or central government to any particular scheme.

The choice of scheme upon which a full feasibility study is carried out would of course be the developer's and may bring in more factors such as personal preference for one use over another, a subjectivity which would not be expected from an independent consultant.

To define a concept

In my opinion, where one of the primary reasons for commissioning a hotel feasibility study is to define the concept—providing the answer to the question 'what should I build?'—then it is in these circumstances that the services of a consultant are being used to the full, and the contents of the feasibility study are the most comprehensive. Many clients, justifiably, do not require a feasibility study to define a concept. For example, a hotel operator whose portfolio contains only branded deluxe hotels, and who is looking for development opportunities, will have little interest in a feasibility study which concludes that there is a market opportunity in a specific location for only a three-star operation. In this example, the concept is already defined (although advice may be required on the size of ancillary facilities such as conference rooms). Such an investigation and conclusion may well, however, be required by a developer seeking advice, or by a local authority wishing to promote hotel development in their area.

A hotel feasibility study can certainly define the most appropriate concept for a specific location, indicating not only how big the box should be, but also how it should be divided up between facilities—the standard, scale and mix of those facilities—down to the smallest detail, if required. Detailed interior design is one aspect that could be excluded from this process, as this is such a subjective subject, but the objective aspects—for example a style of decor required in order to attract certain markets—can indeed be included. An extreme example could be: 'Unless all interior finishes are pink, levels of occupancy will be low!'

Mechanical and pro-active studies

This examination of the primary reasons for commissioning hotel feasibility studies has developed a further general categorization of studies into those which can be described as **mechanical** and those which are **pro-active**. Inevitably, some will defy such a categorization, but most will fall under one or the other heading, and this will be decided by a combination of who the client is, and the initial brief to the consultant.

Mechanical studies are those which a client commissions because third parties require it of him. The client would not otherwise have commissioned a study, and therefore has no personal use *per se* for the information or recommendations therein. The source of finance may require a prospective borrower to provide an independent feasibility study in support of the application for funds, and this is the most common circumstance in which a mechanical study is prepared. Bankers, certainly, are less willing now than in the past to accept project appraisals prepared by the developer or his essential advisers such as the architect or quantity surveyor, and are less willing to lend on projects unless such appraisals have been well organized and have been carried out by independent professional organizations.

A **pro-active** study is one where the client who commissions it requires information to be provided in addition to projections of the return on investment. As discussed previously, the study may be required to define the concept of the hotel, or to provide marketing and operational information. It is of note that whether the study is to be essentially mechanical or pro-active does not necessarily depend on the reason for commissioning the study. In the previously quoted example where a study is used to support an application for finance, if the source of finance (for example a bank) itself commissions the study, what was a mechanical study for the borrower becomes a pro-active study for the lender.

In these circumstances, the type of study prepared is very much a question of the attitude of the client. Thus, although within our definition all feasibility studies have a common purpose (to appraise a development proposal), the style and content of a study, while adhering to a general framework, will depend upon the objectives of the client, of the third party to whom the study is transmitted, on the attitude of the client and on the initial brief to the consultant. The last can range from 'prepare a feasibility study on this previously defined hotel concept' to 'what shall I do with this site?'

Who writes the study?

Avoiding any discussion regarding the cost effectiveness of using consultants to undertake tasks, the answer to this question must depend on the reason(s) for commissioning the feasibility study. A firm such as mine specializes in the tourism and hotel industries, and the greater part of our assignments are hotel feasibility studies: but the consultancy profession cannot claim to be the only persons capable of undertaking this work. There is no reason why the developer, or operator, or lending institution or public-sector grant-aiding body cannot prepare a feasibility study themselves, using internal resources. It all depends on what the study is to be used for, and who is doing the work.

Most major hotel operators are quite capable, and have the necessary resources to do so, of defining an appropriate concept for a new project. Some developers will be able to derive an optimum land usage. All banks can project levels of cash flow before debt service. An appraisal of a development proposal is within the capabilities of many. A professional consultant can, however, offer to the process of preparing a feasibility study three qualities, one or more of which is missing from all other parties to the development. These are independence, objectivity and experience (measured in terms of personal experience as well as support services such as a comprehensive data bank). The extent to which these three are essential ingredients in the hotel feasibility study will depend, again, on the objectives of the client/person who has need of a study, and on the third party to whom the study is transmitted.

Timing of the hotel feasibility study

All too often, in my opinion, the preparation of a hotel feasibility study is viewed as a defined step on the development ladder, which once used, is no longer required. This occurs most often when the study is 'mechanical' as previously defined. This may be because the client already has the resources to attract an operator, to define the concept, and identify market opportunities; in short he can satisfy these objectives without commissioning a 'pro-active' study but needs a feasibility study, probably to support an application for finance. The client is therefore using a consultant for the latter's independence and experience, but is, from his point of view, discounting the benefits of objectivity totally. This objectivity can reveal elements of a project, desirable for its success, which someone closer to it might miss. It has been said of our feasibility studies in one particular country where we do a substantial amount of work that clients do not even look at the report, but pass it straight to a source of finance for consideration. An exaggeration, I am sure, but if true a source of regret.

Kendell suggests the following phased project development process (Kendell, 1982):

1. Preliminary concept (sometimes including financing arrangements)
2. Market study
3. Revised concept
4. Revised costings
5. Financial evaluation project
6. Sensitivity analyses

7. Financing arrangements
8. Detailed design and planning

In this model, 2, 5 and 6 are consecutive phases of the feasibility study. I would add a loop to the model, to allow for a reversion to step 3 after step 6 when necessary. The results of the financial analysis, using some measurement of feasibility such as IRR, can therefore be used to revise the concept. Omitting a restaurant from the scheme, for example, may result in such cost savings as outweigh the loss of revenue from not having the facility, and will therefore increase the IRR. In step 7, the finance plan should be arranged so as to be most appropriate for the derived concept's cash flow.

I would also suggest that a stage in this process is missing—selection of the operator for the hotel (where one is involved at the beginning of the development process). This does, however, tend to be a classic 'chicken and egg' situation. From a developer's point of view, should he reach preliminary agreement with an operator before commissioning a feasibility study, and thereby run the risk of missing out on market opportunities which that operator cannot or will not exploit? Or should he have a completed feasibility study prior to seeking an operator, and run the risk of not finding an operator willing to participate in the project? The choice must be dependent on the specific circumstances of any project and of the developer of that project and therefore, while it must be considered in the development process, cannot be assigned a rigid place in the order.

The negative feasibility study

We as a firm, and I am sure most other specialist consultancy practices, have on occasion all been accused of rarely, if ever, producing a negative feasibility study, that is, one which recommends the project is not pursued. That is a misconception. Our appraisal of a development proposal sometimes does result in the conclusion that the concept, *as defined*, is inappropriate and this is reported, often verbally, to the client: we are then very often instructed to continue work and define a concept for which we can produce a full feasibility study. Few clients have any need for a full study which concludes at the end that the whole exercise has been a waste of time. It is rare for us to undertake work on a site for which there is no potential for some form of tourism use, as such sites are generally rejected prior to entering the formal development process.

The decision that a feasibility study is negative is a difficult one to make, and essentially subjective. Common sense dictates that a proposed hotel projected to achieve only 40 per cent occupancy is likely to be financially non-viable, but what if the projection is for 55 per cent occupancy? A minimum financial result of any hotel project must be its capability to cover debt service, but how much debt service? And when? The answers to such questions may make or break a project at 55 per cent occupancy (or even at 40 per cent). In our work, our general approach is not 'this project is financially non-viable', but 'what can be done to make this project viable?' The answer may lie in decreasing (or even increasing) the number of bedrooms proposed, or reducing the scale of the public areas.

Principles of a hotel feasibility study

In the following section, I outline the general framework around which a hotel feasibility study should be constructed, according to the objectives of that study, and the other factors which determine the detail of the structure. Before that, however, there are two principles which any hotel feasibility study must adhere to in order for it to be valid.

First, the contents of the study must be current, relevant and focused. Everything contained therein must have some impact upon the proposed hotel operation, or must be instrumental in assisting the reader in making a decision based upon that study. General background information on a country or area is therefore relevant where the reader may be unfamiliar with such information, but even then the choice of background information must be focused. It has been said that the skill of the consultant lies not so much in what he puts into a study, but in what he leaves out.

Second, the work of the team undertaking the feasibility study must begin with an assessment of the suitability of the site for development. Much time and effort can be wasted in assessing the local hotel market and other relevant aspects if it has not been established from the outset that the site will be suitable at the time the hotel is in operation, for some type of hotel development, and what that might be. That location is of vital importance to a hotel operation cannot be ignored in carrying out a feasibility study.

Certainly there are other principles to consider, but I believe that these two are of paramount importance—and it is alarming how often they are omitted.

Steps in undertaking a hotel feasibility study

While the point has already been made that there is no such thing as a standard feasibility study, the experience of professional consultants shows that there are common elements without which any study will be deficient. The demands of the specific study, and the commissioning clients, will dictate the degree to which any element is covered, and the manner in which it is investigated and reported, but none can readily be omitted.

(i) Evaluation of the proposed site for the hotel—its position and general description, topology and topography, soil considerations, access to utilities and infrastructure, environmental considerations and its general suitability for the proposed project. For some of this, input from other professionals such as civil engineers will be required.

(ii) Transportation and accessibility, relating to the general and specific location.

(iii) Assessment of the economic and social climate in the location in which the project is to be sited to identify future economic development and whether there are likely to be future fiscal or social constraints that could influence occupancy rates. This will also encompass, where practicable, an evaluation of relevant influences.

(iv) Market evaluation, where there is a market to evaluate. Pioneer projects cannot benefit from local market demand trends, and the consultant must therefore look elsewhere for data to support projections. This could include an evaluation of similar, but non-competitive, hotels in other locations.

(v) Sources and characteristics of demand, existing and potential, for rooms, food and beverage and other facilities.

(vi) Evaluation of competitive situation and planned additions.

(vii) Future demand and likely market share/demand potential.

(viii) Evaluation and derivation of design concept and recommended facilities.

(ix) Projected operating statements.

(x) Cash flow projections (although these are often prepared by the client or other parties).

Conclusions

This chapter has sought not to teach the reader how to prepare hotel feasibility studies, but to explain the structure surrounding them, in terms of the need for such studies, who prepares them and other considerations. I hope by this means to have made the whole process somewhat clearer, both to those who in one way or another have had contact with that process, and also to those who have not. But there may still be a misapprehension as to what an appraisal of a development proposal actually results in. The recommendations contained in a study will detail an appropriate development concept on a particular site— whether this is the most appropriate development proposal will depend upon the client's brief. The financial projections, based upon that development proposal (which must be closely defined by the report), will represent the view of the author of that study as to what can reasonably be expected; the methods used to calculate those projections, and the conditions upon which they depend, must also be carefully detailed. These financial projections do not represent forecasts, in that they will not have the degree of certainty required by forecasts (they are also generally too far in the future to be accurate in that respect); nor do the financial projections represent budgets for management to work with once the hotel is open, for the same reason. They do represent an evaluation, under present and projected future conditions as defined by the report, of how the consultant, who should have depth and breadth of knowledge of the subject, views the development in financial terms.

This leads to my final point, which is that any feasibility study is a perishable product. The future can never be predicted with guaranteed accuracy and although the consultant will bring his experience into the equation when doing so, and will conscientiously research all the factors which might impact on future projections, unforeseen events can and will happen. Such things might be the unexpected closure of a major employer and generator of room demand, perhaps because the firm has been taken over and operations moved elsewhere; or a natural disaster, such as an earthquake, which destroys half the existing hotel stock in a moment.

The findings of a hotel feasibility study should therefore be subject to examination at regular intervals to assess the impact of any changes in the bases and conditions of the recommendations and projections which have been built up on those factors.

References

Doswell, R., Gamble, P., 1979, *Marketing and Planning Hotels and Tourism Projects*, Barrie & Jenkins, London.

Kendell, P. J., 1982, 'Recent experiences in project appraisal', *Tourism Management*, December 1982: 227–35.

Laventhol and Horwath, 1984, *Hotel/Motel Development*, ULI, Washington DC.

14 Hotel developments in South-East Asia and China

P. Reynolds

Introduction

The tourism industry world-wide, despite dramatic growth in the post-war period and its obvious economic importance, has received only scant attention in academic literature, with little being documented about its development and effects. Wu (1982), of the University of Sydney's Department of Town and Country Planning, bemoans this lack of knowledge, emphasizing that the situation is particularly acute in Asia. There has been very little published research into the growth and patterns of hotel development in the area, or the part that multinational corporations have played within the tourism sector. Only one large-scale study, undertaken by the UN Centre on Transnational Corporations has been published (UNCTC, 1982). Much of the detail of this report is now irrelevant due to the highly active and volatile nature of the hospitality industry in South-east Asia and China.

The purpose of this short chapter is not therefore so much to review current and published research but to outline current trends in the area, and also to help as a guide for future researchers.

Surveys and profiles of hotel companies and resultant analyses, which include details of tourist arrivals, length of stay, hotel expansion and stock, are regularly published (WTO, ATT, EIU, *et al.*). Bailey (1986, 1987) has done valuable work in surveying the development of hotels and hotel groups in South-east Asia, but little academic research has been done into the spread and development of the Multinational Corporation (MNC) in the area, especially in relation to existing theories of multinational growth.

Aggregate growth in the tourism market has been considerable in recent years. Measured in terms of international receipts, tourism has grown at the rate of 170 per cent over the period 1974 to 1980, in comparison with a growth in general merchandise trading of only 140 per cent. In 1983, international receipts totalled US$96.2 billion, making tourism the second largest item in world trade after oil (Waters, 1984). The countries of the Asia–Pacific region received almost 10 per cent of this total in 1983, demonstrating the highest growth rate of any geographical region (American Express, 1984).

Several articles (notably HRI, 1987), have reported a sharp rise in hotel construction, proceeding simultaneously, but often outpacing, the growth in the tourism market. This has resulted in considerable surplus capacity, of which Thailand in 1983 and Singapore in 1986/7 have been recent examples. China now looks as if it will become the next victim of a chronic oversupply of hotel rooms.

One of the many reasons for this growth is clearly the long-term market strategy of the participating Hotel Management Companies (HMCs). Other factors include the strong recoveries of the economies of the Pacific-rim nations and China since 1983. In fact several of these countries have reported GNP increases which were among the world's highest (HKSB).

Fiscal incentives or tax holidays have encouraged HMCs to operate in certain areas. Along with cheap labour and low construction costs, cheap land is still available in primary market areas throughout the region. These factors, coupled with the development of regional airlines and a drop in air fares, has contributed to a massive increase in tourism in the region, with predictions that tourist numbers will rise 7 per cent to 10 per cent per year over the next decade (HRI, 1987).

A more pessimistic or realistic view is offered by Bailey (1986) and others, who have cautioned that the number of tourists, although rising, is not up to predictions. This, coupled with the oversupply problem, is leading to a decline in the profits of HMCs in the area which is reflected in results from National Tourist Offices and market analysts (Pannell Kerr Foster, 1987; Horwarth and Horwarth, 1986). These analytical reports have not deterred the HMCs from even greater planned expansion throughout the region, as the following national profiles suggest.

China

Since the early 1980s, and with the implementation of China's open-door policy, MNCs have been investing in the country, capitalizing on China's tourist drawing potential, cheap labour costs, high GDP and the obvious need for deluxe hotels (Bailey, 1986).

Most hotel chains have at least one project in China—either completed or in the pipeline. This propagation and success of new hotels has led to greater interest among investors willing to take the same route to what was originally perceived to be a low-risk, high-return property investment.

The government stepped in and announced a 30 per cent tax on new service industry building in a bid to slow down the growth (SCMP, 1987). However this ruse appears to have had little effect on the construction programme despite the fact that the original demand from tourists and visiting business people appears to be satisfied.

Areas of intense hotel building include Beijing, where 10,000 new hotel rooms will be completed before 1989; Xi'an, where the famed terracotta warriors were uncovered, will have six hotels and 2,620 rooms by the end of 1988; Guilin, with 24 new hotels planned to be finished by 1990 and Shanghai will have at least an extra 4,000 deluxe rooms in the next two years (ATT, March 1986).

Hong Kong

Hong Kong's hotels have enjoyed occupancy rates of over 80 per cent for over ten years (ATT, January 1985: 11). The current building programme, which saw nine hotels or hotel construction sites change hands in 1987, will bring an extra 6,000 rooms to the market by 1990 but will not alter the situation significantly (SCMP, 20/3/88). The extra supply may in fact alleviate a current room shortage at certain times of the year even with expected arrivals rising to 4.4 million during 1987, an increase of 17 per cent over 1986 (ATT, February, 1988: 14).

Hong Kong has a special pivotal role in MNC development and strategy in South-east Asia, for apart from acting as the gateway to China for many hotel groups, it hosts the headquarters of many multinational groups such as the world's number one and two hotel MNCs, Holiday Inn and Sheraton, as well as being the base for other MNCs' regional offices.

Thus in Hymer's (1971) framework of the spatial effects of multinational corporations, Hong Kong ranks in the level II position relative to the United States-based MNCs in the industry, and in the level I position with the powerful, newly emerged home groups such as Mandarin Oriental, Regent International and New World Hotels International.

It is also illuminating to compare the growth and profitability of the hotel industry in Hong Kong with the steady decline in Singapore.

Singapore

After many years of falling average room rates, overbuilding and serious room glut which was heightened by the recent opening of the three-hotel, 2,000-room Marina complex, the situation in Singapore is poised for an upturn with occupancy rates up to 63.3 per cent and arrivals up 13.3 per cent in 1987 after an average growth of 5.3 per cent in 1986. In spite of this Singapore still has 23,000 rooms to fill, so strenuous efforts are being made by the country's tourist office to continue to improve results; but the gap is still vast, and it will take many years of improved arrival rates to make a significant difference.

Korea

The Asian games in 1986 and the Olympics in 1988 have added to Korea's strength. In Seoul, 13 new hotels with an extra 4,000 rooms have been added to the stock of 12,000 rooms for the Olympics (*Asia Travel News*, March, 1987). The major boost in the area seems to be the convention trade, with delegate attendance up 700 per cent between 1981 and 1985. This was underscored by the opening of the 5,000-seat Korea Trade Convention Centre in early 1988.

Malaysia

The hotel business in Malaysia has had a hard time in the past years. During the period 1985–6 occupancy dropped 9.4 per cent to 54.6 per cent (ATT, February 1988: 44) with room gluts in all key destinations, yet chains continued to expand their operations.

In 1986 eight international HMCs opened in Kuala Lumpur which led to the Malayan Association of Hotels calling for a five-year freeze on hotel building in the area. Out of a total of 38,000 rooms for the whole of the country, Kuala Lumpur and the Petaling Jaya region account for 6,000.

There are signs however, that the tourist economy is picking up, which has renewed hope for the city hotels where demand is closely linked to the business climate. To foster this upturn a new cultural and tourism ministry has been set up with a budget of US$40 million allocated in 1988 for tourism and culture promotion.

Thailand

Thailand has placed great reliance on its tourism market. This can be illustrated by foreign exchange receipts of US$1 billion in 1982, a figure which exceeded the export earnings of rice, traditionally the country's leading export item (Waters, 1984).

Visitors increased in 1987 by 14 per cent to a total of 3.2 million and after several years of oversupply occupancy rates in Bangkok are again above 80 per cent. Much of the increased awareness of Thailand in the tourist's mind is due to a successful 'Visit Thailand Year' in 1987.

The growth area for hotels has shifted from Bangkok to the island of Phuket where there has been an increase in rooms from 4,754 to 1986 to over 7,500 at present mostly from MNC chains (ATT, September 1987).

Indonesia

Since the decline of oil prices, the Indonesian government has put more emphasis on non-oil/gas exports including tourism. As hotels in Jakarta are particularly reliant on oil-related business, and other economic activity that a healthy oil industry brings, prospects are not good for the city's hotels. The situation in the island of Bali is buoyant with visitors up by 29 per cent on 1986 figures and building going on in Nusa Dua in the south of the island.

Conclusions

One similarity exhibited by all multinational HMCs in the area is the reluctance towards any form of financial involvement. The predominant form of control throughout the hotel sector is contractual. This was first investigated by McQueen (1983) supported by the UN report (UNCTC, 1982) in which it was stated that in developed countries hotels associated with MNCs owned 48 per cent of the hotel rooms. In developing countries however the ratio dropped to 18 per cent, in other words, of all hotels in developing countries which were associated with MNCs, 82 per cent exhibited no financial involvement on the part of the MNCs. The principal form of control was found to be management contract which accounted for 63 per cent of cases in all developing countries and 60 per cent of all MNC-associated hotels in Asia. These figures are pre-1982. The situation has now dramatically changed. For instance, all MNCs in China must be run by management contract. Which leaves the question, who, in capital scarce economies, is investing in the hotel sector? And why should the owners of these assets be willing to relinquish control to foreign corporations?

Research into tourism and its effects within South-east Asia has been continuing for some years at several centres; but research into the interlinked but separate area of hotel development in South-east Asia and China appears not to have advanced so swiftly. To redress this situation, research work at both Hong Kong Polytechnic and Hong Kong University now includes inter-country comparisons, and studies into the penetration and development strategies of hotel groups, both indigenous and multinational.

References

American Express Publishing Corporation, 1984, *World Tourism Overview*, New York.
ATT, Asia Travel Trade, Singapore.
Bailey, M., 1986, 'International hotel chain expansion in Asia', *Travel and Tourism Analyst*, March, pp. 19–32.
Bailey, M., 1987, 'Hotel chains in Asia', *Travel and Tourism Analyst*, March, pp. 45–55.
EIU, Economist Intelligence Unit, *International Tourism Reports*, Economist Publications Ltd, London.
Horwarth and Horwarth, 1987, *Hong Kong*. H & H, Hong Kong.
HRI, 1987, *Hotels and Restaurants International*, Cahners Publishing, Co., Washington, April, pp. 44–56; October, pp. 40–60.
HRSB, Hong Kong and Shanghai Banking Corporation, *Business Profile Series*, Hong Kong.
Hymer, S., 1971, 'The multinational corporation and the law of uneven development', in Bhagwati, J. W. (ed.), *Economics and World Order*, Macmillan, New York, pp. 113–40.
McQueen, M., 1983, 'Appropriate policies towards multinational hotel development in developing countries', *World Development* II(2): 141–52.
Pannell Kerr Foster, 1987, *Trends in the Hotel Industry 1987*, Pkf Hong Kong.
SCMP, 1987, *South China Morning Post*, Hong Kong, 12 July, p. 10.
UNCTD, 1982, *Transnational Corporations in International Tourism*, United Nations, New York.

Waters, S. R., 1984, 'The big picture—1984', in *Travel World Yearbook*, Child and Waters Inc., New York.

WTO, 'World tourism 1983–1984: monograph on tourism in East Asia and the Pacific' MON/AP/85, Madrid.

Wu, C. T., 1982, 'Issues of tourism and socioeconomic developments', *Annals of Tourism Research* 9(3): 317–30.

15 An overview of the contract catering industry in the United Kingdom: a view from the industry
G. Hawkes

Introduction

As recently as the 1930s the majority of industrial workers ate sandwiches made at home for their midday meal. Employers offered no catering facilities. The traditions of the early rural stages of the industrial revolution when workers were expected to be self-sufficient, living in their own communities took a long time to fade away. In wartime, the home was no longer able to provide food as effectively as government-supported central kitchens. The Second World War acted as a major catalyst, introducing the canteen as the focal eating point for the whole nation. After the war, contract catering grew slowly. Employers at a time of full employment saw the provision of services like food as a way of attracting and keeping employees. The provision of subsidized food at the workplace became a recognized employee benefit.

In the 1980s the catering industry is changing again with the terms 'staff restaurant' and 'dining-room' replacing canteen. There is a growing demand for style and quality of service in the workplace on a par with that of a restaurant outside. The trend towards healthy eating has given the caterer a boost as an expert in dietary matters. Employers see the provision of a lunch-time experience as an effective form of internal public relations, establishing their credentials as caring and well organized.

Gardner Merchant has experienced the whole range of change in British catering. The company can trace its roots back to 1886 and through many aspects of the development of the food industry—as a butcher and then a victualler to the Navy in 1914; a series of coffee shops; outside caterers in 1939; to contract catering. The company is now the largest contract caterer in the United Kingdom, accounting for some 30 per cent of the contracted market. With one hundred years of catering experience in the United Kingdom and two decades of working overseas, with 34,000 employees working on 4,000 contracts world-wide, the company has a very special perspective on the past, present and future of the catering industry.

Historical development of industrial catering

It would be fashionable to castigate the employers of the early industrial revolution for not providing their employees with a meal at their place of work, but this would be unfair judgement taken out of context of the time. The tradition of rural communities, from where the first industrial workers migrated, was one of self-reliance. Workers in the early industrial revolution were happy to bring a packed meal to be eaten during a short midday break, or during their natural labours at the bench or loom, just as they had been accustomed to do when working as agricultural labourers.

In the Victorian age the era of the paternalistic industrial employer began—along with those who were purely exploitative. The former saw that the provision of food in the workplace, along with other benefits, was good for business. A well-fed worker was perceived to be more productive than an unfed one. A loyal worker who looked to his workplace rather than his home for basic sustenance was more likely to be prepared to commit himself to the purposes of his employer than someone relying on home. The enlightenment of the Victorian paternalists was self-interested in the best sense of the term. Cadburys, Lever Brothers, Frys, Rowntrees, Colman's and others were happy with the concept of meal breaks and later the idea of low-cost lunches provided by the company. It was not long before they set up some of the earliest canteens.

Legislation led to the spread of canteens from the few enlightened employers to the rest. From the mid-nineteenth century onwards, the government reacted to growing public concern about the living and working conditions of industrial workers. Employers were encouraged to look after the welfare of employees. In due course workers ate better food at work than they did at home. The significance of government legislation as a factor improving the diet of workers was much clearer in wartime. Most government factories established at the end of the 1930s were built with canteen facilities. In 1940, the Government Factory Canteen Order made it compulsory for factories employing more than 250 people to provide dining-rooms where wholesome meals at reasonable prices were available.

Wartime meant food rationing. The scarcity of energy and food supplies made the provision of meals from a central kitchen at the workplace economic sense. The contract catering industry was called in by employers to help them meet the rquirements of government legislation. An interesting by-product of these changes from domestic to public eating facilities was a significant increase in the overall health of the population. Present-day problems of unbalanced diet, obesity and other food related disorders were minimal, if they existed at all.

If the demands of war forced the expansion of contract catering, the coming of peace led to a period of relative stagnation. The period between the late 1940s through to the 1960s was one of little growth for the British contract catering industry. It was almost as if rationing and the use of a canteen had become synonymous with wartime austerity and the dictatorship of the paternalist state pilloried by George Orwell. Trends in industrial development in the 1960s and 1970s were also not conducive to the expansion of contract catering. The decline in heavy industry in favour of light industry and service industries accelerated in these years. The latter companies employ fewer people on one site. They have a more mobile and independent work-force usually with access to off-site facilities. Management of these smaller firms are less prepared to invest in canteen or non-earning overheads as they see it.

In this context it is not surprising that in the 1980s, the contract catering industry in the United Kingdom still has only 40 per cent of the potential commercial market. There are signs, however, of a significant shift in management practice which augurs well for the expansion of contract catering in the future. There is a growing trend in management thinking to sub-contract all activities other than the core business activity to specialists. Supplying food to the work-force should no longer be the direct concern of management of non-catering companies.

Once again government, but this time in peacetime, is acting as the catalyst in encouraging the public sector to use contract caterers on a large scale and in new ways. The political idea of privatization has created the prospect of major new market opportunities. The management of the new privatized companies is more accountable to deliver profits to satisfy the City and their new share-holders. The introduction of catering contractors allows them to introduce lower manning levels without reducing the quality of service, allowing significant cost savings in the first year of operation as a private entity.

The same drive to reduce the cost of ancillary services like catering has encouraged the government to introduce contractors into services they directly finance (like health, defence and local government). These services are unlikely to be sold off. Instead services are either contracted out completely or put out to competitive tender. The scale of this new business opportunity is huge. The local government market alone, which will come on stream in August 1989, will add a further 30,000 potential catering opportunities. The catering market worked by contract caterers could triple in the next five years. A close look at the different market segments shows how social and economic change is working in favour of the spread of contract catering.

The primary contract catering markets

The private sector

In the United Kingdom the main market for contract catering is in industrial and commercial locations with 200 or more employees. This category of contract includes some interesting developments where smaller companies share facilities on an industrial estate or within an office building. Currently there are estimated to be some 20,000 sites in the United Kingdom employing more than 200 people, of which some 40 per cent would be using contract caterers to provide facilities.

The next most significant market is location with between 50 and 200 people on site. There are about 40,000 of these. Normally they rely on a delivered food service or vending rather than canteens. But a growing exception to the rule that the lower the number of employees, the lower the investment in catering facilities is emerging with the dining-room concept. This in-house restaurant facility supplied by a contract caterer is being used by the more sophisticated small company employing high-calibre staff. It is used for both internal and external marketing purposes. Quality contract catering matching the highest restaurant standards in both gastronomic terms and service is replacing the canteen as the growth market. The financial services sectors in the City, corporate headquarters and sales and marketing centres which entertain a constant flow of visitors are the main clients in this growing low-turnover, high-profit market.

Contract caterers know that these smaller secondary-niche markets are growing faster than the primary single-site markets. The economy is tending to favour the formation of new industries and small businesses. An alert contract caterer can exploit these new markets as effectively as those of large single sites. A new development in France shows how economies of scale can be applied to the small company sector. Developers of a major trading estate, science park or office complex, include a large catering facility in the central plans. This facility is let on a long-term contract to one central supplier who offers catering services to all employees on the site. Gardner Merchant is now operating many of these units through its French subsidiary in both the Paris and Lyons region. The essential idea behind this French development is applicable to the United Kingdom. Employee care is a top priority for the new high-technology companies in search of scarce technologists and technicians. The supply of a top quality lunch-time experience is an important part of the employee package. The French type of central catering facility on a trading estate makes it possible to provide good food at a reasonable cost.

Catering contractors have little control over the factors changing their market. The demand for a different type of catering service reflects deep-seated developments in society and the economy. The decline in employment in heavy industry leading to the overnight closure of large industrial centres immediately affected all suppliers including contract caterers. There was nothing to be done to keep their business. The contract catering industry has to be market-led and able to respond with imagination to thrive profitably amid all this change.

The public sector

The public sector appears as a major future market in the United Kingdom. The Conservative government with a mandate until 1991 is committed to the involvement of the private sector to reduce public expenditure across all government financed institutions. Hospitals, universities, local government, prisons, colleges of further education, schools, Ministry of Defence establishments as well as the police and fire service make up an impressive list of potential business. In the United Kingdom there are in excess of 2,500 National Health Service (NHS) hospitals alone.

Progress after four years of involvement within this public sector market has been disappointing for caterers. The difficulty has arisen from the dislike by government of cost plus contracts. The contract catering industry has all its contracts in the commercial world as 'management fee contracts', the term they use for cost plus. Experience has shown that both parties gain from contracts which recharge all costs incurred, allow for a small fixed profit or management fee, and are controlled by an open-book accountancy system. Despite extensive lobbying, the government has continued to favour fixed-price contracts for all ancillary services including catering. The contract caterering industry has agreed to respond to fixed-price tender contracts, but only if there is no in-house tender. All fixed-price tender invitations with an in-house bid have been rejected by the vast majority of catering contractors.

The Ministry of Defence market is attractive despite the contracts being let on a fixed price because the service is contracted out with no in-house bid. A central contract unit has made sure that the flow of contracts are put out in line with the resources of contractors to respond. The NHS market, very much bigger than the Ministry of Defence Market, has been disappointing. The choice of competitive tendering linked with fixed-price contracts has led to few catering contractors competing. Gardner Merchant has restricted its tendering activity to large district-wide management-fee contracts.

The local government market is likely to be slow to develop. The Department of the Environment has followed the example of the Department of Health and Social Security and opted for competitive tendering. Fixed-price contracts are favoured. Many catering companies will be unwilling to tender for fixed-price contracts. It will take time for the political orientation of the market to be replaced by a true commercial partnership.

The public-service catering market is evolving into new niche markets in the same way as the commercial and industrial markets. The latest development is to merge catering with older ancillary services to create a hotel services contract. The advantage to the client is a higher rate of saving in terms of management time and overall cost. The contractor gains because of the higher value of the contract being managed essentially by the same management team. But there is one main problem facing contractors. How can they offer a hotel service without the operational experience of other ancillary services like cleaning? Contractors can make alliances with other specialist companies. Alternatively they can set up their own operation to offer all the staff needed. The advantages to the client of the hotel-type contract are so clear that it is likely to spread from the Ministry of Defence and a few NHS health authorities to the whole public-sector market.

The problems of these government markets are their size. Catering contracts worth £1 billion are on offer. Even if only a very small proportion of these are won by contractors, the strain on the skilled management and specialist backup service of the industry will be intense. The opportunities for new business in commercial, industrial and public-sector markets in the United Kingdom is matched by the opportunities abroad, especially in Europe after 1992.

The European market

The contract catering industry is likely to be as changed by 1992 as any other industry. The creation of a single European market will remove any legislative barriers to British contract caterers expanding into other European markets. For example in West Germany, the government restricts the expansion of contract caterers of the British type by legislation. The allowance for feeding workers is fixed by law. Any expenditure over this figure is taxed very heavily. In other countries, however, the barriers will be more cultural than legislative. A caterer will need to be very sensitive to special attitudes towards food and its consumption. Is the main meal at lunch time or in the evening? Do they prefer to eat hot or cold foods? How long do they take for a lunch break? Is it normal for lunch time to be used by management to influence attitudes of employees? What hours of working are normal?

The answers to these questions vary from one European market to another, but can also vary from region to region within some countries. For the French, eating is a way of life. Italians eating at work regard it as topping up the fuel levels. As one might expect, in northern Europe, heavier meals with a large meat content tend to be the norm. In southern Europe, where there is a hot climate, it is not unusual for the working day to be organized with either a finish in mid-afternoon, when employees prefer to go home to eat, or a long two- or three-hour break at midday when employees tend to go off-site.

An additional problem with working in Europe is the difficulty of managing a European group with a wide range of different nationalities each with different attitudes and management skills. A recent resarch study by MORI looking at national stereotypes found that each European nation was perceived in a similar way by the other European nations. Business managers, when asked to select the best European national for each job function in an ideal corporation tended to agree: the Germans were selected for administration, Swedes for design, British for marketing, and so on. These national characteristics need to be considered when building an international management team.

A responsive management strategy is needed to handle these cultural differences. A caterer has to be flexible and fit in with local realities rather than to try to change them. Experience of regional variation in the British market reinforces this point of view.

The effect of the European Community's drive for a single European market in 1992 will be to increase Gardner Merchant's home market from perhaps 50,000 opportunities to perhaps 350,000. The company, along with other larger contract caterers, will have to increase the sophistication of its management to cope with the complexities of working on a European scale.

Gardner Merchant's approach to its market

Introduction

The provision of skilled catering management rather than just the food and drink which people eat at their place of work is what Gardner Merchant offers to clients. The objective of the company is to establish a clear competitive advantage over its rivals. There are three salient features to Gardner Merchant's service.

First, Gardner Merchant exploits its large size to achieve substantial buying power, reducing the cost of food to clients. With food absorbing up to 60 per cent of contract costs, this competitive advantage for Gardner Merchant is significant in winning contracts. Second, Gardner Merchant has invested in an extensive range of support services: for example, developing its own computerized catering management systems, notably Caterfax. Food, stock control, menu planning, recipe costing and management information are available to the manager of every contract. Among the specialist skills the company offers are design and planning of kitchens and dining areas; consultancy advice on the management of existing catering facilities for self-caterers; and (through the vending operations division), a wide range of food and drink for consumption 24-hours-a-day. Dietetics is of increasing importance and around 15 full-time professional dieticians are located throughout the regions to offer specialized dietary advice to clients, particularly those with special requirements such as in the educational and health sectors. Finally there is a major investment in all aspects of personnel, including recruitment and training, to supply the insatiable demand for skilled catering management operatives to manage all the new contracts being won in the UK and abroad.

Personnel development

Gardner Merchant invests the equivalent of 10 per cent of annual profits into training the 34,000 people employed world-wide. The centre-piece of this investment is the only residential management training college in the industry. In 1988, to meet the expanded needs of the company, the training school moved to a refurbished period property in Kenley, Surrey. The new complex combines the function of corporate headquarters and an international catering management-training course. The latter consists of 32 bedrooms, three kitchens, dining facilities and five fully equipped lecture rooms which are used in training programmes to run throughout the year. The Kenley management training centre is linked to a well-developed programme of on-the-job training. This is organized by local training departments near to the place of work.

An ambitious training initiative of this kind needs more than excellent facilities to succeed. A coherent company philosophy is needed to motivate staff to put what they learn in training sessions into practice in the work place.

Gardner Merchant believes that the best catering management is based on two key personal attributes: independence of mind and a fierce ambition to provide the best service possible. Local catering management needs to have the right attitudes to search out ways to improve on old methods of working. They want management prepared to take calculated chances. The company, they believe, will succeed if staff are more frightened to miss an opportunity than to make a mistake. To this extent employees at Gardner Merchant even at senior level are left in no doubt that they can fail with honour and continue to prosper in the company. This adventurous company philosophy, unusual in a large multinational, is not only disseminated by management training but also by the developed organization of the company. Power and responsibility are deliberately passed down to small management units. Younger members of management are given experience of decision-making early in their careers. The intention is to encourage future management to think flexibly as though they were in a small organization and to solve their own problems in line with local circumstance. As a result Gardner Merchant employees work harder to achieve success as they become personally identified with the success or failure of their operations, almost as though it was their own business.

The result has been an unusually stable work-force. Staff turnover among the top 1,000 managers averages under 6 per cent per annum. This stability makes it possible for the company to rely on promoting people from within to meet the growing demand for new quality management to manage new contracts. The rapid growth of the company helps keep employees loyal to the company. There is nowhere else to go in catering management to achieve the same rate of advancement.

In the UK there is a planned programme to recruit the best college and school leavers interested in catering as a career. Two hundred graduates are recruited each year from catering colleges with some 300 young people direct from relevant school craft-training schemes. The objective is to keep these new recruits through their future career, rising through the ranks to senior management positions. Within Gardner Merchant they will find enough opportunity in different types of catering jobs with origins of training to satisfy their professional ambitions.

The rapid growth of the business over the last 10 years seems to suggest that a combination of investment in training and the devolved management structure does allow a large catering company to perform in the eyes of clients with the sensitivity normally associated with a much smaller organization.

International expansion

The notable feature of Gardner Merchant's recent growth has been expansion overseas. Europe and the Middle East were the first targets. In the Netherlands Gardner Merchant has risen to become market leader and it also has a substantial business in Belgium. Recently France has become another country where a significant operation has been established.

The United States shows the biggest potential for growth in the immediate future. Catering contracts are held with many major organizations including General Electric, Chase Manhattan, Exxon, Perkin Elmer and Merill Lynch. With its headquarters in Connecticut, the American operation is expanding from its original New York, New Jersey and Connecticut base to cover the main eastern seaboard from Boston to Miami.

From the Gulf to Australia and Singapore, the Gardner Merchant catering management team are building up their business. Even in the Falkland Islands, Gardner Merchant is dominant. A wholly-owned subsidiary, Kelvin Catering, provides catering, homekeeping and other ancillary services to the armed forces on the island.

The success of Gardner Merchant overseas has been a tribute to the strength of its management systems. The flexibility given to local management and the relentless emphasis on a quality approach to catering management has overcome the natural barriers between cultures. This success overseas suggests a future as large as the company management is prepared to contemplate.

Conclusion

Catering is not an easy business. The supply of quality meals with a quality service day after day is difficult to organize. On top of these organizational demands come the problems of meeting the changing fashions in eating. Food is subject to fashion in the same way as music and clothes. The successful catering operation will recognize the need to respond immediately to what people want. There should be no reluctance to change. At Gardner Merchant, we try to stay one step ahead—but well in touch for example with international cuisine, fast foods and healthy eating.

The future in catering over the next 30 years will probably see an even faster rate of change in food tastes than in the past. There is little doubt about the large potential for growth both in the United Kingdom and overseas. The decline in the supply of young people available to enter the catering industry is likely to accelerate the swing from in-house to contract caterers.

Amid all this change and growth, Gardner Merchant will stay calm, adhering steadfastly to its simple tenets of a philosophy outlining the essence of good catering management. A contract caterer is essentially providing catering management and not the food and drink. The success of the business depends upon the quality of the management. Anything the clients want will be provided to specification, provided they are able to pay for it. Against this prescription, the future looks bright.

16 New developments in computer technology and their application to the hospitality industry

P. R. Gamble

Introduction

While the hospitality industry is not noted for its innovative uses of computer technology, it may be worth recalling at the outset that its connections with computing stretch back to the beginnings of the modern commercial machine. The very first commercial computer, the Ferranti Mark 1, was installed at Manchester University in February 1951. However, following the work of Professor Maurice Wilkes at the University of Cambridge, a device known as the LEO Mark 1 was installed for a 'true' commercial operation later that same year, just beating Remington-Rand's Univac machine.

The Lyons Electronic Office (LEO), named for the British company J. Lyons Catering which installed it, weighed in with half a ton of mercury and over 7,000 valves. Even so, it was considerably smaller than the archetypal ENIAC devised by Eckert and Mauchly at Princeton in 1946 which required 15,000 square feet of space and a floor loading capable of supporting 30 tons. Thus Leo marked the beginning of a trend for smaller computers, capable of delivering greater performance which has continued to the present.

It was during the 1960s that hotels began to make use of (expensive) minicomputers for applications other than accounting. In 1964, IBM and Hilton opened the world's first 'fully computerised hotel', the New York Hilton. Unfortunately, the computer systems in this hotel were closed down some nine days after opening, an experience which coloured IBM's perception of the hospitality market and which, due to IBM's ensuing loss of interest in the topic, probably slowed the rate of development. On the other side of the Atlantic, Lyons successfully ran the reservation systems for large London hotels like the 450-room Strand Palace Hotel and the 800-room Cumberland Hotel on DEC PDP8 computers throughout the sixties.

However, it was not until the late 1970s and the advent of the micro-computer that computer-based technology became important for the hospitality industry. The world's first Property Management System (PMS) to run on a microcomputer was installed in 1978 by Hoskyns Services, at that time a British division of the Martin Marietta aerospace group, in the Seven Hills Hotel, Cobham, England. In the United States no microcomputers were recorded in lodging properties in 1980 (Chervenak, Keane and Co., 1988). By mid-1983 there were 600 and by 1987 there were over 30,000. Indeed, by 1988 Chervenak and Keane estimated that there were over 3,000 relevant techno-logy products on the American market alone. For all practical purposes therefore, progress in computer technology in the hospitality industry dates back just over ten years and it is this period which is interesting to consider.

Current applications in the hospitality industry

Broadly, current applications of computer technology in the hospitality industry can be grouped into three main areas, operational, guest services and management information (Gamble, 1984; Godowski, 1987; Kasavana and Cahill, 1987). The overall functionality of these applications is similar across a range of different hospitality organizations though the technology used to support them may vary. Large, city-centre hotels tend to use minicomputers for their PMS work; elsewhere, microcomputers are employed.

Operational applications

The two main specialist operational areas concern accommodation manage-ment and food and beverage management. Front office systems usually incorporate reservations, registration and billing because these three elements are linked by the high proportion of data which they use in common. In addition, such systems may incorporate a guest history system, a room status system and extend to cover the greater proportion of the accounting system. There is a very high usage rate of such computer systems in hotels with over 250 rooms, probably approaching 100 per cent in most western countries. The most usual configuration is that of dual minicomputers able to support a large number of terminals. Typically, such systems have direct links to other hotel systems such as telephones, in-room entertainment, security and so on which may be run off the central system or supported by dedicated small computers. Hotels under 250 rooms or so are more likely to use microcomputer hardware for similar applications. Penetration rates for these hotels are lower, depending on market sector.

Food and beverages are much less significant in terms of their contribution to profitability and perhaps because of this have attracted less interest from hospitality managers. Overall, penetration rates are probably less than 2 per cent and very few of these occur in the commercial restaurant sector. The most comprehensive application is known as a Catering Information System or CIS. A CIS bases its reports on a file of recipes which are priced up to the minute for every ingredient cost change. The computer is then used to calculate menu costings and summarize stores requisitions based on production forecasts. It may also be used for menu planning. In addition, stock control is possible for both main stores and a number of kitchens.

For beverage areas, specialist control systems may be installed which link sensors to optics and metered pumps. In turn, these are connected to a micro-computer or to an electronic cash register. It is also quite feasible to install low-level control systems, especially in relation to beverages using a standard data-base manager or even a spreadsheet.

Billing and accounting

The hospitality industry generally makes use of standard applications for accountancy and billing though the accounting system will often be custom-ized to support the American Hotel Motel Association Uniform System of Accounts which is now widely adopted internationally. Although standard Point of Sale (POS) devices are quite likely to be used for billing, there have been developments in what might be called waiter communication systems. Based on microcomputers, these systems support terminals on each waiter station with links to both the kitchen and the cashier. They allow waiters to place orders or to cash up without leaving their station. Although they can be extended to function as a CIS this is not common. They have been quite successful and are installed on a widespread basis by several major catering chains.

Guest services

The term 'guest services' might be taken to encompass communications, security, vending and audio-visual services and engineering.

Communications

Primarily this refers to telephone systems where microcomputer support provides for more accurate billing, some improvements in guest service through better call routing and more management information. Other services may also be supported via telephone computers, especially in older hotels where the retrofit costs of new wiring can be high. Thus security, room status or even room heating may be serviced by this approach.

Security systems

Concerns about personal safety in large cities have supported growth in the application of electronic security systems. Controlled by a small computer in the front office these can be operated by magnetic cards, magnetic keys or digital pads. In addition to improved security and a new promotional channel, the slim, plastic keys lend themselves to vending by machine. Thus budget hotels in particular are able to offer a self check-in service based on a credit card and a vending machine. At the other extreme, high security hotels in Las Vegas and the Middle East have used retinal pattern scanners to regulate the movement of both staff and guests. Other back of house security systems may be based on motion detectors, closed circuit TV, watch tour systems, infra red and seismic sensors.

Vending and audio-visual services

It is convenient to group those services provided directly into the guest's room under this heading. Vending services, usually in the form of mini-bars, owe little to computer technology other than a form of monitored billing. Similarly, wake-up services or alarm systems may be controlled by a microprocessor or a telephone computer.

Of more interest are in-room entertainment systems. Principally these involve video cassette films and extra television channels supported by satellite and cable systems. Sometimes these may be directly billed by computer. Where there is an interface between the television systems and the main PMS, in-room televisions may be used to support self check-out, messaging and room-service orders.

Satellite systems are also used as the basis of teleconferencing services and one major American chain has made successful use of private satellite channels both for these applications and for its central reservation system. More down-to-earth videotex television services controlled by computers are employed for in-house advertising, national news and information and even for reservation systems. Probably the most successful application in this respect is the French Minitel service.

Engineering

Most engineering applications are based entirely on microprocessors. These fall into two distinct categories. Energy control devices are widely used in all types of hospitality organizations because of their demonstrably rapid pay-back periods. Many types of device are involved, ranging from full building automation systems linked into the PMS, through load cyclers, peak power demand controllers, chiller optimization controls, automatic shut-off systems, soft-start lighting, down to simple time switches.

Microprocessor controlled catering equipment provides for consistency and quality control by incorporating more functionality into the catering equipment itself. In this way service standards can be maintained without worrying too much about the need for heavy training costs and close, skilled supervision. Microprocessor-controlled catering equipment costs about five times as much as its conventional equivalent but provides for more consistent quality with low-training and direct labour costs.

Management information

A scheme of description which presents a review of management information after dealing with operational applications and guest services may not appear to conform to a logical order of priority. The work of Porter and Millar (1985) is particularly important in this context since they have argued that information systems may shape the nature of the organizations of which they are part. In doing so the information systems may transform both the nature of the organization and the nature of the products and services that they provide. Porter and Millar offer this as an important new source of competitive differential.

Many writers have reviewed the effect of technology on organizations. Perhaps inspired by Woodward's (1959) early work, researchers have sought to demonstrate relationships between size, structure, technology (Aldrich, 1972; Pugh, 1973; Blau *et al.*, 1976; Hunt, 1979) and, to a lesser extent leadership style (Argyris, 1972). Some of this discussion in relation to computers is neatly summarized by Robey (1977). At the time of writing it is difficult to demonstrate the workings of some kind of exogenous technological imperative which shapes and alters organizations. Such changes as occur may well be ascribed to political effects (Warwick, 1975; Watson, 1980; Wilkinson, 1983). There is no evidence to indicate that hotels, as organizations, differ in this respect.

However, as service industries, hotels share common characteristics with other organizations examined by Porter and Millar in which both the information intensity of the value chain is high and the information content of the product is high. Examples include banks, airlines and newspapers. It will be noticed that in these industries, as in hotels, the operational systems by which day to day activities are regulated are identical to those systems from which management information is derived.

In the hotel industry, this has had the effect of allowing custodial processing, such as the need to record reservations, to dominate and overwhelm potential interest in the information requirements of tactical and limited strategic planning. Thus research has indicated (Gamble, 1986) that accounting and finance applications predominate. The most common application in hospitality organizations in use by almost half of all hospitality managers (47 per cent) is computerized billing. Those applications employed by one-fifth of managers or more include all types of ledger accounts, payroll and budgeting. The third major area in the high-usage group is inventory applications: either inventories of sales in the form of reservations or inventories of raw materials in the form of stock control and inventory. On considering intentions and possible future applications, all the indications are for more of the same. Yet this mismatch between where gains are expected and where computers are actually used is not unusual. PA Management Consultants (1985), revealed what was described as a 'disturbing mismatch' between the expectations of top managers and their companies' Information Technology (IT) strategies.

Using a survey based on 156 chief executives of *The Times'* top 1,000 companies, they found that while 61 per cent of chief executives expected to obtain improved information and communications, only 31 per cent explicitly targeted this kind of improvement in their corporate strategy. Fifty-two per cent expected more support for management from IT, and 32 per cent expected more support for sales strategy. However, only 22 per cent and 13 per cent respectively have addressed these issues when applying IT to their corporate needs. Elsewhere, Galliers (1986) found that in only 20 per cent of cases were information systems planned in relation to business needs and that in only 10 per cent of cases was information system planning fully integrated with business planning.

Trends in microcomputing

As suggested by the trend from ENIAC to LEO, computer hardware has continued to offer an increasingly powerful capability in what tends to be an ever smaller box. Thus over the last 35 years there has been a move away from the $1m mainframe computer to the application of time-shared minicomputers now used in larger hotels. By 1988, the performance delivered by high-end microcomputers has overlapped that of minicomputers to an extent that embarrasses even their manufacturers. Indeed market research company Romtec (1987) has forecast a fall in the value of the British minicomputer market from just over £1 billion in 1988 to £440 million in 1991. During this period, sales of multiuser microcomputers are expected to grow by 462 per cent to just under £1.7 billion.

In terms of hardware, the trends reflect a demand for faster and more powerful processors capable of high-volume, rapid calculations necessary to support high-resolution graphics displays. This kind of device is epitomized in business application terms by IMB's PS/2 70-A21, a 32-bit device based on an Intel 80386 running at 25MHz. Such a microcomputer, linked with a multisynch analog graphics display and a laser printer is capable of a speed and quality of performance unmatched by many minicomputers.

To exploit this capability, IBM is expecting its multiuser, multitasking operating system OS/2, launched in 1988, to become the new business standard thus replacing its current microcomputer operating system, PC-DOS. OS/2 will run several jobs simultaneously, link into communication networks and provide access to huge amounts of memory. In hospitality computing, this would allow the PMS to switch instantly between reservations, registration and billing. Alternatively, at a personal level, it would allow a manager to refer quickly to a personal diary viewed through a convenient screen window, without interrupting the calculation of the large spreadsheet that formed the engine of the current business plan.

Such an operating system would support three important trends in software developments (Pilcher, et al., 1987). The first of these, high-quality graphics, is turning even text-based applications such as word processing into an application that requires extensive use of pictorial representation. Thus word processors are beginning to give way to Desk Top Publishing (DTP) software that integrates graphics with text and provides for complete on-screen formatting of output.

The second trend is towards increased connectivity. In local terms this means that the software should be able to link into computer networks, bulletin boards, other corporate computers and public information services. Commercially it might be expected that hospitality computer systems will be able to link easily into corporate reservation systems and, perhaps more importantly, airline reservation systems. New airline reservation systems scheduled for introduction in 1988, such as Galileo and Amadeus, emulate and extend the functions of the existing American Airlines' Sabre system. These systems will have enormous power within the distribution channel to regulate the sales of hotel beds, airline seats, car rentals, theatre tickets, restaurant meals and other travel-related services.

The third important trend is toward the application of what Searle (1985) calls weak Artificial Intelligence techniques (AI) into business applications. Searle defines weak AI as work which provides insight into how people perform certain intellectual tasks (as distinct from strong AI which purports to emulate thinking). Commercial examples include a data-base manager that allows users to formulate queries on screen, independent of query syntax or index structures within the data-base and then attempts to interpret the request by generating its own retrieval program.

Clearly, advances in software are much more important for managers than advances in hardware. After all, hardware simply drives software. Nevertheless, the two are closely related. Thus a measure of the rate of change might be gained by reflecting that one year after the launch of the IBM PS/2 range in April 1987 the market share of 80386-based products was, according to Romtec, less than 3 per cent in unit terms. Indeed, in unit terms the market was dominated by more 'traditional' machines of a type first available over five years before.

Trends in hospitality computing

Many researchers believe that artificial intelligence is the key to exploiting the power and performance of modern microcomputers in management terms through the creation of expert systems. An expert system seeks to capture the knowledge that experts use to solve problems and, through organizing that knowledge symbolically on a computer, makes it available as a resource for solving problems. Such systems seek to deal not only with quantitative data, for which computers are well known, but also rule-based or even qualitative data which forms an important part of some decisions (Winston, 1984). Thus it has been suggested by Luconi et al. (1986) that expert systems represent the new challenge for managers. However, a comprehensive review of commercial AI applications (Rauch-Hindin, 1988) reveals no major developments specific to the hospitality industry.

There are few projects actually using these techniques in commercial hospitality management. An experimental microcomputer expert system to support front office decision-making was reported initially by Gamble and Smith (1986). In the food area, Nissan (1987) has described a program which may give advice on the design of menus, based on knowledge of suitable foods, medical and social constraints and actual food availability.

However, the first commercial implementation of these techniques is described by Smith (1987). This involves a yield mangement system based on expert-system techniques which was installed at the Balsams Grand Resort Hotel in Dixville Notch, New Hampshire and the Royal Sonnesta Hotel in Boston. Essentially, the program enhances conventional statistical approaches with a rule-based system design to maximize revenue yield by assisting reservation clerks to make critical accept/refuse decisions for short-stay reservations. The system, which holds data on guests who have visited the hotel over the last 16 years, is reported to have increased profitability and reduced training time.

Concluding remarks

It is clearly important not to confuse advances in technology with advances in the diffusion of innovations. New computers or new software do not make new managers. The diffusion of innovations may depend on leadership style (Mytinger, 1968), environmental complexity (Feller and Menzel, 1977), the character of the innovation itself (Rogers and Shoemaker, 1971) or even the extent of informal communication between organizations (Martilla, 1971). An interesting review by Rothwell (1977) emphasizes the significance of good communications within and between organizations and the importance of marketing users' needs, demand pull rather than technology push.

There is clearly an inertia in the market-place associated with existing investments in hardware and software. At the same time, there is some inertia in hospitality managers themselves. Kiechel (1984) has commented on the reluctance of hospitality executives to introduce computers and Whittaker (1987) has referred to what she calls barriers of will by managers. It must be accepted that managers themselves still form a major constraint on the implementation of new computing techniques for operating and managing hotels. None the less, it is important to view this observation in context. Other studies by Gamble (1988), while supporting the view that the formal training available to hospitality managers is less than that available to other types of manager, did not discover significant differences in their attitudes to information technology.

The notion that management development and training is the key to implementing new techniques is not inconsistent with studies of many industries. Fried (1987) has noted that many types of manager do not understand the nature and potential of expert systems. However external pressures resulting from new industry structures, political initiatives such as European harmonization and related technological changes in airline systems may

radically alter the nature of the international hospitality market. Since existing computer technology offers many forsaken opportunities, some changes in the rate and nature of management development may be expected.

References

Aldrich, H. E., 1972, 'Technology and organizational structure: re-examination of the findings of the Aston Group', *Administrative Science Quarterly*, 17: 26–43.

Argyris, C., 1972, *The Applicability of Organizational Sociology*, Cambridge University Press, Cambridge.

Blau, P. M., Falbe, C. M., McKinley W. and Tracy, P. K., 1976, 'Technology and organization in manufacturing', *Administrative Science Quarterly*, 21; 20–40.

Chervenak, Keane & Co. Inc., 1988, 'GKC report', *The Hotel Technology Newsletter*, 5(1): 3.

Feller, I., and Menzel, D. C., 1977, 'Diffusion milieus as a focus of research on innovation in the public sector', *Policy Sciences*, 8: 49–68.

Fried, L., 1987, 'The dangers of dabbling in expert systems', *Computerworld*, XXI: 65–6, 69–72.

Galliers, R., 1986, 'A failure of direction', *Business Computing & Communications*, July/August: 32–8.

Gamble, P. R., 1984, *Small Computers and Hospitality Management*, Hutchinson, London.

Gamble, P. R., 1986, *Computers and Innovation in the Hospitality Industry: A Study of Some Factors Affecting Management Behaviour*, unpublished PhD Thesis, University of Surrey.

Gamble, P. R., 1988, 'Attitudes to computers by managers in the hotel industry', *Behaviour and Information Technology*, 7(3): 305–21.

Gamble, P. R., and Smith, G., 1986, 'Expert front office management by computer', *International Journal of Hospitality Management*, 5(3): 109–14.

Godowski, S., 1987, *Microcomputers in the Hotel and Catering Industry*, Heinemann, London.

Hunt, J. W., 1979, *Managing People at Work*, McGraw Hill, London.

Kasavana, M. and Cahill, J., 1987, *Managing Computer Systems in the Hospitality Industry*, CBI, New York.

Kiechel, W., 1984, 'To compute and not to compute: why executives don't', *The Cornell Hotel and Restaurant Administrative Quarterly*, February: 9–11.

Luconi, F. L., Malone, T. W., and Scott Morton, M. S., 1986, 'Expert systems: the next challenge for managers', *Sloan Management Review*, Summer: 3–13.

Martilla, J. A., 1971, 'Word-of-Mouth Communication in the industrial adoption process', *Journal of Marketing Research*, 8: 173–8.

Mytinger, R. E., 1968, *Innovation in Local Health Services*, US Government Printing Office, Washington DC.

Nissan, E., 1987, 'The wining and dining project II—Fidel Gastro, an expert system for gastronomy and terminal food processing', *International Journal of Hospitality Management*, 6(4): 207–15.

PA Management Consultants, 1985, *Survey of Chief Executives and their Perception of Office Automation*, Royston.

Pilcher, O. L., Lubrano, C. R. and Theophano, R., 1987, 'The promise of application software', *Byte*, 12(7): 33–5.

Porter, M. E. and Millar, V. E., 1985, 'How information gives you competitive advantage', *Harvard Business Review*, July/August: 149–60.

Pugh, D. S., 1973, 'The measurement or organization structures: does context determine form?' *Organizational Dynamics* (Spring): 19–34.

Rauch-Hindin, W. B., 1988, *A Guide to Commercial Artificial Intelligence*, Prentice Hall, Englewood Cliffs.

Robey, D., 1977, 'Computers and management structure: some empirical findings re-examined', *Human Relations*, 30(11): 963–76.

Rogers, E. M. and Shoemaker, F. F., 1971, *Communication of Innovations: A Cross Cultural Approach*, Collier-Macmillan, New York.

Romtec, 1987, *Annual Market Review*, Romtec, Maidenhead.

Rothwell, R., 1977, 'The characteristics of successful innovators and technically progressive firms', *R&D Management*, 7(3): 191–206.

Searle, J., 1985, *Minds, Brains and Science*, BBC, London.

Smith, C., 1987, 'The eloquent system helps the Balsams Grand Resort Hotel give personalized service while increasing occupancy rates', *The Texas Instruments Artificial Intelligence Letter*, III(9): 2–5.

Warwick, D. P., 1975, *A Theory of Public Bureaucracy*, Harvard University Press, Cambridge, Mass.

Watson, T. J., 1980, *Work and Industry*, Routledge and Kegan Paul, London.

Whittaker, M., 1987, 'Overcoming the barriers to successful implementation of information technology in the UK hotel industry', *International Journal of Hospitality Management*, 6(4): 229–35.

Wilkinson, B., 1983, *The Shopfloor Politics of New Technology*, Heinemann, London.

Winston, P. H., 1984, *Artificial Intelligence*, Addison Wesley, Reading, Mass.

Woodward, J., 1959, *Management and Technology*, HMSO, London.

17 Advances in catering technology

D. Kirk

Definition and scope

Catering technology is a relatively new discipline. It could be said that it came of age and gained international standing at the three symposia organized by the Hotel and Catering Research Centre (Glew, 1977, 1980 and 1985). Because of their importance, the reports of these symposia have been taken as the starting-point for this review.

Another important aspect of catering technology, which partly stems from its newness, is the low level of fundamental research work in this area. It may be considered that, because of the very applied nature of the catering industry, fundamental research is not required and that most knowledge that is required can be assimilated through technology transfer from related disciplines such as food science, chemical engineering and control engineering. For example, the report on the COST project (European Cooperation in Scientific and Technical Research) has much relevance to catering technology (Zeuthen *et al.*, 1983). However, this is to deny the unique nature of many catering problems. The situation is compounded by the relatively low level of funding for catering research both from government sources and from industry. Research into catering technology is low in priority for the major sources of research funding. Coupled with this is the fact that for effective catering technology research there is a need for interdisciplinary teams if the potential benefits are to be achieved (Fawcett and McDowell, 1987).

This chapter examines developments in catering technology in two parts. The first part considers reasons for the adoption of catering technology and its implications from a business point of view and in relation to demands from customers. The second part is concerned with the nature of technological developments and with a review of papers which have made a significant contribution to the scientific understanding of the catering process.

The adoption of catering technology

Technology and the catering industry

In recent years there has been considerable debate about the role of technology in the catering industry and about its relevance in an industry which has a large service element. This debate is summarized by Pine (1987). He points to the 'low technology' view of catering held by many people in the industry. On the one hand this leads to a resistance to technological change from some people in the industry. On the other hand, Pine points to the danger of making staff merely adjuncts to technology:

technology should not simply be viewed as equipment and machines or in terms of a larger design concept dealing with the configuration of various pieces of equipment and processes, but should encompass wider organisational, social and even psychological considerations of all people who will be affected by or involved with that equipment and design.

The service area in particular has been the subject of debate about the appropriateness of technology. The service area is concerned with a number of operational and managerial functions (Nevett, 1985):

(a) buffer stock holding between production and customer;
(b) merchandizing of food and beverages;
(c) delivery of food to the customer with minimum deterioration of quality;
(d) financial, quality and quantity control.

Nevett discusses the likely impact on customers arising from the use of technology in the hotel and catering industries. Jones (1986) considers a number of developments in the design of service systems:

(a) the application of production line technologies incorporating batch or mass production techniques; tasks are de-skilled and technology is used to provide a fast and efficient service. Jones uses as an example of this the fast food operation;
(b) a decoupling of the technical core from the delivery system. The decoupling may be in terms of time and/or location. In a catering context he sees this as a separation of back-of-house and front-of-house activities. It may also be seen in terms of systems such as cook-freeze, cook-chill and *sous-vide*.

With these changes in the ways of designing and/or viewing catering operations, it is useful to be able to categorize alternative systems. A system of classification of institutional foodservice systems can be described in terms of

purchasing (B):	raw material, semi-processed, fully processed;
manipulation (M):	mechanical alteration prior to cooking;
processing (K):	chemical or physical process which may be in bulk or non-bulk;
preservation (P):	freezing or chilling;
reheat (H):	microwave, convection, infra-red, integral heat and contact plate heating;
distribution (D):	assembly and transport; cold tray and hot tray.

They argue that this **BMKPHD** classification system can be used to describe and analyse both conventional systems as well as developments such as cook-freeze and cook-chill.

Another aspect of foodservice which has had an impact on the development of technology in the industry is that of 'showmanship' where food preparation is converted into a front-of-house activity. This, and the need for much greater flexibility in the use of space in the hotel and catering industry has led to the need for flexible services and mobile equipment (DES, 1986).

Nutrition and healthy eating

There has been great debate, particularly in the developed world, about the unsatisfactory nature of the modern diet which has led to the demand for diets with lower fat (particularly saturated), sugar, salt, fewer additives and preservatives and an increase in fibre (Dennis, 1987).

Because of concern about the effects of diet on health, there has been considerable debate in the industry on the need for healthier menus (Scobie, 1987; Loughridge and Boyar, 1987; Chin *et al.*, 1988) and for nutritional labelling on menus (Lefebvre, 1987).

Hygiene

Outbreaks of food poisoning associated with catering continue to be an area of international concern. An analysis of causes of food poisoning in the United Kingdom between 1970 and 1984 (Gilbert, 1987) indicates the following as the major causes:

preparing too far in advance	57%
storage at ambient temperature	38%
inadequate cooling	30%
inadequate reheating	26%

Of these cases, 38 per cent were due to *Salmonella* species, 35 per cent to *Clostridium perfringens* and 11.2 per cent to *Staphylococcus aureus*. In addition to these familiar organisms, Gilbert discusses the rise in the number of cases associated with less common agents which are occurring world-wide, many of which are associated with refrigerated foods. Given the increase in the size of the chilled food chain and the increased use of chilled storage in catering there is cause for concern. As an example, cases of food poisoning in the United States caused by *Lysteria monocytogenes* have increased from 20 in 1979 to 108 in 1985.

Microbiological quality control is difficult to apply to the catering industry in the same way as it is handled in the food industry, where there is a reliance on product testing. Collinson *et al.* (1987) evaluated nearly 20 catering units in the United Kingdom to compare their standards of operation with those defined in the statement of Good Manufacturing Practice by the Institute of Food Science and Technology. Their results showed a bimodal distribution with units with either very poor or very good food control, and few in the middle. The best controls were found in operations which used technological systems such as cook-freeze or cook-chill. The poor control establishments were predominantly upper-market licensed restaurants and hotels. The authors argue that good catering practice should be based on good written procedures linked with documentation to show whether or not these practices have been followed.

One technique which has been found to be of use in catering is that of HACCP (hazard analysis and critical control point). Rather than relying on testing of products HACCP relies on the analysis of all steps in the process in order to identify critical stages on which control must be concentrated. Snyder (1986) has argued that, for HACCP to be used in the catering industry, the analysis must include the management aspects of the operation. He also uses this as an argument for proper education and demonstration of competence before licensing of all caterers.

Productivity gains

One of the main reasons cited for the use of technology in the catering industry is to improve productivity and to reduce costs. As an example, one of the major reasons for introducing cook-chill was stated to be a reduction in labour costs (Walker and Light, 1988). In a survey of some 78 cook-chill units in the United Kingdom, Walker and Light show that, where objectives such as this are clearly identified at the outset, there was a reasonable level of success in achieving these objectives. However they do point to another barrier to the use of technology from labour and union organizations. Shepherd (1987), in her report for the London Food Commission, points to some of the technological problems associated with cook-chill but is equally concerned about the effects on levels of employment in the industry.

Energy management

The cost of energy in catering has been one inducement for technological developments. Consumption of energy in catering is evaluated by Unklesbay and Unklesbay (1982) and by the Energy Efficiency Office (1984). The latter have shown that significant savings can be made (of the order of 30 per cent), through good management. Developments in the design of equipment have reduced the energy consumption per kg of food; this has also improved the environment in the kitchen. Work has also been done on the recovery of heat from extractors (Jones, 1986) and refrigeration (Fretton, 1982).

Developments and applications of catering technology

Prime cooking

A large proportion of prime cooking takes place on the hob or boiling table which is very energy inefficient and causes environmental problems in kitchens. Newborough and Probert (1988) consider improvements which could be made in the use of existing electric hobs. They also consider design improvements which could lead to energy savings of 40 per cent. Adams and Palin (1986) investigated the induction hob and found that 10 to 20 per cent savings in energy consumption were possible.

The use of forced convection ovens as a replacement for natural convection is now firmly established in the catering industry, but the advantages and disadvantages from the use of these ovens is under-researched. Hseih and Matthews (1986) have investigated the effect of air temperature and oven load on cooking time, yield and energy consumption. They show that oven position is important in convection ovens; this has implications for batch cooking in convection ovens. They also showed that there must be a trade-off between cooking times, energy consumption and yields. Higher oven temperatures gives shorter cooking times but higher energy consumptions and lower yields. An increase in temperature from 105°C to 135°C resulted in a reduction of cooking time of 27 per cent but the energy consumption rose by 6 per cent and the yield fell from 78 per cent to 72 per cent. An increase from 105°C to 165°C resulted in a 34 per cent reduction in cooking time but caused the energy consumption to rise by 19 per cent and the yield to fall 69 per cent.

Because of the importance of short cooking times in many catering operations, cooking by broiling, griddling and grilling is of great importance. Dagerskog and Osterstrom (1979) carried out fundamental research into the nature of food heating using infra-red radiation. Comparisons of infra-red and conventional grilling/broiling have been carried out by Vandermey and Khan (1987). They found that there were no significant differences in sensory properties, texture or thiamin retention between the two methods. Infra-red steaks had a higher moisture content and a lower fat content than conventional steaks. Cooking losses were 28.3 per cent in the infra-red grill and 24.2 per cent in the conventional grill. Development work has been carried out in Sweden on the development of a griddle plate which uses electric resistance elements in the form of a thin foil located between two layers of electrically insulating material. Experiments have shown that these heating elements give griddle plates which have greater temperature uniformity and are easier to control and to divide up into heating zones (Andersson, 1986).

Research into the mechanism of heat transfer during conduction heating, as is found in griddles, has been carried out by Housova and Topinka (1985). They investigated reasons for variations in the heat flux and the heat transfer coefficient to meat patties at the contact surface. They found that recipe formulation had a considerable effect on heat transfer coefficients as did the pressure applied to the contact surface. Plate temperature had a less significant effect. Heat transfer coefficients varied between 200 and 1200 W m-2 K-1.

Frying is an important part of the modern catering industry, and an important aspect of the development of modern facilities has been the importance of oil-filtration on a regular basis. Handel *et al*. (1986) have demonstrated the importance of daily oil-filtration and cleaning of the deep fat fryer on the life of frying oil and on the quality of the fried food product.

Holding and regeneration systems

In Sweden there has been much research into nutritional and sensory changes in food during periods of warm-holding. The overall conclusion of these studies was that warm-holding times should be kept to a minimum and a temperature of 60°C to 65°C used. They have also advocated the use of nitrogen or carbon dioxide rather than air as a means of improving sensory quality during warm-holding (Andersson, 1986).

Frozen foods form a part of most modern catering operations, be it food which has been prepared on site and frozen, or food which is bought in from a food processor. Because of its importance to the food industry, there has been much research on the freezing of foods, but less on the problems of thawing foods. Lind and Hulthen (1986) have reported on research carried out in Sweden on improving the techniques used in catering for thawing foods. They report that special thawing equipment is often not used and that thawing times are lengthy and handling problems considerable. They describe the development of a pilot scale thawing tunnel to investigate the parameters affecting the thawing process. They were able to show that an air velocity of 3 m/s, an air humidity of 75 per cent and an air temperature of +8°C gave the best results for meat loaves and fish blocks.

The use of rapid chilling and storage between +3°C and −1°C (cook-chill) is now firmly established as a part of the possible systems for use in catering. Walker and Light (1988) discuss the success of cook-chill in terms of its ability to meet the primary objectives of users. Most users (65 per cent) stated that their main objective was to reduce labour costs, followed by improved productivity (11 per cent). The report states that the most successful cook-chill operations were those that had clear goals, thorough planning and effective training. Another interesting fact to emerge from this research is that there are few pure cook-chill systems in the United Kingdom, with 52 per cent of the units in the sample producing less than half of their food by cook-chill. One concern about the use of chilled storage is its effect on nutrients and here evidence is conflicting. Shepherd (1987) points to the losses of nutrients associated with chilled storage and this is confirmed by data summarized by Hunt (1984) and Mottishaw (1987). However, these comparisons are all made against freshly cooked foods and, in many cases, cook-chill is used to replace hot food holding and hot food distribution systems where nutrient loss was very high (Yorkshire Regional Health Authority, 1987). In these situations cook-chill can lead to an improvement in nutrient retention and food quality. An important aspect of cook-chill systems is the rate of chilling. Rollin *et al*. (1979) provide a model for predicting cooling times for cook-chill foods.

Work carried out by Thomas and Brown (1987), indicates that the additional consumption and cost of electricity caused by the use of cook-chill and cook-freeze for hospital foodservice is insignificant (0.74 kWh per tray). This included chilling, freezing, storage and reheating.

There has been much discussion in the trade press about the value of in-pack pasteurization together with vacuum and low-temperature storage (the *sous-vide* process), but there is still a need for scientific evidence for lengthy storage periods. Work in the Food and Hospitality Research Centre at the Dorset Institute of Higher Education shows promising results for this technology from a microbiological and organoleptic viewpoint (Young *et al*., 1988; Schafheitle *et al*., 1988; Schafheitle and Light, 1988).

Food service

One area where technology has been applied to the service element of the catering operation is the use of mechanized vending for the service of food and drink. Light *et al*. (1987a) report on a survey of full meal vending machines in the United Kingdom. Based on this survey, they report that good practice, in the form of hygienic preparation, rapid chilling and adequate control of the chilled food chain was sometimes lacking. They also report on the poor temperature control in a high proportion of chilled food vending machines (Light *et al*., 1987b).

Conclusion

This brief review of catering technology indicates some of the reasons for using, and some of the reasons mitigating against the use of technology in catering. It also evaluates some of the research which is taking place. It can be seen that catering technology is at its strongest in those areas where there are direct links or clear parallels between the catering and food processing industries. It is also strong where there are public health implications. Given the size of the modern catering and foodservice industries the level of fundamental and applied research into catering technology is low and underfunded. Associated with this is a lack of structure and focus to the research which is taking place. There is evidence that some sectors of the catering industry are moving towards higher levels of capital investment in catering technology (Pine and Ball, 1987), although there are not always clear correlations between high technology and high productivity.

References

Adams, A., Palin, M., 1986, 'An investigation into the efficiency of induction cooking and a comparison of its performance with other cooking methods', *Journal of Foodservice Systems*, 4(1): 59–66.

Andersson, Y., 1986, 'Foodpreparation in the foodservice business—fundamental and applied research work done at SIK', *Journal of Foodservice Systems*, 4(2): 69–80.

Chin, J., McCall, I., and Struzik, J., 1988, 'Reducing fat and cholesterol in foodservice', *Journal of Foodservice Systems*, 4(4): 277–300.

Collison, R., West, A., and Sawyer, C., 1987, 'Good catering practice', *Food Science and Technology Today*, 1(4): 244–7.

Collinson, R., Colwill, J., 1986, 'The analysis of food waste results and related attributes of restaurants and public houses', *Journal of Foodservice Systems*, 4(1): 17–30.

Dagerskog, M., Osterstrom, L., 1979, 'Infra red radiation for food processing I: a study of the fundamental properties of infra-red radiation', *Lebensmittel Wissenschaft und Technologie*, 12(4): 237–42.

Dennis, C., 1987, 'Trends in food manufacturing and catering practice', Symposium on Microbiological and Environmental Health Problems Relevant to the Food and Catering Industries, Campden Food Preservation Research Association, 19–21 January, pp. 131–48.

Department of Educational Science, 1986, *Adaptable Teaching Kitchens in Further Education*, DES Building Bulletin 65, HMSO, London.

Energy Efficiency Office, 1984, *Energy Consumption in Catering*, Department of Energy, London.

Escueta, E. S., Fielder, K. M., Reisman, A., 1986, 'A new hospital foodservice classification system', *Journal of Foodservice Systems*, 4(2): 107–16.

Fawcett, S. L., McDowell, D. A., 1987, 'Assessment of the potential of commercially available enzymes in meat and tenderisation', *Journal of Foodservice Systems*, 4(3): 133–42.

Fretton, K., 1982, *Hot Water from Refrigeration*, Electricity Council Conference on Cost Effective Catering, University of Sussex, 22–25 March.

Gilbert, R. J., 1987, *Foodborne Infections and Intoxications—Recent Problems and New Organisms*, Symposium on Microbiological and Environmental Health Problems Relevant to the Food and Catering Industries, Campden Food Preservation Research Association, 19–21 January, pp. 1–22.

Glew, G., 1977, *Catering Equipment and Systems Design*, Elsevier Applied Science Publishers, London.

Glew, G., 1980, *Advances in Catering Technology*, Elsevier Applied Science Publishers, London.

Glew, G., 1985, *Advances in Catering Technology III*, Elsevier Applied Science Publishers, London.

Handel, A. P., Dumper, A. N., and Hamouz, F. L., 1986, 'Effect of deep-fat fryer cleaning procedures on oil life and food quality', *Journal of Foodservice Systems*, 4(2): 117–24.

Housova, J., Topinka, P., 1985, 'Heat transfer during contact cooking of minced meat patties', *Journal of Food Engineering*, 4(3): 169–88.

Hsieh, J., Matthews, M. E., 1986, 'Energy use, time and product yield of turkey rolls at three oven loads and cooking temperatures in a convection oven', *Journal of Foodservice Systems*, 4(2): 97–106.

Hunt, C., 1984, 'Nutrient losses in cook-freeze and cook-chill catering', *Human Nutrition: Applied Nutrition*, 38A: 50–9.

Jones, M., 1980, *Ventilation and the Extraction of Waste Heat*, Electricity Council Conference on Cost Effective Catering, University of York, 24–27 March.

Jones, P., 1986, *Hierarchy of operational types in the catering industry*, IAHMS symposium on Catering Management, Oxford Polytechnic, November, pp. 67–80.

Lefebvre, C., 1987, 'A case history of nutritional information on menus', *Journal of Foodservice Systems*, 4(3): 153–8.

Light, N., Young, H., and Youngs, A., 1987a, 'A qualitative survey of the use of chilled vending machines as a means of food service in the UK', *Food Science and Technology Today*, 1(4): 247–51.

Light, N., Young, H., and Youngs, A., 1987b, 'Operating temperatures in chilled food vending machines and risk of growth of food poisoning organisms', *Food Science and Technology Today*, 1(4): 252–6.

Lind, I., Hulthen, B., 1986, 'Thawing of food in catering', *Journal of Foodservice Systems*, 4(2): 81–96.

Loughridge, J. R., Boyar, A. P., 1987, 'Menu Manhattan', *Journal of Foodservice Systems*, 4(3): 187–214.

Mottishaw, J., 1987, 'Nutritional aspects of the cook-chill process', Seminar presentation to the Institution of Environmental Health Officers, 3–4 June in Yorkshire Regional Health Authority, *Interim report by the regional expert group on the safety of the cook-chill system*, 30 September, 1987, pp. 33–8.

Nevett, W., 1985, 'Operations management perspectives and the hospitality industry', *International Journal of Hospitality Management*, 4(4): 173–8.

Newborough, M., Probert, S. D., 1988, 'Energy conscious design improvements for electric hobs, *Journal of Foodservice Systems*, 4(4): 233–58.

Pine, R., 1987, *Management of Technological Change in the Catering Industry*, Avebury, Aldershot.

Pine, R., Ball, J., 1987, 'Productivity and technology in catering operations', *Food Science and Technology Today*, 1(3): 174–6.

Rollin, J. L., Mathews, E. M., and Lund, D. B., 1979, 'Cook/chill foodservice systems', *Journal of the American Dietetic Association*, 75(4): 440–5.

Schafheitle, J., Light, N., Hudson, D., Williams R., and Barrett, J., 1988, 'A pilot study on the use of *sous-vide* vacuum cooking as a production system for high quality foods in catering', *International Journal of Hospitality Management*, 7(1): 21–8.

Schafheitle, J., Light, N., 1988, *An Investigation of the Technical, Microbiological and Sensory Parameters for Cooked, Chilled food production and storage using the method of vacuum (sous-vide) cooking* (forthcoming).

Scobie, P., 1987, 'Catering for health', *Nutrition and Food Science*, 107: 10–11.

Shepherd, J., 1987, *The Big Chill*, London Food Commission.

Snyder, O. P., 1986, 'Applying the hazard analysis and critical control points system in foodservice and foodborne illness prevention', *Journal of Foodservice Systems*, 4(2): 125–31.

Thomas, C. J., Brown, N. E., 1987, 'Use and cost of electricity for selected processes specific to a hospital cook-chill/freeze food-production system', *Journal of Foodservice Systems*, 4(3): 159–70.

Unklesbay, N., Unklesbay, K., 1982, *Energy Management in Foodservice*, AVI, Westport.

Vandermey, P. A., Khan, M. A., 1987, 'Thiamin retention and sensory quality of infrared and conventionally broiled beef loin steaks for foodservice use', *Journal of Foodservice Systems*, 4(3): 143–52.

Walker, A., Light, N., 1988, 'Is cook-chill being put to its best use?', *Hospitality*, 86 February: 15–17.

Yorkshire Regional Health Authority, 1987, *Interim Report by the Regional Expert Group on the Safety of the Cook-Chill System*, 30 September.

Young, H., Youngs, A., and Light, N., 1988, *The effects of the growth of naturally occurring microflora in cooked, chilled foods used in the catering industry*, forthcoming.

Zeuthen, P., Chefetel, J. C., Eriksson, C., Jul, M., Leniger, H., Linko, P., Varela, G., and Vos, G., 1983, 'Thermal processing and quality of foods', Seminar Proceedings, Athens, 14–18 November, Elsevier Applied Science Publishers, London.